Learning Docker

Second Edition

Build, ship, and scale faster

Jeeva S. Chelladhurai
Vinod Singh
Pethuru Raj

BIRMINGHAM - MUMBAI

Learning Docker

Second Edition

First published: June 2015

Second edition: May 2017

Production reference: 1290517

Published by Packt Publishing Ltd.
Livery Place
35 Livery Street
Birmingham
B3 2PB, UK.
ISBN 978-1-78646-292-3

www.packtpub.com

Credits

Authors
Jeeva S. Chelladhurai
Vinod Singh
Pethuru Raj

Copy Editor
Tom Jacob

Reviewer
Werner Dijkerman

Project Coordinator
Kinjal Bari

Commissioning Editor
Kartikey Pandey

Proofreader
Safis Editing

Acquisition Editor
Prachi Bisht

Indexer
Mariammal Chettiyar

Content Development Editor
Radhika Atitkar

Graphics
Kirk D'Penha

Technical Editor
Bhagyashree Rai

Production Coordinator
Melwyn Dsa

About the Authors

Jeeva S. Chelladhurai has been working as a DevOps specialist at the IBM Global Cloud Center of Excellence (CoE) in India for the past 8 years. He has more than 20 years of experience in the IT industry. In various capacities, he has technically managed and mentored diverse teams across the globe in envisaging and building pioneering telecommunication products. He specializes in DevOps and cloud solution delivery, with a focus on data center optimization, Software-defined Environments (SDEs), and distributed application development, deployment, and delivery using the newest Docker technology. Jeeva is also a strong proponent of agile methodologies, DevOps, and IT automation. He holds a master's degree in computer science from Manonmaniam Sundaranar University and a graduate certificate in project management from Boston University. He has been instrumental in crafting reusable assets for IBM solution architects and consultants in Docker-inspired containerization technology. He can be reached at his LinkedIn page: `https://www.linkedin.com/in/JeevaChelladhurai`

Vinod Singh held various positions across development, architecture, and engagement with clients throughout his career.

Currently, he is a senior cloud architect with IBM's cloud flagship offering Bluemix, supporting customers across the world. Vinod's experience with networking and data communication spans software design, development, and testing. The cloud, cognitive computing, and Linux are his passions, and he feels cognitive computing is once again going to change the world.

Vinod is a regular speaker at IBM's internal conferences, IEEE conferences, and technology meetups. Vinod's latest day job revolves around IBM Bluemix, Kubernetes, Docker, IBM Watson and Amazon AWS. He can be reached at LinkedIn page: `https://www.linkedin.com/in/vinod-singh-687b43/` and Twitter @1vinodsingh.

Vinod acknowledges his wife for extraordinary support at home that enables him to run extra mile in professional life.

Pethuru Raj, PhD, has been working as the chief architect in Reliance Jio Cloud and previously worked as a cloud infrastructure architect in the IBM Global Cloud Center of Excellence (CoE), IBM India, Bangalore for four years. Prior to that, he worked as TOGAF-certified enterprise architecture (EA) consultant in Wipro Consulting Services (WCS) Division. He also had a fruitful stint as a lead architect in the corporate research (CR) division of Robert Bosch, Bangalore. He has gained more than 17 years of IT industry experience and 8 years of research experience.

He finished the CSIR-sponsored PhD degree in Anna University, Chennai and continued the UGC-sponsored postdoctoral research in the department of Computer Science and Automation, Indian Institute of Science, Bangalore. Thereafter, he was granted a couple of international research fellowships (JSPS and JST) to work as a research scientist for 3.5 years in two leading Japanese universities. He has published more than 30 research papers in peer-reviewed journals such as IEEE, ACM, Springer-Verlag, and Inderscience. He has authored 7 books thus far and he focuses on some of the emerging technologies such as:

- Software-defined Cloud Environments (SDCEs)
- Big, Fast, Streaming and IoT Data Analytics
- DevOps through Docker-enabled Containerization
- Microservices Architecture (MSA)
- Context-aware Computing
- Edge / Fog and Cognitive Analytics
- Blockchain Technology for IoT Data and Device Security
- Smarter Cities Technologies and Tools

Home page: www.peterindia.net
LinkedIn profile: https://www.linkedin.com/in/peterindia

He gives all honor and glory to the Lord and Savior Jesus Christ.

About the Reviewer

Werner Dijkerman is a system engineer from the Netherlands. He has more than 10 years of experience in IT operations departments in different organizations. He started working with a leading online retailer in the Netherlands and continued in one of the leading software companies for general practitioners. He now works for iWelcome, the only established IDaaS provider in Europe.

Having experience as a Windows and Linux admin, he also knows his way around Java application servers such as Tomcat and JBoss, (No)SQL databases, and monitoring systems. He is very busy with maintaining several free available Docker containers. Finding new ways to monitor Docker, orchestrate containers, and testing containers before it is used on production environments.

He was also a technical reviewer on the book *Zabbix Network Monitoring, Second Edition*, also available from Packt Publishing.

www.PacktPub.com

For support files and downloads related to your book, please visit www.PacktPub.com.

Did you know that Packt offers eBook versions of every book published, with PDF and ePub files available? You can upgrade to the eBook version at www.PacktPub.com and as a print book customer, you are entitled to a discount on the eBook copy. Get in touch with us at service@packtpub.com for more details.

At www.PacktPub.com, you can also read a collection of free technical articles, sign up for a range of free newsletters and receive exclusive discounts and offers on Packt books and eBooks.

https://www.packtpub.com/mapt

Get the most in-demand software skills with Mapt. Mapt gives you full access to all Packt books and video courses, as well as industry-leading tools to help you plan your personal development and advance your career.

Why subscribe?

- Fully searchable across every book published by Packt
- Copy and paste, print, and bookmark content
- On demand and accessible via a web browser

Customer Feedback

Thanks for purchasing this Packt book. At Packt, quality is at the heart of our editorial process. To help us improve, please leave us an honest review on this book's Amazon page at https://www.amazon.com/dp/1786462923.

If you'd like to join our team of regular reviewers, you can e-mail us at customerreviews@packtpub.com. We award our regular reviewers with free eBooks and videos in exchange for their valuable feedback. Help us be relentless in improving our products!

Table of Contents

Preface

There are several technical and business advantages associated with Docker. The longstanding goals of application development, deployment, and delivery automation are accomplished through Docker-enabled containerization, which is being touted as a crucial automation method for the tremendous success of the cloud paradigm. Existing workloads are containerized and cloud-enabled to be stocked in public as well as private repositories. Both business and IT workloads can be easily pampered, packaged, and presented as remotely discoverable, usable, portable, and composable containers. Further on, containers are shipped and run everywhere without any hassle, hitches, and hurdles. The containerization concept has made IT infrastructures and processes agile and adaptive. This means that not only is software engineering sped up, but also the tasks of software configuration, deployment, and delivery are accelerated. Precisely speaking, the unique goals of DevOps are accomplished through the smart use of containers.

Beside a litany of Docker-centric solutions, there is a growing family of third-party tools to make embracing and enabling Docker risk-free, easier, and faster. There are powerful case studies and real-world deployments clearly illustrating that Docker consistently contributes to establishing and sustaining IT environments in minutes rather than in months. The other noteworthy advancements brought by the Docker paradigm include the real-time scalability of application infrastructures and the improved utilization of IT resources brought about by having several application containers within any Docker host. There are container cluster management platforms for efficient container scheduling, and orchestration for quickly producing and sustaining multihost, multicontainer, and microservices-centric distributed applications.

The role and responsibility of the widely deliberated Docker technology in ensuring event-driven, service-oriented, insights-filled, context-aware, cloud-hosted, business-centric, and mission-critical applications is enchanting really and is well articulated in this new edition of the book, in order to adequately empower our readers with all the relevant details of the most popular Docker paradigm.

What this book covers

Chapter 1, *Getting Started with Docker*, talks about the various distinctions of the open-source Docker platform and how it simplifies and speeds up the process of realizing containerized workloads to be readily deployed and run on a variety of operating systems, bare metal servers, and virtual machines. This chapter also has step-by-step details on installing the Docker Engine, downloading a Docker image from the centralized Docker Hub, creating a Docker container out of that image, and troubleshooting the Docker container.

Chapter 2, *Handling Docker Containers*, is dedicated to clearly explaining the various commands required to manage Docker images and containers. This chapter provides the basic Docker terminologies needed to understand the output of Docker commands. Other details covered here include starting an interactive session inside a container, managing your images, running containers, and tracking changes inside containers.

Chapter 3, *Building Images*, describes how Docker images are built. There are several ways and means through which Docker images are built and stored. The other important topics covered in this chapter include a quick overview of a Dockerfile's syntax and a bit of theoretical information on how Docker stores images.

Chapter 4, *Publishing Images*, tells you everything about publishing images on the centralized Docker Hub and how to get the most out of Docker Hub. The other important contents in the chapter include more details about Docker Hub, how to push images to Docker Hub, the automatic building of images, how to create organizations on Docker Hub, and finally private repositories.

Chapter 5, *Running Your Private Docker Infrastructure*, explains how corporates can set up and run their own private repositories. There are a few valid reasons why corporates want to have their own repositories to host some crucial Docker images. This means that publicly available repositories are found unsuitable for storing certain specific images. This chapter has all the information required to set up and sustain private repositories.

Chapter 6, *Running Services in a Container*, illustrates how a web application can be run inside a Docker container as a service and how to expose the service, in order for the outside world to find and access it. How the appropriate Dockerfile is developed to simplify this task is also described in detail.

Chapter 7, *Sharing Data with Containers*, shows you how to use Docker's volumes feature to share data between the Docker host and its containers. The other topics covered here are how to share data between containers, the common use cases, and the typical pitfalls to avoid.

Chapter 8, *Orchestrating Containers*, explains how to do the orchestration of multiple containers towards composite and containerized workloads. It is a well-known truth that orchestration plays a major role in producing composite applications. This chapter includes relevant details about the orchestration process and the toolset made available for enabling the process of orchestration. Finally, you will find a well-orchestrated example of how containers can be orchestrated to bring forth highly reusable and business-aware containers.

Chapter 9, *Testing with Docker*, focuses on testing your code inside Docker images. You will also find out how to run tests inside an ad hoc Docker image. Finally, you will be given details of how to integrate Docker testing into a continuous integration server such as Jenkins.

Chapter 10, *Debugging Containers*, teaches you how to debug applications running inside containers. How Docker ensures that processes running inside containers are isolated from the outside world is also covered.

Chapter 11, *Securing Docker Containers*, explains the security and privacy challenges and concerns, and how they are addressed through the liberal use of competent standards, technologies, and tools. This chapter covers the mechanism for dropping user privileges once inside an image. There is also a brief introduction to how the security capabilities introduced in SELinux come in handy when securing Docker containers.

Chapter 12, *The Docker Platform – Distinct Capabilities and Use Cases*, describes how the Docker platform is becoming an enterprise-grade method for bringing forth a variety of distinct automation in the fields of software engineering and distributed computing. Several industry case studies are included in this chapter in order to address any worries about Docker and to enhance its penetration and participation.

What you need for this book

You need Ubuntu 16.04 to run the examples covered in this book.

Who this book is for

This book is ideal for developers, operations managers, and IT professionals who would like to learn about Docker and use it to build and deploy container-based applications. No prior knowledge of Docker is expected.

Conventions

In this book, you will find a number of text styles that distinguish between different kinds of information. Here are some examples of these styles and an explanation of their meaning.

Code words in text, database table names, folder names, filenames, file extensions, pathnames, dummy URLs, user input, and Twitter handles are shown as follows: "Let's start our Docker journey with the `docker version` subcommand, as shown here:"

A block of code is set as follows:

```
FROM busybox
RUN ls -lh
CMD echo Hello world
```

When we wish to draw your attention to a particular part of a code block, the relevant lines or items are set in bold:

```
FROM busybox
RUN ls -lh
CMD echo Hello world
```

Any command-line input or output is written as follows:

```
$ sudo apt-get install -y docker-engine
```

New terms and **important words** are shown in bold. Words that you see on the screen, for example, in menus or dialog boxes, appear in the text like this: "Now, clicking on the **Start using Jenkins** button will take you to the **Welcome to Jenkins!** page."

 Warnings or important notes appear in a box like this.

 Tips and tricks appear like this.

Reader feedback

Feedback from our readers is always welcome. Let us know what you think about this book—what you liked or disliked. Reader feedback is important to us as it helps us develop titles that you will really get the most out of.

To send us general feedback, simply e-mail feedback@packtpub.com, and mention the book's title in the subject of your message.

If there is a topic that you have expertise in and you are interested in either writing or contributing to a book, see our author guide at www.packtpub.com/authors.

Customer support

Now that you are the proud owner of a Packt book, we have a number of things to help you to get the most from your purchase.

Downloading the example code

You can download the example code files for this book from your account at http://www.packtpub.com. If you purchased this book elsewhere, you can visit http://www.packtpub.com/support and register to have the files e-mailed directly to you.

You can download the code files by following these steps:

1. Log in or register to our website using your e-mail address and password.
2. Hover the mouse pointer on the **SUPPORT** tab at the top.
3. Click on **Code Downloads & Errata**.
4. Enter the name of the book in the **Search** box.
5. Select the book for which you're looking to download the code files.
6. Choose from the drop-down menu where you purchased this book from.
7. Click on **Code Download**.

Once the file is downloaded, please make sure that you unzip or extract the folder using the latest version of:

- WinRAR / 7-Zip for Windows
- Zipeg / iZip / UnRarX for Mac
- 7-Zip / PeaZip for Linux

The code bundle for the book is also hosted on GitHub at `https://github.com/PacktPubl ishing/Learning-Docker-Second-Edition`. We also have other code bundles from our rich catalog of books and videos available at `https://github.com/PacktPublishing/`. Check them out!

Downloading the color images of this book

We also provide you with a PDF file that has color images of the screenshots/diagrams used in this book. The color images will help you better understand the changes in the output. You can download this file from `https://www.packtpub.com/sites/default/files/down loads/LearningDockerSecondEdition_ColorImages.pdf`.

Errata

Although we have taken every care to ensure the accuracy of our content, mistakes do happen. If you find a mistake in one of our books – maybe a mistake in the text or the code – we would be grateful if you could report this to us. By doing so, you can save other readers from frustration and help us improve subsequent versions of this book. If you find any errata, please report them by visiting `http://www.packtpub.com/submit-errata`, selecting your book, clicking on the **Errata Submission Form** link, and entering the details of your errata. Once your errata are verified, your submission will be accepted and the errata will be uploaded to our website or added to any list of existing errata under the Errata section of that title.

To view the previously submitted errata, go to `https://www.packtpub.com/books/conten t/support`and enter the name of the book in the search field. The required information will appear under the **Errata** section.

Piracy

Piracy of copyrighted material on the Internet is an ongoing problem across all media. At Packt, we take the protection of our copyright and licenses very seriously. If you come across any illegal copies of our works in any form on the Internet, please provide us with the location address or website name immediately so that we can pursue a remedy.

Please contact us at `copyright@packtpub.com` with a link to the suspected pirated material.

We appreciate your help in protecting our authors and our ability to bring you valuable content.

Questions

If you have a problem with any aspect of this book, you can contact us at questions@packtpub.com, and we will do our best to address the problem.

1
Getting Started with Docker

Docker is undeniably the most popular technology these days in the **Information Technology (IT)** world. Mainly, there are two principal trends in the Docker landscape. First, the open source Docker platform is being continuously equipped with more correct and relevant features and functionalities in order to make it the most powerful and pioneering IT platform, not only for software developers but also for on-premise and off-premise IT operational teams. The second trend is the unprecedented adoption of the Docker-inspired containerization technology by various IT service and solution providers across the Globe in order to bring forth a growing array of premium offerings to their consumers and clients. The enhanced simplicity in the development of fresh software applications, the automated and accelerated deployment of Docker containers, and the extreme maneuverability of Docker containers are being widely touted as the key differentiators of this unique paradigm's unprecedented success.

In this chapter, we would like to shed more light on Docker, and show why it is being touted as the latest *best thing* for the impending digital idea and insightful economy. We would like to introduce you to the practical side of Docker; in this chapter, we will cover the following topics:

- The key drivers for Dockerization
- Differentiating between containerization and virtualization
- Installing the Docker Engine
- Understanding the Docker setup
- Downloading the first image
- Running the first container
- Troubleshooting Docker containers

The key drivers for Dockerization

The first and foremost driver for Docker-enabled containerization is to competently and completely overcome the widely expressed limitations of the virtualization paradigm. Actually, we have been working on proven virtualization techniques and tools for quite a long time now in order to realize the much-demanded software portability. That is, with the goal of eliminating the inhibiting dependency between software and hardware there have been several right initiatives that include the matured and stabilized virtualization paradigm. Virtualization is a kind of beneficial abstraction, accomplished through the incorporation of an additional layer of indirection between hardware resources and software components. Through this freshly introduced abstraction layer (hypervisor or **Virtual Machine Monitor (VMM)**), any kind of software applications can run on any underlying hardware without any hitch or hurdle. In short, the longstanding goal of software portability is trying to achieve through this middleware layer. However, the much-published portability target is not fully met even by the virtualization technique. The hypervisor software from different vendors gets in the way of ensuring the much-needed application portability. Further, the distribution, version, edition, and patching differences of operating systems and application workloads hinder the smooth portability of workloads across systems and locations.

Similarly, there are various other drawbacks attached to the virtualization paradigm. In data centers and server farms, the virtualization technique is typically used to create multiple **Virtual Machines (VMs)** out of physical machines and each VM has its own **Operating System (OS)**. Through this solid and sound isolation enacted through automated tools and controlled resource-sharing, multiple and heterogeneous applications are being accommodated in a physical machine. That is, the hardware-assisted virtualization enables disparate applications to be run simultaneously on a single physical server. With the virtualization paradigm, various kinds of IT infrastructure (server machines, storage appliances, and networking solutions) become open, programmable, remotely monitorable, manageable, and maintainable. However, because of the verbosity and bloatedness (every VM carries its own OS), VM provisioning typically takes a few minutes and this longer duration is not acceptable for production environments.

The other widely expressed drawback closely associated with virtualization is that the performance of virtualized systems also goes down due to the excessive usage of precious and expensive IT resources (processing, memory, storage, network bandwidth, and so on). Besides the longer runtime, the execution time of VMs is on the higher side because of multiple layers ranging from the guest OS, hypervisor, and the underlying hardware.

Finally, the compute virtualization has flourished, whereas the other closely associated network and storage virtualization concepts are just taking off; precisely speaking, building distributed applications and fulfilling varying business expectations mandate the faster and flexible provisioning, high availability, reliability, scalability, and maneuverability of all the participating IT resources. Computing, storage, and networking components need to work together in accomplishing the varying IT and business needs. This sharply increments the management complexity of virtual environments.

Enter the world of containerization. All the aforementioned barriers get resolved in a single stroke. That is, the evolving concept of application containerization coolly and confidently contributes to the unprecedented success of the software portability goal. A container generally contains an application. Along with the primary application, all of its relevant libraries, binaries, and other dependencies are stuffed and squeezed together to be packaged and presented as a comprehensive yet compact container to be readily shipped, run, and managed in any local as well as remote environments. Containers are exceptionally lightweight, highly portable, rapidly deployable, extensible, and so on. Further on, many industry leaders have come together to form a kind of consortium to embark on a decisive journey towards the systematic production, packaging, and delivery of industry-strength and standardized containers. This conscious and collective move makes Docker deeply penetrative, pervasive, and persuasive. The open source community is simultaneously spearheading the containerization conundrum through an assortment of concerted activities for simplifying and streamlining the containerization concept. These containerization life cycle steps are being automated through a variety of tools.

The Docker ecosystem is also growing rapidly in order to bring in as much automation as possible in the containerization landscape. Container clustering and orchestration are gaining a lot of ground; thus, geographically distributed containers and their clusters can be readily linked up to produce bigger and better application-aware containers. The distributed nature of cloud centers is, therefore, to get benefited immensely with all the adroit advancements gaining a strong foothold in the container space. Cloud service providers and enterprise IT environments are all set to embrace this unique technology in order to escalate the resource utilization and to take the much-insisted infrastructure optimization to the next level. On the performance side, plenty of tests demonstrate Docker containers achieving native system performance. In short, IT agility through the DevOps aspect is being guaranteed through the smart leverage of Dockerization, and this in turn leads to business agility, adaptivity, and affordability.

Differentiating between containerization and virtualization

It is pertinent, and it is paramount for extracting and expounding the game-changing advantages of the Docker-inspired containerization movement over the widely used and fully matured virtualization paradigm. As elucidated earlier, virtualization is the breakthrough idea and game-changing trendsetter for the unprecedented adoption of cloudification, which enables the paradigm of IT industrialization. However, through innumerable real-world case studies, cloud service providers have come to the conclusion that the virtualization technique has its own drawbacks and hence the containerization movement took off powerfully.

Containerization has brought in strategically sound optimizations through a few crucial and well-defined rationalizations and the insightful sharing of compute resources. Some of the innate and hitherto underutilized capabilities of the Linux kernel have been rediscovered. A few additional capabilities too are being embedded to strengthen the process and applicability of containerization. These capabilities have been praised for bringing in the much-wanted automation and acceleration, which will enable the fledgling containerization idea to reach greater heights in the days ahead. The noteworthy business and technical advantages of containerization include bare metal-scale performance, real-time scalability, higher availability, IT DevOps, software portability, and so on. All the unwanted bulges and flabs are being sagaciously eliminated to speed up the roll-out of hundreds of application containers in seconds. The following diagram on the left-hand side depicts the virtualization aspect, whereas the diagram on the right-hand side vividly illustrates the simplifications that are being achieved in containers:

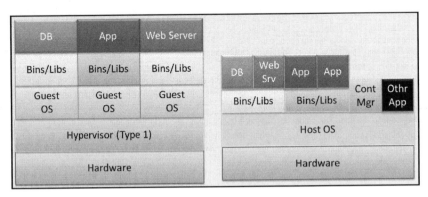

Type 1 Virtualization versus Containerization

As we all know, there are two main virtualization types. In Type 1 virtualization, the hypervisor provides the OS functionalities plus the VM provisioning, monitoring, and management capabilities and hence there is no need for any host OS. VMware ESXi is the leading Type 1 virtualization hypervisor. The production environments and mission-critical applications are run on the Type 1 virtualization.

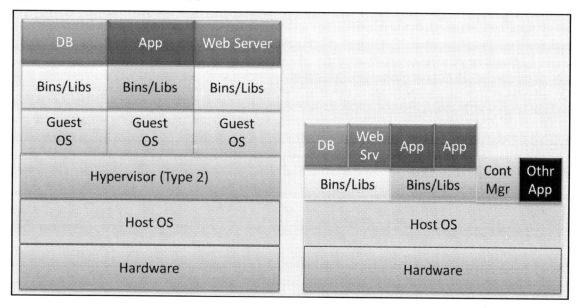

Type 2 virtualization versus Containerization

The second one is the Type 2 virtualization, wherein the hypervisor runs on the host OS as shown in the preceding figure. This additional layer impacts the system performance and hence generally Type 2 virtualization is being used for development, testing, and staging environments. The Type 2 virtualization greatly slows down the performance because of the involvement of multiple modules during execution. Here, the arrival of Docker-enabled containerization brings forth a huge boost to the system performance.

In summary, VMs are a time-tested and battle-hardened software stack and there are a number of enabling tools to manage the OS and applications on it. The virtualization tool ecosystem is consistently expanding. Applications in a VM are hidden from the host OS through the hypervisor. However, Docker containers do not use a hypervisor to provide the isolation. With containers, the Docker host uses the process and filesystem isolation capabilities of the Linux kernel to guarantee the much-demanded isolation.

Docker containers need a reduced disk footprint as they don't include the entire OS. Setup and startup times are therefore significantly lower than in a typical VM. The principal container advantage is the speed with which application code can be developed, composed, packaged, and shared widely. Containers emerge as the most prominent and dominant platform for the speedier creation, deployment, and delivery of microservices-based distributed applications. With containers, there is a lot of noteworthy saving of IT resources as containers consume less memory space.

Great thinkers have come out with a nice and neat comparison between VMs and containers. They accentuate thinking in terms of a house (VM) and an apartment complex. The house, which has its own plumbing, electrical, heating, and protection from unwanted visitors, is self-contained. An apartment complex has the same resources as a house, such as electrical, plumbing, and heating, but they are shared among all the units. The individual apartments come in various sizes and you only rent what you need, not the entire complex. The apartment flats are containers, with the shared resources being the container host.

Developers can use simple and incremental commands to create a fixed image that is easy to deploy and can automate building those images using a `Dockerfile`. Developers can share those images easily using simple, Git-style `push` and `pull` commands to public or private Docker registries. Since the inception of the Docker technology, there is an unprecedented growth of third-party tools for simplifying and streamlining Docker-enabled containerization.

The latest additions to the Docker platform

Containers are primarily presented as the next-generation application delivery platform. Containers are bringing forth a kind of mechanism for efficiently virtualizing the OS for the sole purpose of running applications on a single kernel host. Applications can also include the fast-emerging microservices. The open source Docker platform is now available primarily in two variants:

- **Docker Enterprise Edition (Docker EE)**: This is designed for enterprise development and IT teams who build, ship, and run business-critical applications in production at scale. Docker EE is integrated, certified, and supported to provide enterprises with the most secure container platform in the industry to modernize all applications.

- **Docker Community Edition (Docker CE)**: This is ideal for developers and small teams looking to get started with Docker and experimenting with container-based applications. Docker CE is available on many platforms, from desktop to cloud to the server. Docker CE is available for macOS and Windows and provides a native experience to help you focus on learning Docker. You can build and share containers and automate the development pipeline, all from a single environment.

Windows containers

Docker and Microsoft have entered into a long-lasting partnership to bring the much-needed agility, portability, and security benefits of the Docker platform to every edition of Windows Server 2016. Organizations that upgrade their servers to this new OS will then be able to use containers right from the development to the production environments. Windows uses namespace isolation, resource control, and process-isolation mechanisms to restrict the files, network ports, and running processes that each container can access. This isolation ensures applications running in containers can't interact with or see other applications running on the host OS or in other containers. Microsoft includes two different types of container. The first type is based on the Windows Server core image and is called a **Windows Server container**. The second one is called a **Hyper-V container** and is based on the Windows Nano Server image.

Windows Server containers share the underlying OS kernel. This architecture enables faster startup and efficient packaging while delivering the capability to run a number of containers per host. Containers share the local data and APIs with lower isolation levels between each. These containers are best for homogenous applications that do not require strong isolation and security constraints. Large microservice applications composed of multiple containers can use Windows Server containers for performance and efficiency.

Hyper-V containers offer the best of both worlds: VMs and containers. Since each container gets a dedicated copy of Windows kernel and memory, Hyper-V containers have better isolation and security levels than Windows Server containers. The containers are more secure because the interaction with the host operating system and other containers is minimal. This limited sharing of resources also increases the startup time and the size of packaged containers.

Hyper-V containers are preferred in multi-tenant environments such as public clouds. Here is a summary of Windows container jargon with descriptions:

- **Container Host**: Physical or VM configured with the Windows container feature.
- **Container Image**: A container image contains the base OS, application, and all the application dependencies that are needed to quickly deploy a container.
- **Container OS Image**: The container OS image is the OS.
- **Container Registry**: Container images are stored in a container registry and can be downloaded on demand. A registry can be off- or on-premise.
- **Docker Engine**: It is the core of the open source Docker platform. It is a lightweight container runtime that builds and runs Docker containers.
- **Dockerfile**: `Dockerfile` is used by developers to build and automate the creation of container images. With a `Dockerfile`, the Docker daemon can automatically build a container image.

Microsoft has its own public and official repository available via this URL: `https://hub.docker.com/u/microsoft/`. **Amazon Web Services (AWS)** has begun supporting Windows containers, providing a more direct way for older applications to jump into the cloud.

Windows containers provide the same advantages as Linux containers for applications that run on Windows. Windows containers support the Docker image format and Docker API. However, they can also be managed using PowerShell. Two container runtimes are available with Windows containers, Windows Server containers, and Hyper-V containers. Hyper-V containers provide an additional layer of isolation by hosting each container in a super-optimized VM.

This addresses the security concerns of running containers on top of an OS. Further, it also enhances the container density in a compute instance. That is, by running multiple containers in Hyper-V VMs, you can effectively take your density count to another level and run hundreds of containers on a single host. Windows containers are just Docker containers. Currently, you can deploy Windows containers in Windows Server 2016 (Full, Core, or Nano Server Editions), Windows 10 (Enterprise and Professional Editions), as well as Azure. You can deploy and manage these containers from any Docker client, including the Windows command line when the Docker Engine is installed. You can also manage them from PowerShell, which is open source software.

In this book, we have focused on the Docker CE.

Installing the Docker Engine

The Docker Engine is built on top of the Linux kernel and it extensively leverages Linux kernel features such as namespaces and cgroups. Due to the burgeoning popularity of Docker, it is now being packaged by all the major Linux distributions so that they can retain their loyal users as well as attract new users. You can install the Docker Engine using the corresponding packaging tool of the Linux distribution, for example, using the `apt-get` command for Debian and Ubuntu, and the `yum` command for Red Hat, Fedora, and CentOS. Alternatively, you can use the fully automated install script, which will do all the hard work for you behind the scenes.

If you are a Mac or Microsoft Windows user, you can run Docker on Linux emulations (VMs). There are multiple solutions available to run Docker using Linux VM, which is explained in a later subsection. Docker and Microsoft are working towards supporting native Windows containers to run a native Windows application, which is outside the scope of this book.

 For all practical purposes, we have chosen the Ubuntu 16.04 LTS (Xenial Xerus) (64-bit) Linux distribution.

Installing Docker on Ubuntu

Docker is currently supported only on 64-bit architecture Linux and the Linux kernel must be 3.10 or later. At the time of writing this book, the latest version of the Docker was 17.03.0-ce. The following steps prescribe the installation procedure of the Docker Engine on Ubuntu Linux 16.04 in detail:

1. First, the best practice for installing any software in Ubuntu begins with the resynchronization of the package repository. This step will essentially update the package repository in line with the latest published packages, thus we will ensure that we always get the latest published version using the command shown here:

   ```
   $ sudo apt-get update
   ```

Downloading the example code

You can download the example code files from your account at
http://www.packtpub.com for all the Packt Publishing books you have
purchased. If you purchased this book elsewhere, you can visit
http://www.packtpub.com/support and register to have the files e-
mailed directly to you.

2. Add the Docker package repository path for Ubuntu 16.04 to your APT sources,
   as shown here:

```
$ sudo sh -c "echo deb https://apt.dockerproject.org/repo \
ubuntu-xenial main > /etc/apt/sources.list.d/docker.list"
```

3. Add the **GNU Privacy Guard** (**GPG**) key by running the following command:

```
$ sudo apt-key adv --keyserver \
 hkp://p80.pool.sks-keyservers.net:80 --recv-keys \
 58118E89F3A912897C070ADBF76221572C52609D
```

4. Resynchronize with the package repository using the following command:

```
$ sudo apt-get update
```

5. Install Docker and start the Docker service:

```
$ sudo apt-get install -y docker-engine
```

6. Having installed the Docker Engine, let's verify our installation by running
   docker --version as shown here:

```
$ docker --version
Docker version 17.03.0-ce, build 60ccb22
```

Hurrah!! We have successfully installed Docker version 17.03.0 community edition.

Installing Docker using an automated script

In the previous section, we installed the Docker Engine by manually configuring the GPG key, APT repository, and so on. However, the Docker community has taken a step forward by hiding all these details in an automated install script. This script enables the installation of Docker on most popular Linux distributions, either through the `curl` command or through the `wget` command, as shown here:

- For the `curl` command:

```
$ sudo curl -sSL https://get.docker.io/ | sh
```

- For the `wget` command:

```
$ sudo wget -qO- https://get.docker.io/ | sh
```

 The preceding automated script approach enforces AUFS as the underlying Docker filesystem because AUFS is preferred over `devicemapper`. This script probes the AUFS driver, and then installs it automatically if it is not found in the system. In addition, it also conducts some basic tests upon installation for verifying the sanity.

Installing Docker on the Mac

On a Mac system, you can run Docker on Linux VM. Tools such as Vagrant and Docker Toolbox are quite handy to emulate Linux on Mac and in turn run Docker on it. Docker recently released Docker on Mac as a Beta, using the `xhyve` hypervisor to provide the Linux emulation. The `xhyve` hypervisor virtualizes the Docker Engine environment and Linux kernel-specific features for the Docker daemon.

 It is always recommended that you use Docker for Mac for supported OS X versions 10.10.3, Yosemite or newer.

The following steps describe the installation of Docker for Mac:

1. Download Docker for Mac from the link
   `https://download.docker.com/mac/beta/Docker.dmg`.

2. Double-click to download `Docker.dmg` and move it, as shown here:

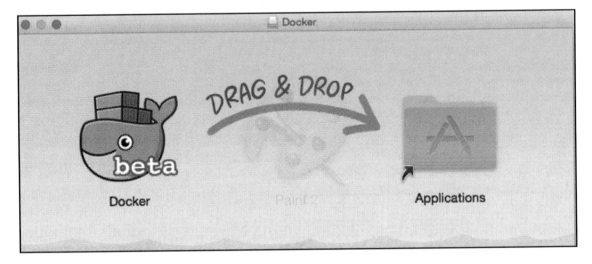

3. Now, double-click on `Docker.app` in `Applications` and it will install all Docker components. During installation, it will ask for the machine's administrative password to install the software.

4. Upon successful installation, the whale icon will appear in the top status bar:

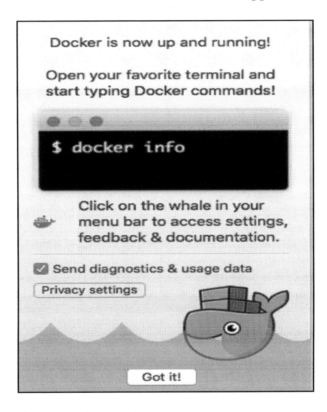

5. Finally, verify the Docker versions:

```
$ docker --version
Docker version 17.03.0-ce, build 60ccb22
$ docker-compose --version
docker-compose version 1.11.2, build dfed245
$ docker-machine --version
docker-machine version 0.10.0, build 76ed2a6
```

Installing Docker on Windows

As with the Mac, on Windows, you can also run Docker on Linux VMs using tools such as Vagrant and Docker Toolbox. Recently, Docker released a Beta version of Docker for Windows, which uses Hyper-V to virtualize the Docker Engine and Linux kernel-specific features that are essential to run the Docker Engine.

At the time of writing this book, Docker on Windows is supported only on 64-bit Windows 10 Enterprise and Education (1511 November update, Build 10586 or later). In the future, Docker will support more versions of Windows 10. Be aware that the Hyper-V package must be enabled.

It is always recommended that you use Docker native if you have a supported Windows 10 operating system. The following steps are required to install Docker on Windows:

1. Download the Docker for Windows installer from
   `https://download.docker.com/win/beta/InstallDocker.msi`.

2. Double-click on `InstallDocker.msi`; the installation wizard will start. It will ask for the Windows administrative password to complete the installation:

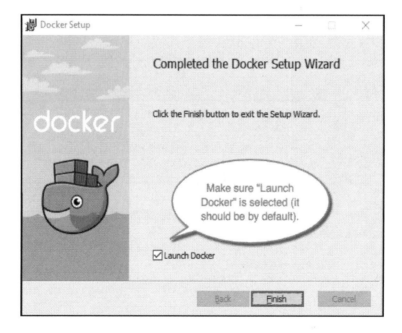

3. Docker starts automatically and the whale will appear in the status bar:

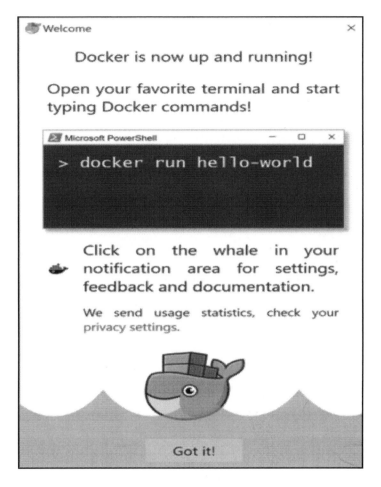

4. Finally, verify the Docker versions:

```
$ docker --version
Docker version 17.03.0-ce, build 60ccb22
$ docker-compose --version
docker-compose version 1.11.2, build dfed245
$ docker-machine --version
docker-machine version 0.10.0, build 76ed2a6
```

For other versions of Windows, you can install Docker Toolbox
from `https://docs.docker.com/toolbox/overview/`. The Docker Toolbox runs
Boot2Docker, a lightweight Linux VM on the Oracle VirtualBox hypervisor and installs the
Docker Engine on top of it.

Understanding the Docker setup

It is important to understand the Docker components and their versions, storage, and the
execution drivers, the file locations, and so on. Incidentally, the quest for understanding the
Docker setup will also reveal whether the installation was successful or not. You can
accomplish this using two Docker subcommands: `docker version` and `docker info`.

Let's start our Docker journey with the `docker version` subcommand, as shown here:

```
$ sudo docker version
Client:
 Version:      17.03.0-ce
 API version:  1.26
 Go version:   go1.7.5
 Git commit:   60ccb22
 Built:        Thu Feb 23 10:57:47 2017
 OS/Arch:      linux/amd64

Server:
 Version:      17.03.0-ce
 API version:  1.26 (minimum version 1.12)
 Go version:   go1.7.5
 Git commit:   60ccb22
 Built:        Thu Feb 23 10:57:47 2017
 OS/Arch:      linux/amd64
 Experimental: false
```

Although the `docker version` subcommand lists many lines of text, as a Docker user you
should know what these following output lines mean:

- The client version
- The client API version
- The server version
- The server API version

Here, both the client and server are of community edition 17.03.0 and the client API and the
server API of version 1.26.

If we dissect the internals of the `docker version` subcommand, then it will first list the client-related information that is stored locally. Subsequently, it will make a REST API call to the server over HTTP to obtain server-related details.

Learn more about the Docker environment using the `docker info` subcommand:

```
● ● ● ●    ubuntu4docker — ubuntu@ubuntu-xenial: ~ — ssh ‹ vagrant s...
$ sudo docker info
Containers: 0
 Running: 0
 Paused: 0
 Stopped: 0
Images: 0
Server Version: 17.03.0-ce
Storage Driver: aufs
 Root Dir: /var/lib/docker/aufs
 Backing Filesystem: extfs
 Dirs: 0
 Dirperm1 Supported: true
Logging Driver: json-file
Cgroup Driver: cgroupfs
Plugins:
 Volume: local
 Network: bridge host macvlan null overlay
Swarm: inactive
Runtimes: runc
Default Runtime: runc
Init Binary: docker-init
containerd version: 977c511eda0925a723debdc94d09459af49d082a
runc version: a01dafd48bc1c7cc12bdb01206f9fea7dd6feb70
init version: 949e6fa
Security Options:
 apparmor
 seccomp
  Profile: default
Kernel Version: 4.4.0-66-generic
Operating System: Ubuntu 16.04.2 LTS
OSType: linux
Architecture: x86_64
CPUs: 2
Total Memory: 992.2 MiB
Name: ubuntu-xenial
ID: GMHP:5H3Z:CLSD:ZJMY:3KTP:6270:BNFN:GSCX:QUOJ:CNGE:GIH3:SPIO
Docker Root Dir: /var/lib/docker
Debug Mode (client): false
Debug Mode (server): false
Registry: https://index.docker.io/v1/
WARNING: No swap limit support
Experimental: false
Insecure Registries:
 127.0.0.0/8
Live Restore Enabled: false
$
```

As you can see, in the output of a freshly installed Docker Engine, the number of Containers and Images is invariably nil. The Storage Driver has been set up as aufs, and the directory has been given the /var/lib/docker/aufs location. The runtime has been set to runc. This command also lists details, such as Logging Driver, Cgroups Driver, Kernel Version, Operating System, CPUs, and Total Memory.

Client-server communication

On Linux installations, Docker is usually programmed to carry out the server-client communication using the Unix socket (/var/run/docker.sock). Docker also has an IANA-registered port, which is 2375. However, for security reasons, this port is not enabled by default.

Downloading the first Docker image

Having installed the Docker Engine successfully, the next logical step is to download the images from the Docker Registry. The Docker Registry is an application repository that hosts various applications, ranging from basic Linux images to advanced applications. The docker pull subcommand is used to download any number of images from the registry. In this section, we will download a sample hello-world image using the following command:

```
$ sudo docker pull hello-world
Using default tag: latest
latest: Pulling from library/hello-world
78445dd45222: Pull complete
Digest:
sha256:c5515758d4c5e1e838e9cd307f6c6a0d620b5e07e6f927b07d05f6d12a1ac8d7
Status: Downloaded newer image for hello-world:latest
```

Once the images have been downloaded, they can be verified using the docker images subcommand, as shown here:

```
$ sudo docker images
REPOSITORY     TAG      IMAGE ID        CREATED        VIRTUAL SIZE
hello-world    latest   48b5124b2768    6 weeks ago    1.84 kB
```

Running the first Docker container

Now you can start your first Docker container as shown here:

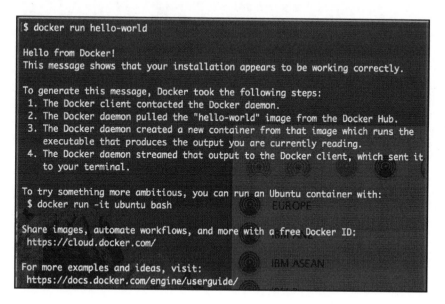

```
$ docker run hello-world

Hello from Docker!
This message shows that your installation appears to be working correctly.

To generate this message, Docker took the following steps:
 1. The Docker client contacted the Docker daemon.
 2. The Docker daemon pulled the "hello-world" image from the Docker Hub.
 3. The Docker daemon created a new container from that image which runs the
    executable that produces the output you are currently reading.
 4. The Docker daemon streamed that output to the Docker client, which sent it
    to your terminal.

To try something more ambitious, you can run an Ubuntu container with:
 $ docker run -it ubuntu bash

Share images, automate workflows, and more with a free Docker ID:
 https://cloud.docker.com/

For more examples and ideas, visit:
 https://docs.docker.com/engine/userguide/
```

Cool, isn't it? You have set up your first Docker container in no time. In the preceding example, the `docker run` subcommand has been used to create a container from the `hello-world` image.

Troubleshooting Docker containers

Most of the times you will not encounter any issues when installing Docker. However, unexpected failures might occur. Therefore, it is necessary to discuss the prominent troubleshooting techniques and tips. Let's begin by discussing troubleshooting know-how in this section. The first tip is that Docker's running status should be checked using the following command:

```
$ sudo service docker status
```

If the Docker service is up-and-running, the `Active` column (the third from the top) will list the status of the Docker service as `active (running)`, as shown next:

```
 docker.service - Docker Application Container Engine
   Loaded: loaded (/lib/systemd/system/docker.service; enabled; vendor preset: enabled)
   Active: active (running) since Thu 2017-02-23 10:52:39 UTC; 2 days ago
     Docs: https://docs.docker.com
 Main PID: 29327 (dockerd)
    Tasks: 22
   Memory: 31.6M
      CPU: 1min 18.943s
   CGroup: /system.slice/docker.service
           ├─29327 /usr/bin/dockerd -H fd://
           └─29336 docker-containerd -l unix:///var/run/docker/libcontainerd/docker-containerd
```

However, if the `Active` column shows `inactive` or `maintenance` as the status, your Docker service is not running. In such cases, restart the Docker service, as shown here:

```
$ sudo service docker restart
```

If you are still experiencing issues with the Docker setup, then you must extract the Docker log, using the `journalctl -u docker` command, for further investigation.

Summary

In a way, Docker containers are the lightweight, loosely-coupled, and nimble cousins of VMs. As elucidated before, containers enable packaging an application along with all of its dependencies compactly and shipping it elsewhere, running it smoothly in development, test, and production environments. Docker harnesses some powerful kernel-level features intelligently and provides a growing ecosystem of tools for realizing and running containers in an automated fashion. The end result is a potential game-changer for distributed application developers and system administrators. With hybrid clouds as the toast of worldwide enterprises for their IT needs, the Docker platform is a blessing in disguise for enterprise IT teams. Containers are typical sandboxes, isolating processes from each other. Docker does a nice and neat job of advancing the containerization paradigm for a slew of purposes such as lightweight packaging, frictionless shipping, faster deployment, and more rapid delivery of software applications.

The next chapter throws more light on the operational aspects of Docker containers, especially the sagacious handling of containers in order to produce real-world Dockerized applications.

2
Handling Docker Containers

In the previous chapter, we explained the stimulating and sustainable concepts that clearly articulated Docker's way of crafting futuristic and flexible application-aware containers. We discussed all the relevant details of bringing Docker containers into multiple environments (on-premise as well as off-premise). You can easily replicate these Docker capabilities in your own environments to get a rewarding experience. Now, the next logical step for us is to understand container life cycle aspects in a decisive manner. You are to learn the optimal utilization of your own containers as well as those of other third-party containers in an efficient and risk-free way. Containers are to be found, accessed, assessed, and leveraged toward bigger and better distributed applications.

In this chapter, we will dig deeper and describe the critical aspects of container handling at length. A number of practical tips and execution commands for leveraging containers will also be discussed for the benefit of readers.

In this chapter, we will cover the following topics:

- Clarifying Docker terms
- Working with Docker images and containers
- The meaning of the Docker Registry and its repository
- The Docker Hub Registry
- Searching Docker images
- Working with an interactive container
- Tracking changes inside the containers
- Controlling and housekeeping Docker containers
- Building images from containers
- Launching a container as a daemon

Clarifying Docker terms

For substantially simplifying the understandability of this chapter and for minimizing any kind of ambiguity, frequently used terms are explained in the following section.

Docker images

A **Docker image** is a collection of all the files that make up an executable software application. This collection includes the application plus all the libraries, binaries, and other dependencies such as the deployment descriptor, just needed to run the application everywhere without hitch or hurdle. These files in the Docker image are read-only and hence the content of the image cannot be altered. If you choose to alter the content of your image, the only option Docker allows is to add another layer with the new changes. In other words, a Docker image is made up of layers, which you can review using the `docker history` subcommand, as explained in `Chapter 3`, *Building Images*.

The Docker image architecture effectively leverages this layering concept to seamlessly add additional capabilities to the existing images in order to meet varying business requirements and also increase the reuse of images. In other words, capabilities can be added to the existing images by adding additional layers on top of that image and deriving a new image. Docker images have a parent-child relationship and the bottom-most image is called the **base image**. The base image is a special image that doesn't have any parent:

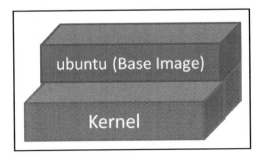

In the preceding diagram, `ubuntu` is a base image and it does not have any parent image.

Ubuntu is a Debian-based Linux operating system. The Ubuntu Docker image is a minimalist bundle of software libraries and binaries that are critical to run an application. It does not include the Linux kernel, device drivers, and various other services a full-fledged Ubuntu operating system would provide.

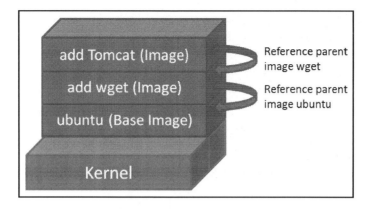

As you can see in the preceding figure, everything starts with a base image and here in this example, it is ubuntu. Further on, the wget capability is added to the image as a layer and the wget image is referencing the ubuntu image as its parent. In the next layer, an instance of the Tomcat application server is added and it refers the wget image as its parent. Each addition that is made to the original base image is stored in a separate layer (a kind of hierarchy gets generated here to retain the original identity). Precisely speaking, any Docker image has to originate from a base image and an image gets continuously enriched in its functionality by getting fresh modules, and this is accomplished by adding an additional module as a new layer on the existing Docker image one by one, as vividly illustrated in the preceding figure.

The Docker platform provides a simple way for building new images or extending existing images. You can also download the Docker images that other people have already created and deposited in the Docker image repositories (private or public). Every image has a unique ID, as explained in the following section.

Docker containers

Docker images are a read-only template of the application stack bundle and they don't have any state associated with them. The Docker container is spun off from the Docker image and it adds a read-write layer on top of the static image layers. If we try to draw a comparison with the object-oriented programming paradigm, Docker images are typically classes, whereas Docker containers are objects (instances of the classes).

The Docker image defines the behavior of the Docker container such as what process to run when the container is started. In the previous chapter, when you invoked `docker run hello-world`, the Docker Engine launched a new container from the `hello-world` Docker image and it went on to output quite a lot of information on the screen. From this example, it is quite evident that Docker images are the basic building block for Docker containers and Docker images prescribe the behavior of Docker containers.

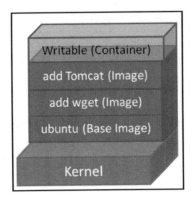

As clearly illustrated in the preceding figure, when the container is spun-off, a writeable (read-write) layer is added on top of the image in order to maintain the application state. There could be several read-only images beneath the container layer (writeable).

Docker Registry

A **Docker Registry** is a place where Docker images can be stored in order to be publicly or privately found, accessed, and used by software developers worldwide for quickly crafting fresh and composite applications without any risks. Because all the stored images will have gone through multiple validations, verifications, and refinements, the quality of those images is really high. You can dispatch your Docker image to the registry so that it is registered and deposited using the `docker push` subcommand. You can download Docker images from the registry using the `docker pull` subcommand.

Docker Registry could be hosted by a third party as a public or private registry, like one of the following registries:

- Docker Hub
- Quay
- Google Container Registry
- AWS Container Registry

Every institution, innovator, and individual can have their own Docker Registry to stock up their images for internal and/or external access and usage.

Working with Docker images

In the previous chapter, we demonstrated the typical *Hello World* example using the `hello-world` image. Now, there is a need for a closer observation of the output of the `docker pull` subcommand, which is the de facto command to download Docker images. Now, in this section, we will use the `busybox` image, one of the smallest but a very handy Docker image, to dive deep into Docker image handling:

```
$ sudo docker pull busybox
Using default tag: latest
latest: Pulling from library/busybox
8ddc19f16526: Pull complete
Digest: sha256:a59906e33509d14c036c8678d687bd4eec81ed7c4b8ce907b888c607f6a1e0e6
Status: Downloaded newer image for busybox:latest
$
```

If you pay close attention to the output of the `docker pull` subcommand, you will notice the `Using default tag: latest` text. The Docker image management capability (the local image storage on your Docker host or on a Docker image registry) enables storing multiple variants of the Docker image. In other words, you could use tags to version your images.

By default, Docker always uses the image that is tagged as `latest`. Each image variant can be directly identified by qualifying it with an appropriate tag. An image can be tag-qualified by adding a colon (`:`) between the tag and the repository name (`<repository>:<tag>`). For demonstration, we will pull the `1.24` tagged version of `busybox` as shown here:

```
$ sudo docker pull busybox:1.24
1.24: Pulling from library/busybox

385e281300cc: Pull complete
a3ed95caeb02: Pull complete
Digest: sha256:8ea3273d79b47a8b6d018be398c17590a4b5ec604515f416c5b797db9dde3ad8
Status: Downloaded newer image for busybox:1.24
```

Awesome! Isn't it? We are able to pull a specific version of `busybox`; in this case, it is `busybox:1.24`. The `docker pull` command also supports the `-a` option to download all available image variants. Use this option cautiously because you might end up filling up your disk space.

So far, we downloaded a few Docker images from the repository, and now they are locally available in the Docker host. You can find out the images that are available on the Docker host by running the `docker images` subcommand:

```
$ sudo docker images
REPOSITORY          TAG           IMAGE ID          CREATED
SIZE
hello-world         latest        c54a2cc56cbb      3 weeks ago
1.848 kB
busybox             latest        2b8fd9751c4c      4 weeks ago
1.093 MB
busybox             1.24          47bcc53f74dc      4 months ago
1.113 MB
```

Evidently, we have three items in the preceding list and to gain a better understanding of these, we need to comprehend the information that is printed out by the `docker images` subcommand. Here is a list of the possible categories:

- `REPOSITORY`: This is the name of the repository or image. In the preceding example, the repository names are `hello-world` and `busybox`.
- `TAG`: This is the tag associated with the image, for example `1.24` and `latest`. One or more tags can be associated with one image.

- `IMAGE ID`: Every image is associated with a unique ID. The image ID is represented using a 64 hex digit long random number. By default, the `docker images` subcommand will only show 12 hex digits. You can display all the 64 hex digits using the `--no-trunc` flag (for example: `sudo docker images --no-trunc`).
- `CREATED`: This indicates the time when the image was created.
- `SIZE`: This category highlights the virtual size of the image.

The Docker Hub

In the previous section, when you ran the `docker pull` subcommand, the `busybox` image got downloaded mysteriously. In this section, let's unravel the mystery around the `docker pull` subcommand and how the Docker Hub immensely contributed toward this unintended success.

The good folks in the Docker community have built a repository of images and they have made it publicly available at a default location, `index.docker.io`. This default location is called the **Docker Hub**. The `docker pull` subcommand is programmed to look for images at this location. Thus, when you pull a `busybox` image, it is effortlessly downloaded from the default registry. This mechanism helps in speeding up the spinning of Docker containers. The Docker Hub is the official repository that contains all the painstakingly curated images that are created and deposited by the worldwide Docker development community. This so-called cure is implemented for ensuring that all the images stored in the Docker Hub are secure and safe through a host of quarantine tasks. There are additional mechanisms, such as creating the image digest and having content trust, which gives you the ability to verify both the integrity and the publisher of all the data received from a registry over any channel.

There are proven verification and validation methods for cleaning up any knowingly or unknowingly introduced malware, adware, viruses, and so on, from these Docker images. The digital signature is a prominent mechanism of the utmost integrity of the Docker images. Nonetheless, if the official image has been either corrupted or tampered with, then the Docker Engine will issue a warning and then continue to run the image.

In addition to the official repository, the Docker Hub Registry also provides a platform for third-party developers and providers for sharing their images for general consumption. The third-party images are prefixed by the user ID of their developers or depositors. For example, `thedockerbook/helloworld` is a third-party image, wherein `thedockerbook` is the user ID and `helloworld` is the image repository name. You can download any third-party image using the `docker pull` subcommand, as shown here:

```
$ sudo docker pull thedockerbook/helloworld
```

Apart from the preceding repository, the Docker ecosystem also provides a mechanism for leveraging images from any third-party repository hub other than the Docker Hub Registry, and it also provides the images hosted by the local repository hubs. As mentioned earlier, the Docker Engine has been programmed to look for images at `index.docker.io` by default, whereas in the case of third-party or the local repository hub we must manually specify the path from where the image should be pulled. A manual repository path is similar to a URL without a protocol specifier, such as `https://`, `http://`, and `ftp://`. The following is an example of pulling an image from a third-party repository hub:

```
$ sudo docker pull registry.example.com/myapp
```

Searching Docker images

As we discussed in the previous section, the Docker Hub repository typically hosts both official images as well as images that have been contributed by third-party Docker enthusiasts. At the time of writing this book, thousands of curated Docker images (also called the **Dockerized application)** were available for users. Most of them are downloaded by millions of users. These images can be used either as-is or as a building block for user-specific applications.

You can search for Docker images in the Docker Hub Registry using the `docker search` subcommand, as shown in this example:

```
$ sudo docker search mysql
```

The search on `mysql` will list many `mysql` images, but we will limit it to just five lines by piping it with the `head -10` command, as follows:

```
$ sudo docker search mysql | head -10
NAME                    DESCRIPTION                              STARS    OFFICIAL    AUTOMATED
mysql                   MySQL is a widely used, open-source relati...  2759  [OK]
mysql/mysql-server      Optimized MySQL Server Docker images. Crea...  178                 [OK]
centurylink/mysql       Image containing mysql. Optimized to be li...  46                  [OK]
sameersbn/mysql                                                  36                  [OK]
appcontainers/mysql     Centos/Debian Based Customizable MySQL Con...  8                   [OK]
marvambass/mysql        MySQL Server based on Ubuntu 14.04             6                   [OK]
alterway/mysql          Docker Mysql                                   2                   [OK]
drupaldocker/mysql      MySQL for Drupal                               2                   [OK]
azukiapp/mysql          Docker image to run MySQL by Azuki - http:...  2                   [OK]
<
```

As you can see in the preceding search output excerpts, the images are ordered based on their star rating. The search result also indicates whether the image is an official image (curated and hosted by Docker Inc) or not. The search result also indicates whether the image is built using the automation framework provided by Docker Inc. The `mysql` image curated and hosted by Docker Inc has a `2759` star rating, which indicated that this is the most popular `mysql` image. We strongly recommend that you use the images that are officially hosted by Docker Inc for security reasons, otherwise make sure that the images are provided by trusted and well-known sources. The next image in the list is `mysql-server`, made available by the third party, `mysql`, with a `178` star rating. Docker containers are the standard building blocks of distributed applications.

A dynamic repository of Docker images is being realized with the help of the enthusiastic contribution of several community members across the Globe. Software engineers can download the images stocked in the Docker Hub and come out with different images and containers to exceptionally cater for differing business needs. This sort of arrangement is to elegantly automate and accelerate the building, deployment, and usage of software applications. The Docker Hub represents a community effort for providing a great base of images for applications, so that developers and system administrators can focus on building new features and functionalities, while minimizing their repetitive work on commodity scaffolding and plumbing.

Based on the search queries in the Docker Hub Registry and discussions with many of the developer community members, the Docker company, which spearheaded the Docker movement so powerfully and passionately, came to the conclusion that the developer community wanted prebuilt stacks of their favorite programming languages. Specifically, the developers wanted to get to work as quickly as possible, writing code without wasting time and wrestling with environments, scaffolding, and dependencies.

Working with an interactive container

In the first chapter, we ran our first *Hello World* container to get a feel for how the containerization technology works. In this section, we are going to run a container in interactive mode. The docker run subcommand takes an image as an input and launches it as a container. You have to pass the -t and -i flags to the docker run subcommand in order to make the container interactive. The -i flag is the key driver, which makes the container interactive by grabbing the standard input (STDIN) of the container. The -t flag allocates a pseudo-TTY or a pseudo Terminal (Terminal emulator) and then assigns that to the container.

In the following example, we are going to launch an interactive container using the ubuntu:16.04 image and /bin/bash as the command:

```
$ sudo docker run -i -t ubuntu:16.04 /bin/bash
```

Since the ubuntu image has not been downloaded yet, if we use the docker pull subcommand, then we will get the following message and the docker run command will start pulling the ubuntu image automatically with following message:

```
Unable to find image 'ubuntu:16.04' locally
16.04: Pulling from library/ubuntu
```

As soon as the download is completed, the container will get launched along with the ubuntu:16.04 image. It will also launch a Bash shell within the container, because we have specified /bin/bash as the command to be executed. This will land us in a Bash prompt, as shown here:

```
root@742718c21816:/#
```

The preceding Bash prompt will confirm that our container has been launched successfully and it is ready to take our input. If you are wondering about the hex number 742718c21816 in the prompt, then it is nothing but the hostname of the container. In Docker parlance, the hostname is the same as the container ID.

Let's quickly run a few commands interactively and confirm what we mentioned about the prompt is correct, as shown here:

```
root@742718c21816:/# hostname
742718c21816
root@742718c21816:/# id
uid=0(root) gid=0(root) groups=0(root)
root@742718c21816:/# echo $PS1
[e]0;u@h: wa]${debian_chroot:+($debian_chroot)}u@h:w$
root@742718c21816:/#
```

From the preceding three commands, it is quite evident that the prompt was composed using the user ID, hostname, and current working directory.

Now, let's use one of the niche features of Docker for detaching it from the interactive container and then look at the details that Docker manages for this container. Yes, we can detach it from our container using the *Ctrl + P* and *Ctrl + Q* escape sequence. This escape sequence will detach the TTY from the container and land us in the Docker host prompt $; however, the container will continue to run. The docker ps subcommand will list all the running containers and their important properties, as shown here:

```
$ sudo docker ps
CONTAINER ID         IMAGE              COMMAND             CREATED
STATUS               PORTS              NAMES
742718c21816         ubuntu:16.04       "/bin/bash"         About a
minute ago     Up About a minute       jolly_lovelace
```

The docker ps subcommand will list out the following details:

- CONTAINER ID: This shows the container ID associated with the container. The container ID is a 64 hex digit long random number. By default, the docker ps subcommand will show only 12 hex digits. You can display all the 64 digits using the --no-trunc flag (For example, sudo docker ps --no-trunc).
- IMAGE: This shows the image from which the Docker container has been crafted.
- COMMAND: This shows you the command executed during the container launch.
- CREATED: This tells you when the container was created.
- STATUS: This tells you the current status of the container.
- PORTS: This tells you if any port has been assigned to the container.
- NAMES: The Docker Engine auto-generates a random container name by concatenating an adjective and a noun. Either the container ID or its name can be used to take further action on the container. The container name can be manually configured using the --name option in the docker run subcommand.

Having looked at the container status, let's attach back to our container using the docker attach subcommand, as shown in the following example. We can either use the container ID or its name. In this example, we have used the container name. If you don't see the prompt, then press the *Enter* key again:

```
$ sudo docker attach jolly_lovelace
root@742718c21816:/#
```

Docker allows attaching with a container any number of times, which proves to be very handy for screen sharing.

The `docker attach` subcommand takes us back to the container prompt. Let's experiment a little more with the interactive container that is up-and-running using these commands:

```
root@742718c21816:/# pwd
/
root@742718c21816:/# ls
bin   dev home lib64  mnt  proc run  srv tmp  var
boot  etc lib  media  opt  root sbin sys usr
root@742718c21816:/# cd usr
root@742718c21816:/usr# ls
bin  games  include  lib  local  sbin  share  src
root@742718c21816:/usr# exit
exit
$
```

As soon as the Bash `exit` command is issued to the interactive container, it will terminate the Bash shell process, which in turn will stop the container. As a result, we will land on the Docker host's prompt `$`.

Tracking changes inside containers

In the previous section, we demonstrated how to craft a container taking `ubuntu` as a base image, and then running some basic commands, such as detaching and attaching the containers. In that process, we also exposed you to the `docker ps` subcommand, which provides the basic container management functionality. In this section, we will demonstrate how we can effectively track the changes that we introduced in our container and compare it with the image from which we launched the container. Let's launch a container in interactive mode, as in the previous section:

```
$ sudo docker run -i -t ubuntu:16.04 /bin/bash
```

Let's change the directory to `/home`, as shown here:

```
root@d5ad60f174d3:/# cd /home
```

Now, we can create three empty files using the `touch` command, as follows. The first `ls -l` command will show that there are no files in the directory and the second `ls -l` command will show that there are three empty files:

```
root@d5ad60f174d3:/home# ls -l
total 0
root@d5ad60f174d3:/home# touch {abc,cde,fgh}
root@d5ad60f174d3:/home# ls -l
total 0
-rw-r--r-- 1 root root 0 Sep 29 10:54 abc
-rw-r--r-- 1 root root 0 Sep 29 10:54 cde
-rw-r--r-- 1 root root 0 Sep 29 10:54 fgh
root@d5ad60f174d3:/home#
```

The Docker Engine elegantly manages its filesystem and it allows us to inspect a container filesystem using the `docker diff` subcommand. In order to inspect the container filesystem, we can either detach it from the container or use another Terminal of our Docker host and then issue the `docker diff` subcommand. Since we know that any `ubuntu` container has its hostname, which is a part of its prompt, and it is also the container's ID, we can directly run the `docker diff` subcommand using the container ID that is taken from the prompt, as shown here:

```
$ sudo docker diff d5ad60f174d3
```

In the given example, the `docker diff` subcommand will generate four lines, as shown here:

```
C /home
A /home/abc
A /home/cde
A /home/fgh
```

The preceding output indicates that the /home directory has been modified, which has been denoted by C, and the /home/abc, /home/cde, and /home/fgh files have been added, and these are denoted by A. In addition, D denotes deletion. Since we have not deleted any files, it is not in our sample output.

 When we work with an image and if we don't specify that image through an appropriate identity (say, a new name), then the `latest` image (recently generated) will always be identified and used by the Docker Engine.

Controlling Docker containers

So far, we have discussed a few practical examples to clearly articulate the nitty-gritty of Docker containers. In this section, we'll introduce a few basic as well as a few advanced command structures for meticulously illustrating how the Docker containers can be managed.

The Docker Engine enables you to `start`, `stop`, and `restart` a container with a set of `docker` subcommands. Let's begin with the `docker stop` subcommand, which stops a running container. When a user issues this command, the Docker Engine sends **SIGTERM** (-15) to the main process, which is running inside the container. The SIGTERM signal requests the process to terminate itself gracefully. Most processes would handle this signal and facilitate a graceful exit. However, if this process fails to do so, then the Docker Engine will wait for a grace period. After the grace period, if the process has not been terminated, then the Docker Engine will forcefully terminate the process. The forceful termination is achieved by sending **SIGKILL** (-9). The SIGKILL signal cannot be caught or ignored, and hence, it will result in an abrupt termination of the process without a proper clean-up.

Now, let's launch our container and experiment with the `docker stop` subcommand, as shown here:

```
$ sudo docker run -i -t ubuntu:16.04 /bin/bash
root@da1c0f7daa2a:/#
```

Having launched the container, let's run the `docker stop` subcommand on this container using the container ID that was taken from the prompt. Of course, we have to use a second screen/Terminal to run this command, and the command will always echo back to the container ID, as shown here:

```
$ sudo docker stop da1c0f7daa2a
da1c0f7daa2a
```

Now, if we switch to the screen/Terminal where we were running the container, we will notice that the container is being terminated. If you observe a little more keenly, then you will also notice the `exit` text next to the container prompt. This happened due to the SIGTERM handling mechanism of the Bash shell, as shown here:

```
root@da1c0f7daa2a:/# exit
$
```

If we take it one step further and run the `docker ps` subcommand, then we will not find this container anywhere in the list. The fact is that the `docker ps` subcommand, by default, always lists container that is in the running state. Since our container is in the stopped state, it was comfortably left out of the list. Now, you might ask, how do we see container that is in the stopped state? Well, the `docker ps` subcommand takes an additional argument −a, which will list all the containers in that Docker host irrespective of its status. This can be done by running the following command:

```
$ sudo docker ps -a
CONTAINER ID              IMAGE                    COMMAND
CREATED                   STATUS                   PORTS
NAMES
da1c0f7daa2a              ubuntu:16.04             "/bin/bash"
20 minutes ago            Exited (0) 10 minutes ago
desperate_engelbart
$
```

Next, let's look at the `docker start` subcommand, which is used for starting one or more stopped containers. A container can be moved to the stopped state either by the `docker stop` subcommand or by terminating the main process in the container either normally or abnormally. On a running container, this subcommand has no effect.

Let's start the previously stopped container using the `docker start` subcommand by specifying the container ID as an argument, as follows:

```
$ sudo docker start da1c0f7daa2a
da1c0f7daa2a
$
```

By default, the `docker start` subcommand will not attach to the container. You can attach it to the container either using the −a option in the `docker start` subcommand or by explicitly using the `docker attach` subcommand, as shown here:

```
$ sudo docker attach da1c0f7daa2a
root@da1c0f7daa2a:/#
```

Now, let's run `docker ps` and verify the container's running status, as shown here:

```
$ sudo docker ps
CONTAINER ID              IMAGE                    COMMAND
CREATED                   STATUS                   PORTS
NAMES
da1c0f7daa2a              ubuntu:16.04             "/bin/bash"
25 minutes ago            Up 3 minutes
desperate_engelbart
$
```

The `restart` command is a combination of the `stop` and the `start` functionality. In other words, the `restart` command will stop a running container by following the same steps followed by the `docker stop` subcommand and then it will initiate the `start` process. This functionality will be executed by default through the `docker restart` subcommand.

The next important set of container controlling subcommands are `docker pause` and `docker unpause`. The `docker pause` subcommand will essentially freeze the execution of all the processes within that container. Conversely, the `docker unpause` subcommand will unfreeze the execution of all the processes within that container and resume the execution from the point where it was frozen.

Having seen the technical explanation of `pause/unpause`, let's see a detailed example for illustrating how this feature works. We have used two screen/Terminal scenarios. On one Terminal, we have launched our container and used an infinite while loop for displaying the date and time, sleeping for 5 seconds, and then continuing the loop. We will run the following commands:

```
$ sudo docker run -i -t ubuntu:16.04 /bin/bash
root@c439077aa80a:/# while true; do date; sleep 5; done
Thu Oct  2 03:11:19 UTC 2016
Thu Oct  2 03:11:24 UTC 2016
Thu Oct  2 03:11:29 UTC 2016
Thu Oct  2 03:11:34 UTC 2016
Thu Oct  2 03:11:59 UTC 2016
Thu Oct  2 03:12:04 UTC 2016
Thu Oct  2 03:12:09 UTC 2016
Thu Oct  2 03:12:14 UTC 2016
Thu Oct  2 03:12:19 UTC 2016
Thu Oct  2 03:12:24 UTC 2016
Thu Oct  2 03:12:29 UTC 2016
Thu Oct  2 03:12:34 UTC 2016
```

Our little script has very faithfully printed the date and time every 5 seconds with an exception at the following position:

```
Thu Oct  2 03:11:34 UTC 2016
Thu Oct  2 03:11:59 UTC 2016
```

Here, we encountered a delay of 25 seconds because this is when we initiated the `docker pause` subcommand on our container on the second Terminal screen, as shown here:

```
$ sudo docker pause c439077aa80a
c439077aa80a
```

When we paused our container, we looked at the process status using the `docker ps` subcommand on our container, which was on the same screen, and it clearly indicated that the container had been paused, as shown in this command result:

```
$ sudo docker ps
CONTAINER ID                    IMAGE                 COMMAND
CREATED                         STATUS                PORTS              NAMES
c439077aa80a                    ubuntu:16.04          "/bin/bash"
47 seconds ago                  Up 46 seconds (Paused)
ecstatic_torvalds
```

We continued issuing the `docker unpause` subcommand, which unfroze our container, continued its execution, and then started printing the date and time, as we saw in the preceding command, as shown here:

```
$ sudo docker unpause c439077aa80a
c439077aa80a
```

We explained the `pause` and the `unpause` commands at the beginning of this section. Lastly, the container and the script running within it were stopped using the `docker stop` subcommand, as shown here:

```
$ sudo docker stop c439077aa80a
c439077aa80a
```

Housekeeping containers

In many of the previous examples, when we issued `docker ps -a`, we saw many stopped containers. These containers could continue to stay in the stopped status for ages if we chose not to intervene. At the outset, it may look like a glitch, but in reality, we can perform operations, such as committing an image from a container and restarting the stopped container. However, not all stopped containers will be reused again, and each of these unused containers will take up disk space in the filesystem of the Docker host. The Docker Engine provides a couple of ways to alleviate this issue. Let's start exploring them.

During a container startup, we can instruct the Docker Engine to clean up the container as soon as it reaches the stopped state. For this purpose, the `docker run` subcommand supports a `--rm` option (for example, `sudo docker run -i -t --rm ubuntu:16.04 /bin/bash`).

The other alternative is to list all the containers using the -a option of the docker ps subcommand and then manually remove them using the docker rm subcommand, as shown here:

```
$ sudo docker ps -a
CONTAINER ID          IMAGE          COMMAND          CREATED
STATUS                PORTS
NAMES
7473f2568add          ubuntu:16.04  "/bin/bash"   5 seconds ago
Exited (0) 3 seconds ago
jolly_wilson

$ sudo docker rm 7473f2568add
7473f2568add
$
```

Two Docker subcommands, that is, docker rm and docker ps, can be combined together for automatically deleting all the containers that are not currently running, as shown in the following command:

```
$ sudo docker rm $(sudo docker ps -aq)
```

In the preceding command, the command inside $() will produce a list of the full container IDs of every container, running or otherwise, which will become the argument for the docker rm subcommand. Unless forced with the -f option to do otherwise, the docker rm subcommand will only remove the container that is not in the running state. It will generate the following error for the running container and then continue to the next container on the list:

```
Error response from daemon: You cannot remove a running container.
Stop the container before attempting removal or use -f
```

Perhaps we could avoid the preceding error by filtering the containers that are in the Exited state using the filter (-f) option of the docker ps subcommand, as shown here:

```
$ sudo docker rm $(sudo docker ps -aq -f state=exited)
```

Feeling frustrated at typing such a long and complicated chain of commands? Here is the good news for you. The docker container prune subcommand comes in handy to remove all stopped containers. This functionality is introduced in Docker version 1.13 and here is a sample run of the docker container prune subcommand:

```
$ sudo docker container prune
WARNING! This will remove all stopped containers.
Are you sure you want to continue? [y/N] y
Deleted Containers:
9b1aaaf108d3922d1a503fe01e9024302f0434a3b387c450d3b302020966a13e
d43c75065c6147501a7bc62f418fe501eeabaddd8617d77a4b28b5807dfeaa89
1614c44092f1c358cbb248a49430e70b674b52b32b8a193da9bba9b7136d1640

Total reclaimed space: 0 B
```

Building images from containers

So far, we have crafted a handful of containers using the standard base images busybox and ubuntu. In this section, let's see how we can add more software to our base image on a running container and then convert that container into an image for future use.

Let's take ubuntu:16.04 as our base image, install the wget application, and then convert the running container to an image by performing the following steps:

1. Launch an ubuntu:16.04 container using the docker run subcommand, as shown here:

   ```
   $ sudo docker run -i -t ubuntu:16.04 /bin/bash
   ```

2. Having launched the container, let's quickly verify if wget is available for our image or not. We used the which command with wget as an argument for this purpose and in our case, it returns empty, which essentially means that it could not find any wget installation in this container. This command is run as follows:

   ```
   root@472c96295678:/# which wget
   root@472c96295678:/#
   ```

3. Now, let's move on to the next step, which involves the wget installation. Since it is a brand new ubuntu container, before installing wget we must synchronize it with the Ubuntu package repository, as shown here:

   ```
   root@472c96295678:/# apt-get update
   ```

4. Once the Ubuntu package repository synchronization is over, we can proceed toward installing wget, as shown here:

   ```
   root@472c96295678:/# apt-get install -y wget
   ```

5. Having completed the `wget` installation, let's confirm our installation of `wget` by invoking the `which` command with `wget` as an argument, as shown here:

```
root@472c96295678:/# which wget
/usr/bin/wget
root@472c96295678:/#
```

6. Installation of any software would alter the base image composition, which we can also trace using the `docker diff` subcommand introduced in the *Tracking changes inside containers* section. From a second Terminal/screen, we can issue the `docker diff` subcommand, as follows:

```
$ sudo docker diff 472c96295678
```

The preceding command would show a few hundred lines of modification to the `ubuntu` image. This modification includes the update on the package repository, `wget` binary, and the support files for `wget`.

7. Finally, let's move on to the most important step of committing the image. The `docker commit` subcommand can be performed on a running or a stopped container. When a commit is performed on a running container, the Docker Engine will pause the container during the `commit` operation in order to avoid any data inconsistency. We strongly recommend that you perform the `commit` operation on a stopped container. We can commit a container to an image with the `docker commit` subcommand, as shown here:

```
$ sudo docker commit 472c96295678 \
    learningdocker/ubuntu_wget
sha256:a530f0a0238654fa741813fac39bba2cc14457aee079a7ae1f
e1c64dc7e1ac25
```

We committed our image using the `learningdocker/ubuntu_wget` name.

We also saw how to create an image from a container, step by step. Now, let's quickly list the images on our Docker host and see if this newly created image is a part of the image list, using the following command:

```
$ sudo docker images
REPOSITORY                      TAG            IMAGE ID
CREATED                         VIRTUAL SIZE
learningdocker/ubuntu_wget      latest         a530f0a02386
48 seconds ago                  221.3 MB
busybox                         latest         e72ac664f4f0
2 days ago                      2.433 MB
```

```
ubuntu                    16.04          6b4e8a7373fe
2 days ago                194.8 MB
```

From the preceding `docker images` subcommand output, it is quite evident that our image creation from the container was quite successful.

Now that you have learned how to create an image from containers using a few easy steps, we encourage you to predominantly use this method for testing. The most elegant and the most recommended way of creating an image is to use the `Dockerfile` method, which will introduce in the next chapter.

Launching a container as a daemon

We already experimented with an interactive container, tracked the changes that were made to the containers, created images from the containers, and then gained insights in the containerization paradigm. Now, let's move on to understand the real workhorse of Docker technology. Yes that's right. In this section, we will walk you through the steps that are required for launching a container in detached mode; in other words, you will learn about the steps that are required for launching a container as a daemon. We will also view the text that is generated in the container.

The `docker run` subcommand supports the –d option, which will launch a container in detached mode, that is, it will launch a container as a daemon. For illustrating, let's resort to our date and time script, which we used in the `pause/unpause` container example, as shown here:

```
$ sudo docker run –d ubuntu \
    /bin/bash -c "while true; do date; sleep 5; done"
0137d98ee363b44f22a48246ac5d460c65b67e4d7955aab6cbb0379ac421269b
```

The `docker logs` subcommand is used for viewing the output generated by our daemon container, as shown here:

```
$ sudo docker logs \
0137d98ee363b44f22a48246ac5d460c65b67e4d7955aab6cbb0379ac421269b
Sat Oct  4 17:41:04 UTC 2016
Sat Oct  4 17:41:09 UTC 2016
Sat Oct  4 17:41:14 UTC 2016
Sat Oct  4 17:41:19 UTC 2016
```

Summary

In this chapter, we described required insights in the post-implementation phases, primarily regarding the operational aspect of Docker containers. We started the chapter by clarifying important terms, such as images, containers, registry, and repository, in order to enable you to acquire an unambiguous understanding of the concepts illustrated thereafter. We explained how to search for images in the Docker repository. We also discussed the operation and handling of Docker containers, how to track changes inside containers, and how to control and housekeep containers. In the next chapter, we will explain promising and potential techniques and tools for building Docker images in an easy-to-grasp manner.

3
Building Images

In the previous chapter, we explained the image and container handling, and its housekeeping techniques and tips in detail. In addition to that, we described the standard procedure for installing a software package on a Docker container and then converting the container into an image for future usage and maneuvering. This chapter is quite different from the previous ones and is included in this book to clearly describe how Docker images are built using `Dockerfile`, which is the standard way for building highly usable Docker images. Leveraging `Dockerfile` is the most competent way of building powerful images for the software development community.

We will cover the following topics in this chapter:

- Docker's integrated image building system
- A quick overview of the syntax of `Dockerfile`
- The `Dockerfile` build instructions
- A brief overview of the Docker image management

Docker's integrated image building system

Docker images are the fundamental building blocks of containers. These images could be very basic operating environments, such as `busybox` or `ubuntu`, as we found while experimenting with Docker in earlier chapters. Alternatively, the images can craft advanced application stacks for the enterprise and cloud IT environments. As we discussed in the previous chapter, we can craft an image manually by launching a container from a base image, install all the required applications, make the necessary configuration file changes, and then commit the container as an image.

As a better alternative, we can resort to the automated approach of crafting the images using `Dockerfile`, which is a text-based build script that contains special instructions in a sequence for building the correct and relevant images from the base images. The sequential instructions inside `Dockerfile` can include selecting the base image, installing the required application, adding the configuration and the data files, and automatically running the services as well as exposing those services to the external world. Thus, the `Dockerfile`-based automated build system has simplified the image-building process remarkably. It also offers a great deal of flexibility in organizing the build instructions and in visualizing the complete build process.

The Docker Engine tightly integrates this build process with the help of the `docker build` subcommand. In the client-server paradigm of Docker, the Docker server (or daemon) is responsible for the complete build process, and the Docker command-line interface is responsible for transferring the build context, including transferring `Dockerfile` to the daemon.

In order to have a sneak peak into the `Dockerfile` integrated build system, we will introduce you to a basic `Dockerfile` in this section. Then, we will explain the steps for converting that `Dockerfile` into an image, and then launch a container from that image. Our `Dockerfile` is made up of two instructions, as shown here:

```
$ cat Dockerfile
FROM busybox:latest
CMD echo Hello World!!
```

We will discuss these two instructions as follows:

- The first instruction is for choosing the base image selection. In this example, we select the `busybox:latest` image.
- The second instruction is for carrying out the `CMD` command, which instructs the container to execute `echo Hello World!!`.

Now, let's proceed towards generating a Docker image using the preceding `Dockerfile` by calling `docker build` along with the path of `Dockerfile`. In our example, we will invoke the `docker build` subcommand from the directory where we have stored `Dockerfile`, and the path will be specified by the following command:

```
$ sudo docker build .
```

After issuing the preceding command, the `build` process will begin by sending the build context to the daemon and then display the text shown here:

```
Sending build context to Docker daemon 2.048 kB
Step 1 : FROM busybox:latest
```

The `build` process will continue and after completing itself, will display the following:

```
Successfully built 0a2abe57c325
```

In the preceding example, the image was built with the `0a2abe57c325` image ID. Let's use this image to launch a container using the `docker run` subcommand, as follows:

```
$ sudo docker run 0a2abe57c325
Hello World!!
```

Cool, isn't it? With very little effort, we have been able to craft an image with `busybox` as the base image, and we have been able to extend that image to produce `Hello World!!`. This is a simple application, but the enterprise-scale images can also be realized using the same technology.

Now, let's look at the image details using the `docker images` subcommand, as shown here:

```
$ sudo docker images
REPOSITORY      TAG         IMAGE ID        CREATED         SIZE
<none>          <none>      0a2abe57c325    2 hours ago     1.11 MB
```

Here, you may be surprised to see that the image (`REPOSITORY`) and `TAG` name have been listed as `<none>`. This is because we did not specify any image or any `TAG` name when we built this image. You could specify an image name and optionally a `TAG` name using the `docker tag` subcommand, as shown here:

```
$ sudo docker tag 0a2abe57c325 busyboxplus
```

The alternative approach is to build the image with an image name during the `build` time using the `-t` option for the `docker build` subcommand, as shown here:

```
$ sudo docker build -t busyboxplus .
```

Since there is no change to the instructions in `Dockerfile`, the Docker Engine will efficiently reuse the old image that has the `0a2abe57c325` ID and update the image name to `busyboxplus`. By default, the build system applies `latest` as the tag name. This behavior can be modified by specifying the tag name after the image name by having a : separator placed between them. This means that, `<image name>:<tag name>` is the correct syntax for modifying behaviors, wherein `<image name>` is the name of the image and `<tag name>` is the name of the tag.

Once again, let's look at the image details using the `docker images` subcommand, and you will notice that the image (repository) name is `busyboxplus` and the tag name is `latest`:

```
$ sudo docker images
REPOSITORY       TAG        IMAGE ID          CREATED          VIRTUAL SIZE
busyboxplus      latest     0a2abe57c325      2 hours ago
2.433 MB
```

Building images with an image name is always recommended as the best practice.

Having experienced the magic of `Dockerfile`, we will introduce you to the syntax or the format of `Dockerfile` and explain a dozen `Dockerfile` instructions in the subsequent sections.

 By default, the `docker build` subcommand uses `Dockerfile` located at the build context. However, with the `-f` option, the `docker build` subcommand allows us to specify an alternate `Dockerfile` at a different path or name.

A quick overview of the Dockerfile's syntax

In this section, we will explain the syntax or the format of `Dockerfile`. A `Dockerfile` is made up of instructions, comments, parser directives, and empty lines, as shown here:

```
# Comment

INSTRUCTION arguments
```

The instruction line of `Dockerfile` is made up of two components, where the instruction line begins with the `INSTRUCTION` itself, which is followed by the arguments for the instruction. The `INSTRUCTION` can be written in any case, in other words, it is case-insensitive. However, the standard practice or the convention is to use *uppercase* in order to differentiate it from the arguments. Let's relook at the content of `Dockerfile` in our previous example:

```
FROM busybox:latest
CMD echo Hello World!!
```

Here, `FROM` is an instruction that has taken `busybox:latest` as an argument and `CMD` is an instruction that has taken `echo Hello World!!` as an argument.

The comment line

The comment line in `Dockerfile` must begin with the # symbol. The # symbol after an instruction is considered as an argument. If the # symbol is preceded by a whitespace, then the `docker build` system will consider this as an unknown instruction and skip the line. Now, understand the preceding cases with the help of an example to get a better understanding of the comment line:

- A valid `Dockerfile` comment line always begins with a # symbol as the first character of the line:

  ```
  # This is my first Dockerfile comment
  ```

- The # symbol can be part of an argument:

  ```
  CMD echo ### Welcome to Docker ###
  ```

- If the # symbol is preceded by a whitespace, then it is considered as an unknown instruction by the build system:

  ```
  # this is an invalid comment line
  ```

The `docker build` system ignores any empty line in the `Dockerfile` and hence, the author of `Dockerfile` is encouraged to add comments and empty lines to substantially improve the readability of `Dockerfile`.

The parser directives

As the name implies, the parser directives instruct the `Dockerfile` parser to handle the content of `Dockerfile` as specified in the directives. The parser directives are optional and must be at the top of a `Dockerfile`. Currently, escape is the only supported directive.

We use the escape character to escape characters in a line or to extend a single line to multiple lines. On UNIX-like platforms, \ is the escape character, whereas, on Windows, \ is a directory path separator and ` is the escape character. By default, the `Dockerfile` parser considers \ is the escape character and you could override this on Windows using the escape parser directive, as shown here:

```
# escape=`
```

The Dockerfile build instructions

So far, we have looked at the integrated build system, the `Dockerfile` syntax, and a sample life cycle, wherein we discussed how a sample `Dockerfile` is leveraged for generating an image and how a container gets spun off from that image. In this section, we will introduce the `Dockerfile` instructions, their syntax, and a few befitting examples.

The FROM instruction

The `FROM` instruction is the most important one and is the first valid instruction of a `Dockerfile`. It sets the base image for the build process. Subsequent instructions will use this base image and build on top of it. The Docker build system lets you flexibly use the images built by anyone. You can also extend them by adding more precise and practical features. By default, the Docker build system looks for the images in the Docker host. However, if the image is not found in the Docker host, then the Docker build system will pull the image from the publicly available Docker Hub Registry. The Docker build system will return an error if it cannot find the specified image in the Docker host and the Docker Hub Registry.

The `FROM` instruction has the following syntax:

```
FROM <image>[:<tag>|@<digest>]
```

In the preceding code statement, note the following:

- `<image>`: This is the name of the image that will be used as the base image.
- `<tag>` or `<digest>`: Both `<tag>` and `<digest>` are optional attributes and you can qualify a particular Docker image version using either a tag attribute or a digest attribute. The `latest` tag is assumed by default if both tag and digest are not present.

Here is an example of the `FROM` instruction with the `centos` image name:

```
FROM centos
```

In the preceding example, the Docker build system will implicitly default to the `latest` tag because neither a tag nor a digest is explicitly added to the image name. Here is another example of the `FROM` instruction with the `ubuntu` image name and the `16.04` tag qualifier:

```
FROM ubuntu:16.04
```

Next is a classic example of the `FROM` instruction with the `ubuntu` image name and the digest qualifier:

```
FROM
ubuntu@sha256:8e2324f2288c26e1393b63e680ee7844202391414dbd48497e9a4fd997cd3
cbf
```

Docker allows multiple `FROM` instructions in a single `Dockerfile` in order to create multiple images. The Docker build system will pull all the images specified in the `FROM` instruction. Docker does not provide any mechanism for naming the individual images that are generated with the help of multiple `FROM` instructions. We strongly discourage using multiple `FROM` instructions in a single `Dockerfile`, as damaging conflicts could arise.

The MAINTAINER instruction

The `MAINTAINER` instruction is an informational instruction of a `Dockerfile`. This instruction capability enables the authors to set the details in an image. Docker does not place any restrictions on placing the `MAINTAINER` instruction in `Dockerfile`. However, it is strongly recommended that you place it after the `FROM` instruction.

The following is the syntax of the `MAINTAINER` instruction, where `<author's detail>` can be in any text. However, it is strongly recommended that you use the image, author's name, and e-mail address as shown in this code syntax:

```
MAINTAINER <author's detail>
```

Here is an example of the MAINTAINER instruction with the author's name and e-mail address:

```
MAINTAINER Dr. Peter <peterindia@gmail.com>
```

The COPY instruction

The COPY instruction enables you to copy the files from the Docker host to the filesystem of the new image. The following is the syntax of the COPY instruction:

```
COPY <src> ... <dst>
```

The preceding code terms are explained here:

- <src>: This is the source directory, the file in the build context, or the directory from where the docker build subcommand was invoked.
- ...: This indicates that multiple source files can either be specified directly or be specified by wildcards.
- <dst>: This is the destination path for the new image into which the source file or directory will get copied. If multiple files have been specified, then the destination path must be a directory and it must end with a slash (/).

Using an absolute path for the destination directory or a file is recommended. In the absence of an absolute path, the COPY instruction will assume that the destination path will start from the root (/). The COPY instruction is powerful enough for creating a new directory and for overwriting the filesystem in the newly created image.

In the following example, we will copy the html directory from the source build context to /var/www/html, which is in the image filesystem, using the COPY instruction, as shown here:

```
COPY html /var/www/html
```

Here is another example of the multiple files (httpd.conf and magic) that will be copied from the source build context to /etc/httpd/conf/, which is in the image filesystem:

```
COPY httpd.conf magic /etc/httpd/conf/
```

The ADD instruction

The ADD instruction is similar to the COPY instruction. However, in addition to the functionality supported by the COPY instruction, the ADD instruction can handle the TAR files and remote URLs. We can annotate the ADD instruction as COPY on steroids.

The following is the syntax of the ADD instruction:

```
ADD <src> ... <dst>
```

The arguments of the ADD instruction are very similar to those of the COPY instruction, as shown here:

- <src>: This is either the source directory or the file that is in the build context or in the directory from where the docker build subcommand will be invoked. However, the noteworthy difference is that the source can either be a TAR file stored in the build context or be a remote URL.
- ...: This indicates that multiple source files can either be specified directly or be specified using wildcards.
- <dst>: This is the destination path for the new image into which the source file or directory will be copied.

Here is an example for demonstrating the procedure for copying multiple source files to the various destination directories in the target image filesystem. In this example, we have taken a TAR file (web-page-config.tar) in the source build context with the http daemon configuration file and the files for the web pages are stored in the appropriate directory structure, as shown here:

```
$ tar tf web-page-config.tar
etc/httpd/conf/httpd.conf
var/www/html/index.html
var/www/html/aboutus.html
var/www/html/images/welcome.gif
var/www/html/images/banner.gif
```

The next line in the Dockerfile content has an ADD instruction for copying the TAR file (web-page-config.tar) to the target image and extracting the TAR file from the root directory (/) of the target image, as shown here:

```
ADD web-page-config.tar /
```

Thus, the TAR option of the ADD instruction can be used for copying multiple files to the target image.

The ENV instruction

The ENV instruction sets an environment variable in the new image. An environment variable is a key-value pair, which can be accessed by any script or application. Linux applications use the environment variables a lot for a starting configuration.

The following line forms the syntax of the ENV instruction:

```
ENV <key> <value>
```

Here, the code terms indicate the following:

- <key>: This is the environment variable
- <value>: This is the value that is to be set for the environment variable

The following lines give two examples for the ENV instruction, where, in the first line, DEBUG_LVL has been set to 3 and on the second line, APACHE_LOG_DIR has been set to /var/log/apache:

```
ENV DEBUG_LVL 3
ENV APACHE_LOG_DIR /var/log/apache
```

The ARG instruction

The ARG instruction lets you define variables that can be passed during the Docker image build time. The Docker build subcommand supports the --build-arg flag to pass a value to the variables defined using the ARG instruction. If you specify a build argument that was not defined in your Dockerfile, the build would fail. In other words, the build argument variables must be defined in the Dockerfile to be passed during the Docker image build time.

The syntax of the ARG instruction is as follows:

```
ARG <variable>[=<default value>]
```

Here, the code terms mean the following:

- <variable>: This is the build argument variable
- <default value>: This is the default value you could optionally specify to the build argument variable

Here is an example for the ARG instruction:

```
ARG usr
ARG uid=1000
```

Here is an example of the `--build-arg` flag of the `docker build` subcommand:

```
$ docker build --build-arg usr=app --build-arg uid=100 .
```

The environment variables

The environment variables declared using the ENV or ARG instruction can be used in the ADD, COPY, ENV, EXPOSE, LABEL, USER, WORKDIR, VOLUME, STOPSIGNAL, and ONBUILD instructions.

Here is an example of the environment variable usage:

```
ARG BUILD_VERSION
LABEL com.example.app.build_version=${BUILD_VERSION}
```

The USER instruction

The USER instruction sets the startup user ID or username in the new image. By default, the containers will be launched with root as the user ID or UID. Essentially, the USER instruction will modify the default user ID from root to the one specified in this instruction.

The syntax of the USER instruction is as follows:

```
USER <UID>|<UName>
```

The USER instructions accept either <UID> or <UName> as its argument:

- <UID>: This is a numerical user ID
- <UName>: This is a valid username

The following is an example for setting the default user ID at the time of startup to 73. Here, 73 is the numerical ID of the user:

```
USER 73
```

Though it is recommended that you have a valid user ID to match with the /etc/passwd file, the user ID can contain any random numerical value. However, the username must match with a valid username in the /etc/passwd file, otherwise, the docker run subcommand will fail and it will display the following error message:

```
finalize namespace setup user get supplementary groups Unable to find user
```

The WORKDIR instruction

The WORKDIR instruction changes the current working directory from / to the path specified by this instruction. The ensuing instructions, such as RUN, CMD, and ENTRYPOINT will also work on the directory set by the WORKDIR instruction.

The following line gives the appropriate syntax for the WORKDIR instruction:

```
WORKDIR <dirpath>
```

Here, <dirpath> is the path for the working directory to set in. The path can be either absolute or relative. In the case of a relative path, it will be relative to the previous path set by the WORKDIR instruction. If the specified directory is not found in the target image filesystem, then the directory will be created.

The following line is a clear example of the WORKDIR instruction in a Dockerfile:

```
WORKDIR /var/log
```

The VOLUME instruction

The VOLUME instruction creates a directory in the image filesystem, which can later be used for mounting volumes from the Docker host or the other containers.

The VOLUME instruction has two types of syntax, as shown here:

- The first type is either exec or JSON array (all values must be within double-quotes (")):

  ```
  VOLUME ["<mountpoint>"]
  ```

- The second type is the shell, as shown here:

  ```
  VOLUME <mountpoint>
  ```

In the preceding lines, `<mountpoint>` is the mount point that has to be created in the new image.

The EXPOSE instruction

The `EXPOSE` instruction opens up a container network port for communicating between the container and the external world.

The syntax of the `EXPOSE` instruction is as follows:

```
EXPOSE <port>[/<proto>] [<port>[/<proto>]...]
```

Here, the code terms mean the following:

- `<port>`: This is the network port that has to be exposed to the outside world.
- `<proto>`: This is an optional field provided for a specific transport protocol, such as TCP and UDP. If no transport protocol has been specified, then TCP is assumed to be the transport protocol.

The `EXPOSE` instruction allows you to specify multiple ports in a single line.

The following is an example of the `EXPOSE` instruction inside a `Dockerfile` exposing the `7373` port number as a `UDP` port and the `8080` port number as a `TCP` port. As mentioned earlier, if the transport protocol has not been specified, then the `TCP` transport is assumed to be the transport protocol:

```
EXPOSE 7373/udp 8080
```

The LABEL instruction

The `LABEL` instruction enables you to add key-value pairs as metadata to your Docker images. These metadata can be further leveraged to provide meaningful Docker image management and orchestration.

The syntax of the `LABEL` instruction is as follows:

```
LABEL <key-1>=<val-1> <key-2>=<val-2> ... <key-n>=<val-n>
```

The `LABEL` instruction can have one or more key-value pairs. Though a `Dockerfile` can have more than one `LABEL` instruction, it is recommended that you use a single `LABEL` instruction with multiple key-value pairs.

Here is an example of the LABEL instruction:

```
LABEL version="2.0"
      release-date="2016-08-05"
```

The preceding label keys are very simple and this could result in naming conflicts. Hence Docker recommends using namespaces to label keys using the reverse domain notation. There is a community project called **Label Schema** that provides shared namespace. The shared namespace acts as a glue between the image creators and tool builders to provide standardized Docker image management and orchestration. Here is an example of the LABEL instruction using Label Schema:

```
LABEL org.label-schema.schema-version="1.0"
      org.label-schema.version="2.0"
      org.label-schema.description="Learning Docker Example"
```

The RUN instruction

The RUN instruction is the real workhorse during the build, and it can run any command. The general recommendation is to execute the multiple commands using one RUN instruction. This reduces the layers in the resulting Docker image because the Docker system inherently creates a layer for each time an instruction is called in Dockerfile.

The RUN instruction has two types of syntax:

- The first is the shell type, as shown here:

  ```
  RUN <command>
  ```

  Here, <command> is the shell command that has to be executed during the build time. If this type of syntax is to be used, then the command is always executed using /bin/sh -c.

- The second syntax type is either exec or the JSON array, as shown here:

  ```
  RUN ["<exec>", "<arg-1>", ..., "<arg-n>"]
  ```

  Here, the code terms mean the following:

  - <exec>: This is the executable to run during the build time
  - <arg-1>, ..., <arg-n>: These are the variable numbers (zero or more) of arguments for the executable

Unlike the first type of syntax, this type does not invoke /bin/sh -c. Hence, the types of shell processing, such as the variable substitution ($USER) and the wildcard substitution (*, ?) do not happen in this type. If shell processing is critical for you, then you are encouraged to use the shell type. However, if you still prefer the exec (JSON array type) type, then use your preferred shell as the executable and supply the command as an argument.

Consider the example, RUN ["bash", "-c", "rm", "-rf", "/tmp/abc"].

Now, let's look at a few examples of the RUN instruction. In the first example, we will use the RUN instruction for adding a greeting line to the .bashrc file in the target image filesystem, as shown here:

```
RUN echo "echo Welcome to Docker!" >> /root/.bashrc
```

The second example is a Dockerfile, which has the instructions for crafting an Apache2 application image on top of the Ubuntu 14.04 base image. The following steps will explain the Dockerfile instructions line by line:

1. We are going to build an image using ubuntu:14.04 as the base image, using the FROM instruction, as shown here:

```
###########################################
# Dockerfile to build an Apache2 image
###########################################
# Base image is Ubuntu
FROM ubuntu:14.04
```

2. Set the author's details using the MAINTAINER instruction, as shown here:

```
# Author: Dr. Peter
MAINTAINER Dr. Peter <peterindia@gmail.com>
```

3. Using one RUN instruction, we will synchronize the apt repository source list, install the apache2 package, and then clean the retrieved files, as shown here:

```
# Install apache2 package
RUN apt-get update && \
    apt-get install -y apache2 && \
    apt-get clean
```

The CMD instruction

The CMD instruction can run any command (or application), which is similar to the RUN instruction. However, the major difference between these two is the time of execution. The command supplied through the RUN instruction is executed during the build time, whereas the command specified by the CMD instruction is executed when the container is launched from the newly created image. Thus, the CMD instruction provides a default execution for this container. However, it can be overridden by the docker run subcommand arguments. When the application terminates, the container will also terminate along with the application and vice versa.

The CMD instruction has three types of syntax, as shown here:

- The first syntax type is the shell type, as shown here:

  ```
  CMD <command>
  ```

  Here, <command> is the shell command, which has to be executed during the launch of the container. If this type of syntax is used, then the command is always executed using /bin/sh -c.

- The second type of syntax is exec or the JSON array, as shown here:

  ```
  CMD ["<exec>", "<arg-1>", ..., "<arg-n>"]
  ```

  Here, the code terms mean the following:

  - <exec>: This is the executable, which is to be run during the launch of the container
  - <arg-1>, ..., <arg-n>: These are the variable numbers (zero or more) of arguments for the executable

- The third type of syntax is also exec or the JSON array, which is similar to the previous type. However, this type is used for setting the default parameters to the ENTRYPOINT instruction, as shown here:

  ```
  CMD ["<arg-1>", ..., "<arg-n>"]
  ```

  Here, the code terms mean the following:

  <arg-1>, ..., <arg-n>: These are the variable numbers (zero or more) of arguments for the ENTRYPOINT instruction, which will be explained in the next section.

Syntactically, you can add more than one CMD instruction in Dockerfile. However, the build system will ignore all the CMD instructions except for the last one. In other words, in the case of multiple CMD instructions, only the last CMD instruction will be effective.

Here, in this example, let's craft an image using Dockerfile with the CMD instruction for providing a default execution and then launching a container using the crafted image. The following is Dockerfile with a CMD instruction to echo a text:

```
##########################################################
# Dockerfile to demonstrate the behavior of CMD
##########################################################
# Build from base image busybox:latest
FROM busybox:latest
# Author: Dr. Peter
MAINTAINER Dr. Peter <peterindia@gmail.com>
# Set command for CMD
CMD ["echo", "Dockerfile CMD demo"]
```

Now, let's build a Docker image using the docker build subcommand and cmd-demo as the image name. The docker build system will read the instruction from the Dockerfile that is stored in the current directory (.), and craft the image accordingly, as shown here:

```
$ sudo docker build -t cmd-demo .
```

Having built the image, we can launch the container using the docker run subcommand, as shown here:

```
$ sudo docker run cmd-demo
Dockerfile CMD demo
```

Cool, isn't it? We have given a default execution for our container and our container has faithfully echoed Dockerfile CMD demo. However, this default execution can be easily overridden by passing another command as an argument to the docker run subcommand, as shown in the following example:

```
$ sudo docker run cmd-demo echo Override CMD demo
Override CMD demo
```

The ENTRYPOINT instruction

The ENTRYPOINT instruction will help in crafting an image for running an application (entry point) during the complete life cycle of the container, which would have been spun out of the image. When the entry point application is terminated, the container would also be terminated along with the application and vice versa. Thus, the ENTRYPOINT instruction would make the container function like an executable. Functionally, ENTRYPOINT is akin to the CMD instruction, but the major difference between the two is that the entry point application is launched using the ENTRYPOINT instruction, which cannot be overridden using the docker run subcommand arguments. However, these docker run subcommand arguments will be passed as additional arguments to the entry point application. Having said this, Docker provides a mechanism for overriding the entry point application through the --entrypoint option in the docker run subcommand. The --entrypoint option can accept only words as its argument and hence, it has limited functionality.

Syntactically, the ENTRYPOINT instruction is very similar to the RUN and CMD instructions, and it has two types of syntax, as shown here:

- The first type of syntax is the shell type, as shown here:

```
ENTRYPOINT <command>
```

Here, <command> is the shell command, which is executed during the launch of the container. If this type of syntax is used, then the command is always executed using /bin/sh -c.

- The second type of syntax is exec or the JSON array, as shown here:

```
ENTRYPOINT ["<exec>", "<arg-1>", ..., "<arg-n>"]
```

Here, the code terms mean the following:

- <exec>: This is the executable, which has to be run during the launch of the container
- <arg-1>, ..., <arg-n>: These are the variable numbers (zero or more) of arguments for the executable

Syntactically, you can have more than one ENTRYPOINT instruction in a Dockerfile. However, the build system will ignore all the ENTRYPOINT instructions except the last one. In other words, in the case of multiple ENTRYPOINT instructions, only the last ENTRYPOINT instruction will be effective.

In order to gain a better understanding of the ENTRYPOINT instruction, let's craft an image using Dockerfile with the ENTRYPOINT instruction and then launch a container using the crafted image. The following is Dockerfile with an ENTRYPOINT instruction to echo a text:

```
##########################################################
# Dockerfile to demonstrate the behavior of ENTRYPOINT
##########################################################
# Build from base image busybox:latest
FROM busybox:latest
# Author: Dr. Peter
MAINTAINER Dr. Peter <peterindia@gmail.com>
# Set entrypoint command
ENTRYPOINT ["echo", "Dockerfile ENTRYPOINT demo"]
```

Now, let's build a Docker image using the docker build as the subcommand and entrypoint-demo as the image name. The docker build system would read the instruction from Dockerfile stored in the current directory (.) and craft the image, as shown here:

```
$ sudo docker build -t entrypoint-demo .
```

Having built the image, we can launch the container using the docker run subcommand:

```
$ sudo docker run entrypoint-demo
Dockerfile ENTRYPOINT demo
```

Here, the container will run like an executable by echoing the Dockerfile ENTRYPOINT demo string and then it will exit immediately. If we pass any additional arguments to the docker run subcommand, then the additional argument would be passed to the ENTRYPOINT command. The following is the demonstration of launching the same image with the additional arguments given to the docker run subcommand:

```
$ sudo docker run entrypoint-demo with additional arguments
Dockerfile ENTRYPOINT demo with additional arguments
```

Now, let's see an example where we override the build time entry point application with the `--entrypoint` option and then launch a shell (`/bin/sh`) in the `docker run` subcommand, as shown here:

```
$ sudo docker run -it --entrypoint="/bin/sh" entrypoint-demo
/ #
```

The HEALTHCHECK instruction

Any Docker container is designed to run just one process/application/service as a best practice and also to be uniquely compatible with the fast-evolving **Microservices Architecture (MSA)**. The life cycle of a container is tightly bound to the process running inside the container. When the process running inside the container crashes or dies for any reason, the Docker Engine will move the container to the stop state. There is a possibility that the application running inside the container might be in an unhealthy state and such a state must be externalized for effective container management. Here the HEALTHCHECK instruction comes in handy to monitor the health of the containerized application by running a health monitoring command (or tool) at a prescribed interval.

The syntax of the HEALTHCHECK instruction is as follows:

```
HEALTHCHECK [<options>] CMD <command>
```

Here, the code terms mean the following:

- `<command>`: The HEALTHCHECK command is to be executed at a prescribed interval. If the command exit status is 0, the container is considered to be in the healthy state. If the command exit status is 1, the container is considered to be in the unhealthy state.
- `<options>`: By default, the HEALTHCHECK command is invoked every 30 seconds, the command timeout is 30 seconds, and the command is retried three times before the container is declared unhealthy. Optionally, you can modify the default interval, timeout, and retries values using the following options:
  - `--interval=<DURATION> [default: 30s]`
  - `--timeout=<DURATION> [default: 30s]`
  - `--retries=<N> [default: 3]`

Here is an example of the HEALTHCHECK instruction:

```
HEALTHCHECK --interval=5m --timeout=3s
    CMD curl -f http://localhost/ || exit 1
```

If there is more than one HEALTHCHECK instruction in a Dockerfile, only the last HEALTHCHECK instruction will take effect. So you can override the health check defined in the base image. For any reason, if you choose to disable the health check defined in the base image, you could resort to the NONE option of the HEALTHCHECK instructions, as shown here:

```
HEALTHCHECK NONE
```

The ONBUILD instruction

The ONBUILD instruction registers a build instruction to an image and this gets triggered when another image is built using this image as its base image. Any build instruction can be registered as a trigger and those instructions will be triggered immediately after the FROM instruction in the downstream Dockerfile. Thus, the ONBUILD instruction can be used for deferring the execution of the build instruction from the base image to the target image.

The syntax of the ONBUILD instruction is as follows:

```
ONBUILD <INSTRUCTION>
```

Here, <INSTRUCTION> is another Dockerfile build instruction, which will be triggered later. The ONBUILD instruction does not allow the chaining of another ONBUILD instruction. In addition, it does not allow the FROM and MAINTAINER instruction as an ONBUILD trigger.

Here is an example of the ONBUILD instruction:

```
ONBUILD ADD config /etc/appconfig
```

The STOPSIGNAL instruction

The STOPSIGNAL instruction enables you to configure an exit signal for your container. It has the following syntax:

```
STOPSIGNAL <signal>
```

Here, <signal> is either a valid signal name, such as SIGKILL, or a valid unsigned signal number.

The SHELL instruction

The SHELL instruction allows us to override the default shell, that is, sh on Linux and cmd on Windows.

The syntax of the SHELL instruction is as follows:

```
SHELL ["<shell>", "<arg-1>", ..., "<arg-n>"]
```

Here, the code terms mean the following:

- <shell>: The shell to be used during container runtime
- <arg-1>, ..., <arg-n>: These are the variable numbers (zero or more) of the arguments for the shell

The .dockerignore file

In the *Docker's integrated image building system* section, you learned that the docker build process will send the complete build context to the daemon. In a practical environment, the docker build context will contain many other working files and directories, which would never be built into the image. Nevertheless, the docker build system will still send those files to the daemon. So, you may be wondering how you can optimize the build process by not sending these working files to the daemon. Well, the folks behind Docker too have thought about that and have given a very simple solution, using a .dockerignore file.

The .dockerignore file is a newline-separated TEXT file, wherein you can provide the files and the directories which are to be excluded from the build process. The exclusion list in the file can have both the fully specified file/directory name and the wildcards.

The following snippet is a sample .dockerignore file through which the build system has been instructed to exclude the .git directory and all the files that have the .tmp extension:

```
.git
*.tmp
```

A brief on the Docker image management

As we saw in the previous chapter and earlier in this chapter, there are many ways of getting a handle on a Docker image. You could download a full setup application stack from the public repository using the `docker pull` subcommand. Otherwise, you could craft your own application stack either manually using the `docker commit` subcommand or automatically using `Dockerfile` and the `docker build` subcommand combination.

The Docker images are positioned as the key building blocks of the containerized applications that in turn enable the realization of distributed applications, which will be deployed on the cloud servers. The Docker images are built in layers, that is, the images can be built on top of other images. The original image is called the **parent image** and the one that is generated is called the **child image**. The base image is a bundle, which comprises an application's common dependencies. Each change that is made to the original image is stored as a separate layer. Each time you commit to a Docker image, you will create a new layer on the Docker image and each change that is made to the original image will be stored as a separate layer. As the reusability of the layers is facilitated, making new Docker images becomes simple and fast. You can create a new Docker image by changing a single line in `Dockerfile` and you do not need to rebuild the whole stack.

Now that you learned about layers in the Docker image, you may be wondering how one could visualize these layers in a Docker image. Well, the `docker history` subcommand is an excellent and handy tool for visualizing the image layers.

Here, let's see a practical example for understanding layering in the Docker images better. For this purpose, let's follow these steps:

1. Here, we have `Dockerfile` with the instructions for automatically building the Apache2 application image on top of the Ubuntu 14.04 base image. The RUN section of the previously crafted and used `Dockerfile` of this chapter will be reused in this section, as shown here:

```
###########################################
# Dockerfile to build an Apache2 image
###########################################
# Base image is Ubuntu
FROM ubuntu:14.04
# Author: Dr. Peter
MAINTAINER Dr. Peter <peterindia@gmail.com>
# Install apache2 package
RUN apt-get update && \
    apt-get install -y apache2 && \
    apt-get clean
```

2. Now, craft an image from the preceding `Dockerfile` using the `docker build` subcommand, as shown here:

```
$ sudo docker build -t apache2 .
```

3. Finally, let's visualize the layers in the Docker image using the `docker history` subcommand:

```
$ sudo docker history apache2
```

The preceding subcommand will produce a detailed report on each layer of apache2 Docker image, as shown here:

```
IMAGE             CREATED          CREATED BY        SIZE
aa83b67feeba    2 minutes ago     /bin/sh -c apt-get
update &&  apt-get inst           35.19 MB
c7877665c770     3 minutes ago     /bin/sh -c #(nop)
MAINTAINER Dr. Peter <peter       0 B
9cbaf023786c     6 days ago       /bin/sh -c #(nop)
CMD [/bin/bash]                   0 B
03db2b23cf03     6 days ago       /bin/sh -c apt-get
update && apt-get dist-upg        0 B
8f321fc43180     6 days ago       /bin/sh -c sed -i
's/^#s* (deb.*universe)$/        1.895 kB
6a459d727ebb     6 days ago       /bin/sh -c rm -rf
/var/lib/apt/lists/*              0 B
2dcbbf65536c     6 days ago       /bin/sh -c echo
'#!/bin/sh' >  /usr/sbin/polic   194.5 kB
97fd97495e49     6 days ago       /bin/sh -c #(nop)
ADD file:84c5e0e741a0235ef8       192.6 MB
511136ea3c5a     16 months ago    0 B
```

Here, the apache2 image is made up of ten image layers. The top two layers, that is, the layers with the aa83b67feeba and c7877665c770 image IDs are the result of the RUN and MAINTAINER instructions in our Dockerfile. The remaining eight layers of the image will be pulled from the repository by the FROM instruction in our Dockerfile.

Best practices for writing a Dockerfile

An undisputable truth is that a set of best practices always plays an indispensable role in elevating any new technology. There is a well-written section listing all the best practices for crafting a `Dockerfile`. We found it incredible and hence, we wanted to share them for your benefit. You can find them at

`https://docs.docker.com/articles/dockerfile_best-practices/`.

Summary

Building Docker images is a crucial aspect of the Docker technology for streamlining the arduous journey of containerization. As indicated before, the Docker initiative has turned out to be disruptive and transformative for the containerization paradigm, which has been present for a while now. `Dockerfile` is the most prominent one for producing competent Docker images, which can be meticulously used across. We have illustrated all the commands, their syntax, and their usage techniques in order to empower you with all the easy-to-grasp details, and this will simplify the image-building process for you. We have supplied a bevy of examples in order to substantiate the inner meaning of each command. In the next chapter, we are going to discuss the Docker Hub, which is a well-designated store for storing and sharing the Docker images, and we will also discuss its profound contributions towards the penetration of the containerization concept into IT enterprises.

4
Publishing Images

In the previous chapter, you learned how to build Docker images. The next logical step is to publish these images in a public repository for public discovery and consumption. So, this chapter focuses on publishing images on Docker Hub, and how to get the most out of Docker Hub. We will create a new Docker image, using the `commit` command and a `Dockerfile`, build on it, and push it to Docker Hub. The concept of a Docker trusted repository will be discussed. This Docker trusted repository is created from GitHub or Bitbucket, and it can then be integrated with Docker Hub to automatically build images as a result of updates in the repository. This repository on GitHub is used to store the `Dockerfile`, which was previously created. Also, we will illustrate how worldwide organizations can enable their teams of developers to craft and contribute a variety of Docker images to be deposited in Docker Hub. The Docker Hub REST APIs can be used for user management and the manipulation of the repository programmatically.

The following topics are covered in this chapter:

- Understanding Docker Hub
- Pushing images to Docker Hub
- Automatic building of images
- Private repositories on Docker Hub
- Creating organizations on Docker Hub
- The Docker Hub REST API

Understanding Docker Hub

Docker Hub is the central place used for keeping the Docker images either in a public or private repository. Docker Hub provides features, such as a repository for Docker images, user authentications, automated image builds, integration with GitHub or Bitbucket, and managing organizations and groups. The Docker Registry component of Docker Hub manages the repository for Docker images. Also, you can protect your repositories using Docker Security Scanning, which is free as of now. This feature was first enabled in IBM container repositories.

Docker Registry is a storage system used to store images. Automated build is a feature of Docker Hub, which is not open source yet at the time of writing this book. The following diagram shows the typical features:

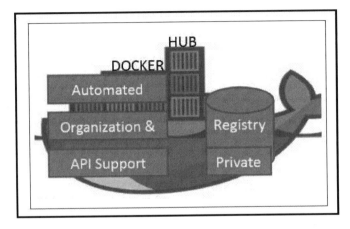

In order to work with Docker Hub, you have to register with Docker Hub, and create an account using the link available at `https://hub.docker.com/`. You can update the Docker Hub ID, e-mail address, and password fields, as shown in the following screenshot:

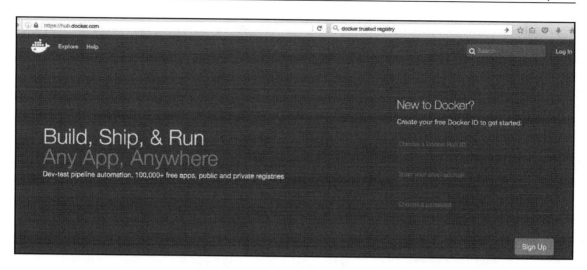

After completing the sign up process, you need to complete the verification received in an e-mail. After the e-mail verification is completed, you will see something similar to the following screenshot when you log in to Docker Hub:

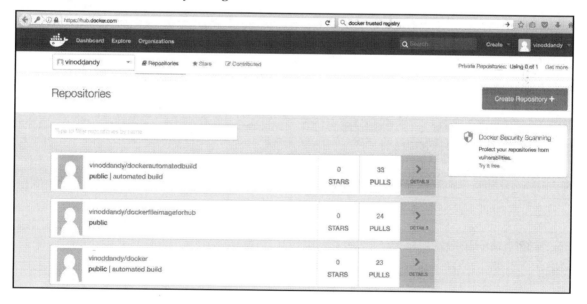

The creation of an account in Docker Hub has completed successfully, and now you can log in to your Docker Hub account from `https://hub.docker.com/login/`, as shown in the following screenshot:

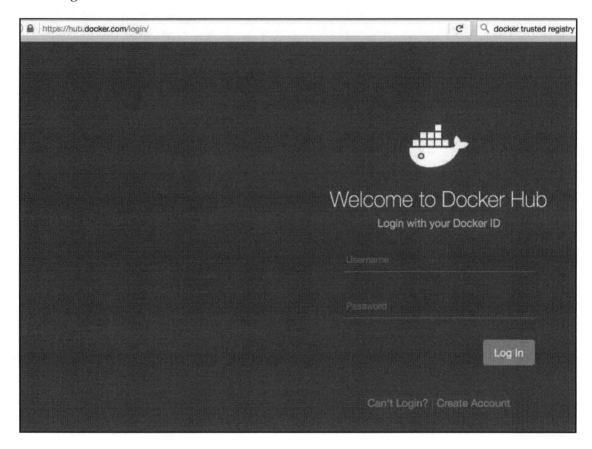

Docker Hub also supports command-line access to Docker Hub using an Ubuntu Terminal:

```
$ sudo docker login
```

Log in with your Docker ID to push and pull images from Docker Hub. If you don't have a Docker ID, head over to `https://hub.docker.com` to create one. Enter your username and password in the Terminal:

```
Username: vinoddandy
Password:
```

After a successful login, the output is as follows:

```
Login Succeeded
```

You can browse the available images in Docker Hub at `https://hub.docker.com/explore/`, as follows:

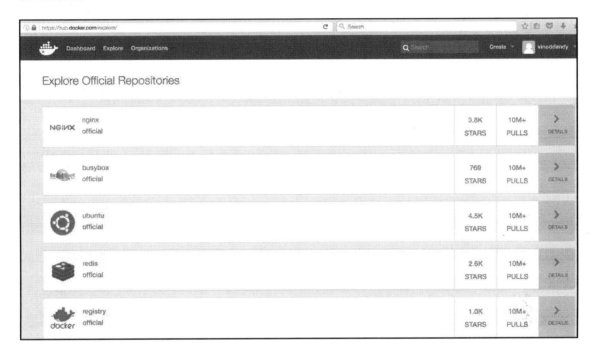

Also, you can see your settings, update your profile, and get details of supported communities, such as Twitter, Stack Overflow, #IRC, Google Groups, and GitHub.

Pushing images to Docker Hub

Here, we will create a Docker image on the local machine and push this image to Docker Hub. You need to perform the following steps in this section:

1. Create a Docker image on the local machine by doing one of the following:

   - Using the `docker commit` subcommand
   - Using the `docker commit` subcommand with `Dockerfile`

2. Pushing this created image to Docker Hub
3. Deleting the image from Docker Hub

We will use the `ubuntu` base image, run the container, add a new directory and a new file, and then create a new image. In `Chapter 3`, *Building Images*, we saw how to create a Docker image using `Dockerfile`. You may refer to that chapter to check for details of the `Dockerfile` syntax.

We will run the container with the `containerforhub` name from the base `ubuntu` image, as shown in the following Terminal code:

```
$ sudo docker run -i --name="containerforhub" -t ubuntu /bin/bash
Unable to find image 'ubuntu:latest' locally
latest: Pulling from library/ubuntu
952132ac251a: Pull complete
Digest:
sha256:f4691c96e6bbaa99d99ebafd9af1b68ace2aa2128ae95a60369c506dd6e6f6ab
Status: Downloaded newer image for ubuntu:latest
root@1068a1fae7da:/#
```

Next, we'll create a new directory and file in the `containerforhub` container. We will also update the new file with some sample text to test later:

```
root@1068a1fae7da:/# mkdir mynewdir
root@1068a1fae7da:/# cd mynewdir
root@1068a1fae7da:/mynewdir# echo 'this is my new container to make image
and then push to hub' > mynewfile
root@1068a1fae7da:/mynewdir# cat mynewfile
this is my new container to make image and then push to hub
root@1068a1fae7da:/mynewdir#
```

Let's build the new image with the `docker commit` command from the container, which has just been created.

 The `commit` command will be executed from the host machine, from where the container is running, and not from inside this container:

```
$ sudo docker commit -m="NewImage for second edition" containerforhub
vinoddandy/imageforhub2
sha256:619a25519578b0525b4c098e3d349288de35986c1f3510958b6246fa5d3a3f56
```

You should use your own username of Docker Hub in place of `vinoddandy` to create the image.

Now, we have a new Docker image available on the local machine with the `vinoddandy/imageforhub2` name. At this point, a new image with `mynewdir` and `mynewfile` is created locally:

```
$ sudo docker images -a
REPOSITORY                 TAG          IMAGE ID         CREATED
SIZE
vinoddandy/imageforhub2    latest       619a25519578
2 minutes ago              126.6 MB
```

We will log in to Docker Hub using the `sudo docker login` command, as discussed earlier in this chapter.

Let's push this image to Docker Hub from the host machine:

```
$ sudo docker push vinoddandy/imageforhub2
The push refers to a repository [docker.io/vinoddandy/imageforhub2]
0ed7a0595d8a: Pushed
0cad5e07ba33: Mounted from library/ubuntu
48373480614b: Mounted from library/ubuntu
latest: digest:
sha256:cd5a86d1b26ad156b0c74b0b7de449ddb1eb51db7e8ae9274307d27f810280c9
size: 1564
```

Now, we'll login to Docker Hub and verify the image in **Repositories**.

To test the image from Docker Hub, let's remove this image from the local machine. To remove the image, first we need to stop the container and then delete the container:

```
$ sudo docker stop containerforhub
$ sudo docker rm containerforhub
```

We will also delete the `vinoddandy/imageforhub2` image:

```
$ sudo docker rmi vinoddandy/imageforhub2
Untagged: vinoddandy/imageforhub2:latest
Untagged:
vinoddandy/imageforhub2@sha256:cd5a86d1b26ad156b0c74b0b7de449ddb1eb51db7e8a
e9274307d27f810280c9
Deleted:
sha256:619a25519578b0525b4c098e3d349288de35986c1f3510958b6246fa5d3a3f56
```

We will pull the newly created image from Docker Hub, and run the new container on the local machine:

```
$ sudo docker run -i --name="newcontainerforhub" -t \
vinoddandy/imageforhub2 /bin/bash
Unable to find image 'vinoddandy/imageforhub2:latest' locally
latest: Pulling from vinoddandy/imageforhub2

952132ac251a: Already exists
82659f8f1b76: Already exists
Digest:
sha256:cd5a86d1b26ad156b0c74b0b7de449ddb1eb51db7e8ae9274307d27f810280c9
Status: Downloaded newer image for vinoddandy/imageforhub2:latest

root@9dc6df728ae9:/# cat /mynewdir/mynewfile
this is my new container to make image and then push to hub
root@9dc6df728ae9::/#
```

So, we have pulled the latest image from Docker Hub and created the container with the new vinoddandy/imageforhub2 image. Make a note that the Unable to find image 'vinoddandy/imageforhub2:latest' locally message confirms that the image is downloaded from the remote repository of Docker Hub.

The text in mynewfile verifies that it is the same image that was created earlier.

Finally, we will delete the image from Docker Hub at https://hub.docker.com/r/vinoddandy/imageforhub2/ and then click on **Settings** and then **Delete**, as shown in the following screenshot:

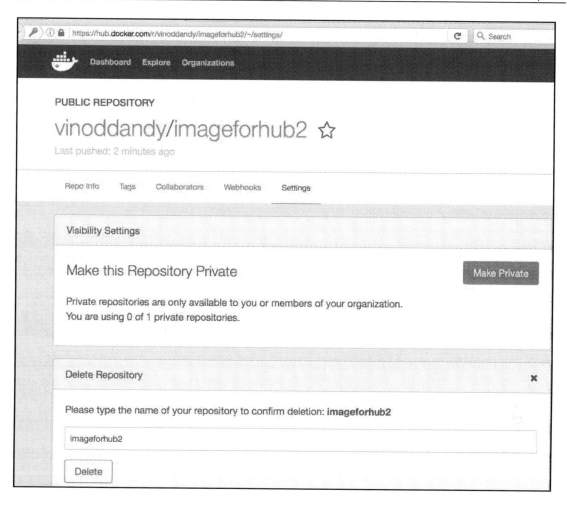

We'll again create this image, but now using the `Dockerfile` process. So, let's create the Docker image using the `Dockerfile` concept explained in `Chapter 3`, *Building Images*, and push this image to Docker Hub.

The `Dockerfile` on the local machine is as follows:

```
##########################################
# Dockerfile to build a new image
##########################################
# Base image is Ubuntu
FROM ubuntu:16.04
# Author: Dr. Peter
MAINTAINER Dr. Peter <peterindia@gmail.com>
# create 'mynewdir' and 'mynewfile'
```

```
RUN mkdir mynewdir
RUN touch /mynewdir/mynewfile
# Write the message in file
   RUN echo 'this is my new container to make image and then push to hub'
 >/mynewdir/mynewfile
```

Now we'll build the image locally using the following command:

```
$ sudo docker build -t="vinoddandy/dockerfileimageforhub1" .
Sending build context to Docker daemon 16.74 MB
Step 1 : FROM ubuntu:16.04
16.04: Pulling from library/ubuntu
862a3e9af0ae: Pull complete
7a1f7116d1e3: Pull complete
Digest:
sha256:5b5d48912298181c3c80086e7d3982029b288678fccabf2265899199c24d7f89
Status: Downloaded newer image for ubuntu:16.04
---> 4a725d3b3b1c
Step 2 : MAINTAINER Dr. Peter <peterindia@gmail.com>
---> Running in 5be5edc9b970
---> 348692986c9b
Removing intermediate container 5be5edc9b970
Step 3 : RUN mkdir mynewdir
---> Running in ac2fc73d75f3
---> 21585ffffab5
Removing intermediate container ac2fc73d75f3
Step 4 : RUN touch /mynewdir/mynewfile
---> Running in c64c98954dd3
---> a6304b678ea0
Removing intermediate container c64c98954dd3
Step 5 : RUN echo 'this is my new container to make image and then push to
hub' > /mynewdir/mynewfile
---> Running in 7f6d087e29fa
---> 061944a9ba54
Removing intermediate container 7f6d087e29fa
Successfully built 061944a9ba54
```

We'll run the container using this image, as shown here:

```
$ sudo docker run -i --name="dockerfilecontainerforhub" -t
vinoddandy/dockerfileimageforhub1 /bin/bash

root@236bfb39fd48:/# cat /mynewdir/mynewfile
this is my new container to make image and then push to hub
```

This text in `mynewdir` confirms that the new image is built properly with a new directory and a new file.

Repeat the login process in Docker Hub and push this newly created image:

```
$ sudo docker login
Login with your Docker ID to push and pull images from Docker Hub. If you
don't have a Docker ID, head over to https://hub.docker.com to create one.
Username (vinoddandy): vinoddandy
Password:
Login Succeeded

$ sudo docker push vinoddandy/dockerfileimageforhub1
The push refers to a repository
[docker.io/vinoddandy/dockerfileimageforhub1]
92e394693590: Pushed
821a2be25576: Pushed
dca059944a2e: Pushed
ffb6ddc7582a: Mounted from library/ubuntu
344f56a35ff9: Mounted from library/ubuntu
530d731d21e1: Mounted from library/ubuntu
24fe29584c04: Mounted from library/ubuntu
102fca64f924: Mounted from library/ubuntu
latest: digest:
sha256:c418c88f260526ec51ccb6422e2c90d0f6fc16f1ab81da9c300160d0e0f7bd87
size: 1979
```

Finally, we can verify the availability of the image on Docker Hub:

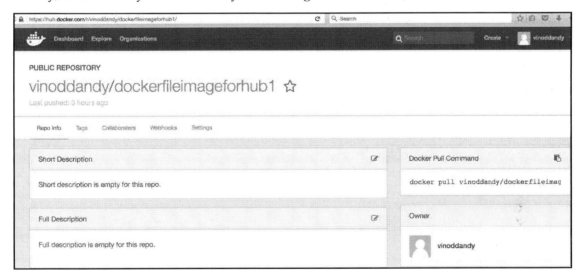

Automating the build process for images

You learned how to build images locally and push these images to Docker Hub. Docker Hub also has the capability to automatically build the image from the `Dockerfile` kept in the repository of GitHub or Bitbucket. Automated builds are supported on both the private and public repositories of GitHub and Bitbucket. The Docker Hub Registry keeps all the automated build images. The Docker Hub Registry is open source and can be accessed from `https://github.com/docker/docker-registry`.

We will discuss the steps needed to implement the automated build process:

1. We first connect Docker Hub to our GitHub account.
2. Log in to Docker Hub from `https://hub.docker.com/login/`, click on **Create**, and then navigate to **Create Automated Build**, as shown in the following screenshot:

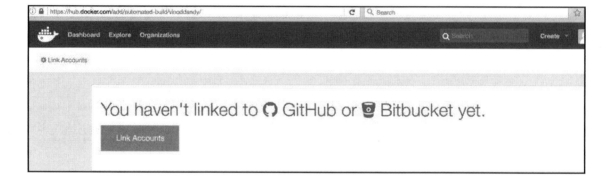

3. We'll now select **Link Accounts**:

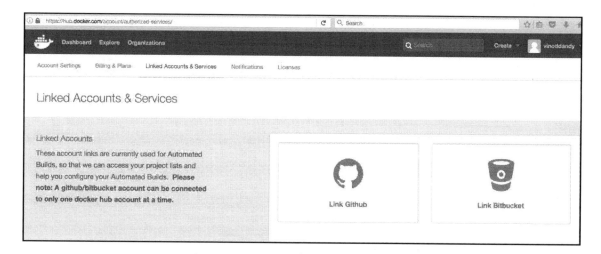

4. Once GitHub is selected, we will select **Public and Private (Recommended)**, as shown here:

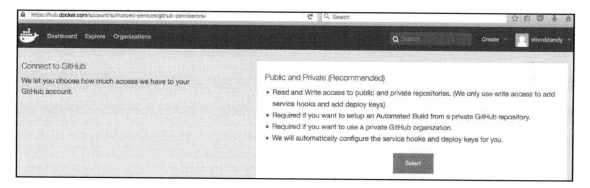

After clicking on **Select**, your GitHub repository will now be shown.

5. Now, provide the GitHub credentials to link your GitHub account with Docker Hub and select **Sign in**:

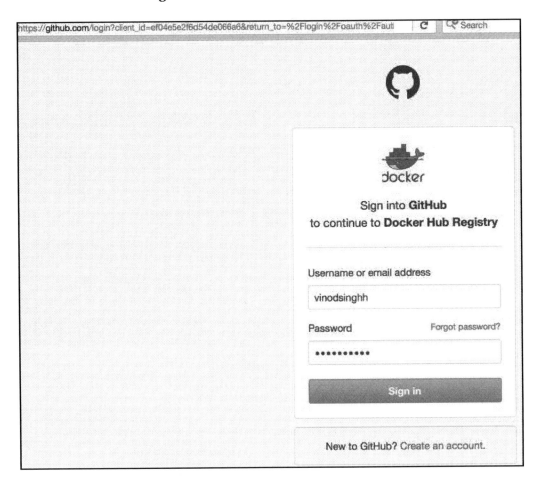

6. After a successful login, the **Linked Accounts & Services** screen looks like the following screenshot:

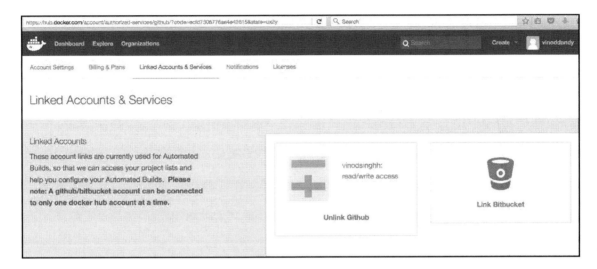

So, whenever the `Dockerfile` is updated in GitHub, the automated build gets triggered and a new image will be stored in the Docker Hub Registry. We can always check the build history. We can change the `Dockerfile` on the local machine and push it to GitHub. Now, we can see the automated build link of Docker Hub at
`https://hub.docker.com/r/vinoddandy/dockerautomatedbuild/builds/`:

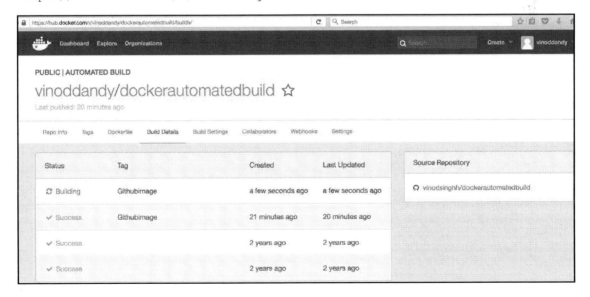

Private repositories on Docker Hub

Docker Hub provides both public and private repositories. The public repository is free to users and the private ones are a paid service. Plans with private repositories are available in different sizes, such as micro, small, medium, or large subscriptions.

Docker has published its public repository code to open source at `https://github.com/doc ker/docker-registry`.

Normally, enterprises will not like to keep their Docker images either in a Docker public or private repository. They prefer to keep, maintain, and support their own repository. Hence, Docker also provides the option for enterprises to create and install their own repository.

Let's create a repository in the local machine using the `registry` image provided by Docker. We will run the registry container on the local machine, using the `registry` image from Docker:

```
$ sudo docker run -p 5000:5000 -d registry
768fb5bcbe3a5a774f4996f0758151b1e9917dec21aedf386c5742d44beafa41
```

In the automated build section, we built the `vinoddandy/dockerfileimageforhub1` image. Let's tag the `224affbf9a65` image ID to our locally created registry image. This tagging of the image is needed for unique identification inside the local repository. This image registry may have multiple variants in the repository, so this tag will help you identify the particular image:

```
$ sudo docker tag 224affbf9a65 \
localhost:5000/vinoddandy/dockerfileimageforhub1
```

Once the tagging is done, push this image to a new registry using the `docker push` command:

```
$ sudo docker push localhost:5000/vinoddandy/dockerfile
imageforhub1
The push refers to a repository
[localhost:5000/vinoddandy/dockerfileimageforhub1
] (len: 1)
Sending image list
Pushing repository localhost:5000/vinoddandy/dockerfileimageforhub1 (1
tags)
511136ea3c5a: Image successfully pushed
d497ad3926c8: Image successfully pushed
-------------------------------------------------
224affbf9a65: Image successfully pushed
```

```
Pushing tag for rev [224affbf9a65] on
{http://localhost:5000/v1/repositories/vinoddandy/dockerfileimageforhub1/ta
gs/latest}
```

Now, the new image is available in the local repository. You can retrieve this image from the local registry and run the container. This task is left for you to complete.

Organizations and teams on Docker Hub

One of the useful aspects of private repositories is that you can share them only with members of your organization or team. Docker Hub lets you create organizations, where you can collaborate with your colleagues and manage private repositories. You will learn how to create and manage an organization next.

The first step is to create an organization on Docker Hub at https://hub.docker.com/organizations/add/, as shown in the following screenshot:

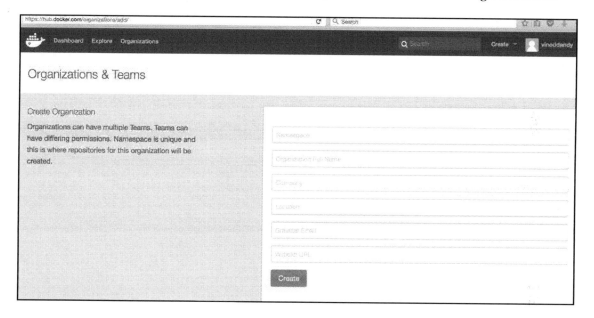

Inside your organization, you can add more organizations, and then add members to it:

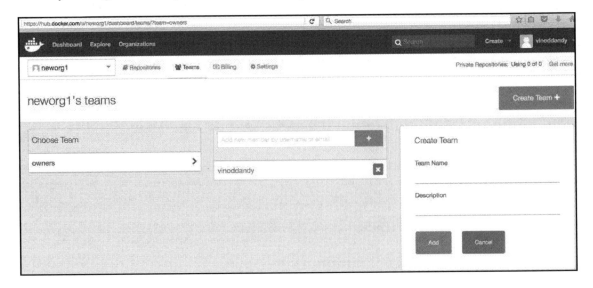

The members of your organization and group can collaborate with the organization and teams. This feature will be more useful in the case of a private repository.

The REST API for Docker Hub

Docker Hub provides a REST API to integrate the Hub capabilities through programs. The REST API is supported for both user and repository management.

User management supports the following features:

- **User Login**: This is used for user login to Docker Hub:

```
GET /v1/users
$ curl --raw -L --user vinoddandy:password
https://index.docker.io/v1/users
4
"OK"
0
```

- **User Register**: This is used for the registration of a new user:

```
POST /v1/users
```

- **Update user**: This is used to update the user's password and e-mail:

  ```
  PUT /v1/users/(username)/
  ```

Repository management supports the following features:

- **Create a user repository**: This creates a user repository:

  ```
  PUT /v1/repositories/(namespace)/(repo_name)/
  $ curl --raw -L -X POST --post301 -H
  "Accept:application/json"  -H "Content-Type:
  application/json" --data-ascii '{"email":
  "singh_vinod@yahoo.com", "password": "password",
  "username":  "singhvinod494" }'
  https://index.docker.io/v1/users
  e
  "User created"
  0
  ```

After you create repositories, your repositories will be listed here, as shown in this screenshot:

- **Delete a user repository**: This deletes a user repository:

  ```
  DELETE /v1/repositories/(namespace)/(repo_name)/
  ```

- **Create a library repository**: This creates a library repository, and it is available only to Docker administrators:

  ```
  PUT /v1/repositories/(repo_name)/
  ```

- **Delete a library repository**: This deletes a library repository, and it is available only to Docker administrators:

  ```
  DELETE /v1/repositories/(repo_name)/
  ```

- **Update user repository images**: This updates the images of a user's repository:

  ```
  PUT /v1/repositories/(namespace)/(repo_name)/images
  ```

- **List user repository images**: This lists the images in a user's repository:

  ```
  GET /v1/repositories/(namespace)/(repo_name)/images
  ```

- **Update library repository images**: This updates the images in a library repository:

  ```
  PUT /v1/repositories/(repo_name)/images
  ```

- **List library repository images**: This lists the images in a library repository:

  ```
  GET /v1/repositories/(repo_name)/images
  ```

- **Authorize a token for a library repository**: This authorizes a token for a library repository:

  ```
  PUT /v1/repositories/(repo_name)/auth
  ```

- **Authorize a token for a user repository**: This authorizes a token for a user's repository:

  ```
  PUT /v1/repositories/(namespace)/(repo_name)/auth
  ```

Summary

Docker images are the most prominent building blocks used for deriving real-world Docker containers that can be exposed as a service over any network. Developers can find and check images for their unique capabilities, and use them accordingly for their own purposes in bringing up highly usable, publicly discoverable, network-accessible, and cognitively composable containers. All crafted images need to be put in a public registry repository. In this chapter, we clearly explained how to publish images in a repository. We also talked about trusted repositories and their distinct characteristics. Finally, we demonstrated how the REST API for the repository can be leveraged to push in and play around with Docker images and user management, programmatically.

Docker images need to be stored in a public, controlled, and network-accessible location to be readily found and leveraged by worldwide software engineers and system administrators. Docker Hub is being touted as the best-in-class method to centrally aggregate, curate, and manage Docker images, originating from Docker enthusiasts (internal as well as external). However, enterprises cannot afford to keep their Docker images in a public domain, and hence the next chapter is dedicated to explaining the steps needed for image deployment and management in private IT infrastructures.

5
Running Your Private Docker Infrastructure

In Chapter 4, *Publishing Images,* we discussed Docker images and clearly explained that Docker containers are the runtime implementations of Docker images. Docker images and containers are plenty these days as the containerization paradigm has taken the IT domain by storm. Therefore, there is a need for worldwide enterprises to keep their Docker images in their own private infrastructure for security considerations. So, the concept of deploying Docker Hub to our own infrastructure has emerged and evolved. Docker Hubs are paramount and pertinent to registering and then depositing the growing array of Docker images. Primarily, Docker Hub is specially made to centralize and centrally manage information on the following:

- User accounts
- Checksums of the images
- Public namespaces

This chapter is developed with a focus on providing all the relevant information to enable you and the Docker container crafters to design, populate, and run your own private Docker Hubs in your own backyards. This chapter covers the following important topics:

- Docker Registry
- Docker Registry use cases
- Running your own Docker Registry and pushing the image to a newly created registry
- Webhook notifications
- Docker Registry HTTP API support

Docker Registry

The Docker Registry implementation has completely changed from the previous version mentioned in the earlier edition of this book. Docker Registry 2.0 is the new implementation for storing and distributing Docker images. It supersedes the previous Docker Registry implementation (`https://github.com/docker/docker-registry`). The new implementation is available at `https://github.com/docker/distribution`. This is open source under the Apache license. The registry is a stateless, highly scalable server-side application that stores and lets you distribute Docker images. The Docker Registry index is deprecated in the new release. Previously, the Docker Registry used index internally to authenticate the user.

Docker Registry 2.0 is completed, new, and implemented in Go and supports the Docker Registry HTTP API v2. The current Docker Hub (`https://hub.docker.com`) is based on the new Docker Registry 2.0 with Docker Engine 1.6 or above. This makes it more reliable and transparent to its users. All cloud providers have adopted this new Docker Registry including AWS and IBM.

The new registry implementation provides the following benefits:

- Faster push and pull
- Secure and efficient implementation
- Simplified deployment
- Pluggable storage backend
- Webhook notifications

The general architecture of Docker Registry shows, as in the following image, how it is integrated with Nginx at frontend and storage at backend:

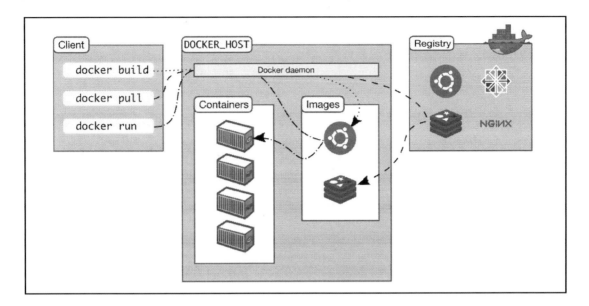

The salient features of the registry are as follows:

- The registry is compatible with Docker Engine version 1.6.0 or higher.
- The default storage driver is the local POSIX filesystem, which is suitable for development or small deployments. It also supports different storage backends (S3, Microsoft Azure, OpenStack Swift, and Aliyun OSS).
- It natively supports TLS and basic authentication.
- In the new version, the registry also supports a robust notification system. The registry supports sending Webhook notifications in response to events happening within the registry. Notifications are sent in response to manifest pushes and pulls and layer pushes and pulls. These actions are serialized into events. The events are queued into a registry-internal broadcast system, which queues and dispatches events to endpoints (`https://docs.docker.com/registry/notifications/#endpoints`).

The latest Docker Registry releases two options:

- Docker Trusted Registry
- Docker Registry

Let's talk about the two options in detail:

- **Docker Trusted Registry (DTR)**: This is the enterprise grade solution from Docker. DTR supports high availability and is installed on the Docker **Universal Control Plane (UCP)** cluster. The details are available at the following website: `https://docs.docker.com/docker-trusted-registry/`.

  DTR supports image management and it has built-in security and access control. It can also be integrated with LDAP and **Active Directory (AD)** and supports **Role Based Access Control (RBAC)**.

  The general architecture of DTR is shown in the following diagram:

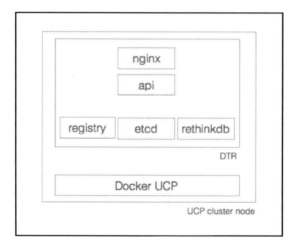

  DTR has a built-in authentication mechanism. DTR running on a node consists of the following containers:

  - `dtr-api-<replica_id>`: Executes the DTR business logic. It serves the DTR web application, and API.
  - `dtr-garant-<replica_id>`: Manages DTR authentication.
  - `dtr-jobrunner-<replica_id>`: Runs cleanup jobs in the background.
  - `dtr-nautilusstore-<replica_id>`: Stores security scanning data.
  - `dtr-nginx-<replica_id>`: Receives HTTP and HTTPS requests and proxies them to other DTR components. By default it listens to ports `80` and `443` of the host.

- dtr-notary-server-<replica_id>: Receives, validates, and serves content trust metadata, and is consulted when pushing or pulling to DTR with content trust enabled.
- dtr-notary-signer-<replica_id>: Performs server-side timestamp and snapshot signing for content trust metadata.
- dtr-registry-<replica_id>: Implements the functionality for pulling and pushing Docker images. It also handles how images are stored.
- dtr-rethinkdb-<replica_id>: A database for persisting repository metadata.

DTR uses the following internal named volumes for persistence of data:

- dtr-ca: The private keys and certificates are stored here
- dtr-etcd: This is used by etcd for storing DTR internal configurations
- dtr-registry: This is the volume where images are stored
- dtr-rethink: This is used by RethinkDB to persist DTR data, such as users and repositories

By default, DTR stores the images on the local filesystem of the host machine. For highly available installations of DTR, it supports cloud storage or network filesystems also. DTR can be configured to support Amazon S3, OpenStack Swift, and Microsoft Azure.

- **Docker Registry**: The registry is a stateless, highly scalable server-side application that stores and distributes Docker images. The registry is open source, under the permissive Apache License (http://en.wikipedia.org/wiki /Apache_License).

In this book, we will focus on the second option of the open source Docker Registry.

Docker Registry use cases

Docker Registry stores the Docker images and provides the basic functionalities of pulling, pushing, and deleting the images. In a typical workflow, a commit to your source revision control system would trigger a build on your CI system, which would then push a new image to your registry if the build is successful. A notification from the registry would then trigger a deployment on a staging environment or notify other systems that a new image is available.

Docker Registry is used when the user needs to do the following:

- Tighten control where images are kept
- Own the images distribution pipeline
- Integrate image storage and distribution with the backend development workflow

The important use cases of registry are as follows:

- **Pull or download an image**: The user requests an image using the Docker client from Docker Registry, the registry in turn responds back to the user with the registry details. Then, the Docker client will directly request the registry to get the required image. The registry authenticates the user with an index internally.
- **Push or upload an image**: A user requests to push the image, gets the registry information, and then pushes the image directly to the registry. The registry authenticates the user and finally, responds to the user.
- **Delete an image**: The user can also request to delete an image from the repository.

  The user has the option to use the registry with or without the index. Using the registry without the index is best suited for storing private images.

In addition to the preceding use cases, Docker Registry also supports version control for images. It can be integrated with **Continuous Integration (CI)** and **Continuous Development (CD)** systems. When a new image is successfully pushed to the registry, then a notification from the registry will trigger a deployment on a staging environment or notify other systems that a new image is available.

In Docker Registry V2, the following new use cases are also supported:

- **Image verification**: Docker Engine would like to run the verified image so it wants to ensure that the image is downloaded from a trusted source and no tampering has occurred. Docker Registry V2 returns a manifest and Docker Engine verifies the manifest's signature before downloading the image. After each layer is downloaded, the Engine verifies the digest of the layer ensuring that the content is as specified by the manifest.
- **Resumable push**: It is possible to lose network connectivity while uploading the image to Docker Registry. Now, Docker Registry has the ability to inform Docker Engine that the file upload has already started. Therefore, Docker Engine will respond by only sending the remaining data to complete the image upload.

- **Resumable pull**: When downloading an image, the connection is interrupted before the completion. Docker Engine keeps the partial data and requests to avoid downloading the repeated data. This is implemented as the HTTP range requests.
- **Layer upload deduplication**: Company Y's build system creates two identical Docker layers from build processes A and B. Build process A completes uploading the layer before B. When process B attempts to upload the layer, the registry indicates that it's not necessary because the layer is already known. If processes A and B upload the same layer at the same time, both the operations will proceed and the first to complete will be stored in the registry (note that we may modify this to prevent dogpile with some locking mechanism).

 This is the reason why Docker Registry V2 needs Docker Engine version 1.6 or above to support these features.

Running Docker Registry and pushing the image

It is fairly easy to install and run Docker Registry, but operating in a production environment requires other non-functional requirements also such as security, availability, and scalability. Also, logging and log processing, systems monitoring, and Security 101 are the required features for production grade systems. Most of the providers use DTR, as explained earlier in the production system. However, Docker Registry is good enough to use in your non-production environment preferably in the intranet environment.

In this section, we will use the Ubuntu 14.04 machine to install, run, and test Docker Registry. Docker Engine will be installed as described in Chapter 1, *Getting Started with Docker*. We will perform the following steps to run our own registry, and finally, push the image:

1. **Running Docker Registry on localhost**: Like most servers, Docker Registry does not need to be installed on client systems where Docker client is running. Docker Registry can be installed to any server which supports Docker and is network reachable. So multiple Docker clients can access the running Docker Registry.

   Docker Registry accepts the connection on TCP port 5000, so this is not blocked by the firewall in your system.

If you push a lot of images to Docker Registry, they will fill up the space quickly, so it is recommended that you configure enough space where the images are kept. On the local file system, the storage path is normally `/var/lib/registry`.

2. **Start the registry**: The following command downloads the registry image from Docker Hub and starts a container in the background:

```
$ sudo docker run -d -p 5000:5000 \
--restart=always --name  registry registry:2
Unable to find image 'registry:2' locally
2: Pulling from library/registry
df53ce740974: Pull complete
9ce080a7bfae: Pull complete
Digest:
sha256:1cfcd718fd8a49fec9ef16496940b962e30e39
27012e851f99905db55f1f4199
Status: Downloaded newer image for registry:2
8e5c4b02a43a033ec9f6a38072f58e6b06b87570ba951b3cce5
d9a031601656e
```

3. **Check Docker Registry is running on localhost**: The following command verifies that Docker Registry is up and running at port `5000` on localhost:

```
$ sudo docker ps -a
CONTAINER ID          IMAGE             COMMAND
CREATED               STATUS            PORTS
NAMES
8e5c4b02a43a          registry:2        "/entrypoint.sh /etc/"
3 minutes ago         Up 3 minutes      0.0.0.0:5000->5000/tcp
registry
```

4. **Get and tag the image**: The most common image to test Docker is the `hello-world` image available from Docker Hub. Pull the image from the local registry:

```
$ sudo docker pull hello-world
Using default tag: latest
latest: Pulling from library/hello-world

c04b14da8d14: Pull complete
Digest:
sha256:0256e8a36e2070f7bf2d0b0763dbabdd677985124
11de4cdcf9431a1feb60fd9
Status: Downloaded newer image for
hello-world:latest
```

The following command tags the image with `localhost:5000`:

```
$ sudo docker tag hello-world
localhost:5000/hello-world
```

Finally, the list of images available on the localhost machine are as follows:

```
$ sudo docker images
REPOSITORY                     TAG      IMAGE ID
CREATED              SIZE
registry                       2        541a6732eadb
2 days ago           33.3 MB
localhost:5000/hello-world     latest   c54a2cc56cbb
12 weeks ago         1.848 kB
hello-world                    latest   c54a2cc56cbb
12 weeks ago         1.848 kB
```

5. **Push the image**: This `hello-world` image can now be pushed to the newly created Docker Registry:

```
$ sudo docker push localhost:5000/hello-world
The push refers to a repository [localhost:5000/
hello-world]
a02596fdd012: Pushed
latest: digest:
sha256:a18ed77532f6d6781500db650194e0f9396ba5f
05f8b50d4046b294ae5f83aa4 size: 524
```

6. **Pull the image**: This `hello-world` image can now be pulled back from the newly created Docker Registry:

```
$ sudo docker pull localhost:5000/hello-world
Using default tag: latest
latest: Pulling from hello-world

Digest:
sha256:a18ed77532f6d6781500db650194e0f9396ba5f0
5f8b50d4046b294ae5f83aa4
Status: Downloaded newer image for localhost:5000/
hello-world:latest
```

7. **Stop Docker Registry and delete**: Now use the following command to stop and delete Docker Registry:

```
$ sudo docker stop registry && sudo docker \
rm -v registry
registry
registry
```

8. **Storage**: Docker Registry retains all the registry data as Docker volume on the host filesystem. The Docker volume can be mounted on the `/var/lib/registry` path, and use the following command to direct Docker Registry to point to this path:

```
$ sudo docker run -d -p 5000:5000 \
--restart=always --name registry -v \
`pwd`/data:/var/lib/registry registry:2
Unable to find image 'registry:2' locally
2: Pulling from library/registry
517dc3530502: Pull complete
Digest: sha256:1cfcd718fd8a49fec9ef16496940b962e30e
3927012e851f99905db55f1f4199
Status: Downloaded newer image for registry:2
5c0ea3042397720eb487f1c3fdb9103ebb0d149421aa114a
8c5a9133f775332a
```

The storage drivers can be configured for `inmemory`, `s3`, `azure`, `swift`, `oss`, and `gcs`:
https://github.com/docker/distribution/blob/master/docs/storage-drivers/index.md.

Running the Docker Registry on localhost with an SSL certificate

In this section, we will emulate the concept of running Docker Registry securely using SSL. In the current scenario of running Docker Registry on localhost, Docker Engine needs to be secured using TLS.

Follow these steps to run Docker Registry securely:

1. **Getting certificates**: We will be using self-signed certificates for TLS certificates. First create the `certs` directory, then run the `openssl` command:

```
$ mkdir certs
$ openssl req -newkey rsa:4096 -nodes -sha256 \
-keyout certs/domain.key -x509 -days 365 -out \
certs/domain.crt
Generating a 4096 bit RSA private key
.....................++
..............................................
.........++
writing new private key to 'certs/domain.key'
-----
You are about to be asked to enter information
that will be incorporated into your certificate
request.
What you are about to enter is what is called a
Distinguished Name or a DN.
There are quite a few fields but you can leave
some blank
For some fields there will be a default value,
If you enter '.', the field will be left blank.
-----
Country Name (2 letter code) [AU]:US
State or Province Name (full name) [Some-State]:
Locality Name (eg, city) []:
Organization Name (eg, company)
[Internet Widgits Pty Ltd]:
Organizational Unit Name (eg, section) []:
Common Name (e.g. server FQDN or YOUR name)
[]:myregistrydomain.com
Email Address []:
$
```

2. Copy the `certs` directory to the certificates directory of Ubuntu 16.04 in the `/usr/local/share/ca-certificates` path. This path is specific to Ubuntu (Debian) systems and you may need to use a different path if using Red Hat systems:

```
$ sudo cp certs/domain.crt \
/usr/local/share/ca-certificates/myregistrydomain.com.crt
$ sudo update-ca-certificates
```

Also copy the `domain.crt` file to `/etc/docker/certs.d/myregistrydomain.com:5000/ca.crt`.

Ensure to create the `certs.d` and `myregistrydomain.com:5000` directories before running the preceding command.

3. Restart Docker Engine:

```
$ sudo service docker restart
```

4. Docker Registry can be started, as follows, in the secure mode:

```
$ sudo docker run -d -p 5000:5000 \
--restart=always --name registry \
>    -v `pwd`/certs:/certs
>    -e REGISTRY_HTTP_TLS_CERTIFICATE=
/certs/domain.crt
>    -e REGISTRY_HTTP_TLS_KEY=/certs/domain.key
>    registry:2
Unable to find image 'registry:2' locally
2: Pulling from library/registry

c0cb142e4345: Pull complete
a5002dfce871: Pull complete
df53ce740974: Pull complete
Digest: sha256:1cfcd718fd8a49fec9ef16496940b962e30e
3927012e851f99905db55f1f4199
Status: Downloaded newer image for registry:2
d7c41de81343313f6760c2231c037008581adf07acceea
0b3372ec2c05a5a321
$
```

5. Now you should be able to push the images from the remote Docker host:

```
docker pull ubuntu
docker tag ubuntu myregistrydomain.com:5000/ubuntu
```

Point your `myregistrydomain.com` to localhost (`127.0.0.1`) by updating `/etc/hosts` by adding `127.0.0.1 myregistrydomain.com`.

```
docker push myregistrydomain.com:5000/ubuntu
docker pull myregistrydomain.com:5000/ubuntu
```

Running Docker Registry with restrictions

The security of Docker Registry is very vital. It is recommended that you run it behind the secure firewall and **Intrusion Protection System (IPS) / Intrusion Defense System (IDS)** in a secure network. Also, it is assumed that registry will only accept a secure connection on HTTPS. In addition to these, Docker Registry can provide access restriction, and the simplest way to implement this is through basic authentication. The basic authentication is standard authentication with web servers using a login name and password:

```
$ mkdir auth
$ sudo docker run --entrypoint htpasswd
registry:2 -Bbn testvinod testpassword > auth/htpasswd
$
```

Here we list out the steps to be done for securely accessing Docker Registry:

1. Since we are running this registry in the secure mode, use a self-signed certificate and enable TLS.

2. Also, restart the Docker process to get the updated configuration.

3. Now rerun the registry and make sure the current running registry is stopped:

```
$ sudo docker run -d -p 5000:5000 --restart=always \
--name registry \
>     -v `pwd`/auth:/auth
>     -e "REGISTRY_AUTH=htpasswd"
>     -e "REGISTRY_AUTH_HTPASSWD_REALM=Registry Realm"
>     -e REGISTRY_AUTH_HTPASSWD_PATH=/auth/htpasswd
>     -v `pwd`/certs:/certs
>     -e REGISTRY_HTTP_TLS_CERTIFICATE=/certs/domain.crt
>     -e REGISTRY_HTTP_TLS_KEY=/certs/domain.key
>   registry:2
```

4. The user needs to log in from a remote machine to test registry user authentication:

```
$ sudo docker login  myregistrydomain.com:5000
Username: testuser
Password:testpassword

Login Succeeded
```

5. Push and pull the images from the remote machine:

```
$ sudo docker pull ubuntu
Using default tag: latest
latest: Pulling from library/ubuntu
cad964aed91d: Pull complete
3a80a22fea63: Pull complete
Digest:
sha256:28d4c5234db8d5a634d5e621c363d900f8f241240ee0a6a978784c978fe9c737
Status: Downloaded newer image for ubuntu:latest
ubuntu@ip-172-30-0-126:~$ sudo docker tag ubuntu
myregistrydomain.com:5000/ubuntu
$ sudo docker push myregistrydomain.com:5000/ubuntu
The push refers to a repository
[myregistrydomain.com:5000/ubuntu]
f215f043863e: Pushed
0c291dc95357: Pushed
latest: digest:
sha256:68ae734b19b499ae57bc8d9dd4c4f90d5ff17cfe801ffbd7b840b120f
d61d3b4 size: 1357
$ sudo docker rmi myregistrydomain.com:5000/ubuntu
Untagged: myregistrydomain.com:5000/ubuntu:latest
Untagged:
myregistrydomain.com:5000/ubuntu@sha256:68ae734b19b499ae57bc8d9dd4c4f90d5ff
17cfe801ffbd7b840b120fd61d3b4
$ sudo docker pull myregistrydomain.com:5000/ubuntu
Using default tag: latest
latest: Pulling from ubuntu
Digest:
sha256:68ae734b19b499ae57bc8d9dd4c4f90d5ff17cfe801ffbd7b840b120fd61d3b4
Status: Downloaded newer image for
myregistrydomain.com:5000/ubuntu:latest
```

Managing Docker Registry with Docker Compose

As Docker Registry grows more complex, dealing with its configuration will be tedious. So it is highly recommended that you use Docker Compose. Docker Compose will be discussed later in Chapter 8, *Orchestrating Containers*.

The `docker-compose.yml` file is created as follows:

```
registry:
 image: registry:2
 ports:
   - 5000:5000
 environment:
   REGISTRY_HTTP_TLS_CERTIFICATE: /certs/domain.crt
   REGISTRY_HTTP_TLS_KEY: /certs/domain.key
   REGISTRY_AUTH: htpasswd
   REGISTRY_AUTH_HTPASSWD_PATH: /auth/htpasswd
   REGISTRY_AUTH_HTPASSWD_REALM: Registry Realm
 volumes:
   - /path/data:/var/lib/registry
   - /path/certs:/certs
   - /path/auth:/auth
```

Now, run the command to run the registry:

```
$ sudo docker-compose up -d
Creating ubuntu_registry_1
```

This ensures Docker Registry is up and running again.

Load balancing consideration

In the enterprise deployments of Docker Registry, the load balancer is required to distribute loads across registry clusters. To make load balancer work correctly, we need to consider storage driver, HTTP secret, and Redis cache (if configured) to be same for the cluster of registries. If any of these parameters are different, the registry will have trouble serving the requests.

For example, the storage driver used for Docker images should be the same across all instances of registry. If a particular mount point is used as a filesystem, it should be accessible and attached to all instances of registries. Similarly, if an S3 or IBM object storage is used, registries should be able to access the same storage resource. The HTTP secret coordinates uploads also must be the same across instances. Actually, configuring different Redis cache for different registry instances may work as of now. However, this is not a good practice and it will be expensive in terms of more requests being redirected to the backend.

Webhook notifications

Docker Registry has the in-built capability of sending notifications based on registry activities:

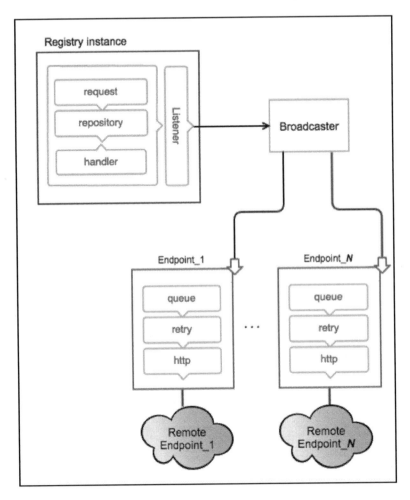

Notifications are sent to the endpoints via HTTP. This complete notification is based on the listener and broadcaster architecture. Each endpoint has its own queue and all actions (push/pull/delete) trigger the events. These events are queued and once the event reaches the end of the queue, it triggers an HTTP request to the endpoint. The events are sent to each endpoint, but the order is not guaranteed.

Events have a well-defined JSON structure and are sent as the body of the notification. One or more events are sent in the structure and are called an **envelope**. An envelope may contain one or more events. The registry is also capable of receiving responses from endpoints. The responses with 2XX or 3XX response codes are considered as valid responses and consider the message delivered.

Docker Registry HTTP API support

Docker Registry has an HTTP interface to interact with Docker Engine. This is used to manage information about Docker images and enable their distribution.

The key update from V1 is the set of changes in the Docker image format and concept of signed manifest. The new, self-contained image manifest simplifies image definition and improves security. This specification will build on that work, leveraging new properties of the manifest format to improve performance, reduce bandwidth usage, and decrease the likelihood of backend corruption.

The complete documentation of the Docker Registry V2 APIs can be found here: `https://github.com/docker/distribution/blob/master/docs/spec/api.md`.

The important APIs are discussed here:

- API version check:

   `GET /v2/`: This API provides version support information based on its response statuses.

   Here is the `curl` command to check the Docker Registry API version:

   ```
   $ curl -i http://localhost:5000/v2/
   HTTP/1.1 200 OK
   Content-Length: 2
   Content-Type: application/json; charset=utf-8
   Docker-Distribution-Api-Version: registry/2.0
   X-Content-Type-Options: nosniff
   Date: Mon, 21 Nov 2016 18:37:06 GMT
   ```

   The supported error codes are `401 Unauthorized` and `404 Not Found`.

- Listing repositories:

 `GET /v2/_catalog`: This API provides the content of repositories.

Here is the `curl` command to get the contents of repository:

```
$ curl -i http://localhost:5000/v2/_catalog
HTTP/1.1 200 OK
Content-Type: application/json; charset=utf-8
Docker-Distribution-Api-Version: registry/2.0
X-Content-Type-Options: nosniff
Date: Mon, 21 Nov 2016 18:36:42 GMT
Content-Length: 33
{"repositories":["hello-world"]}
```

The reader may recall that while starting Docker Registry, we uploaded only one file.

- Pulling an image: The Docker image mainly consists of two parts—a JSON manifest and individual layer files.

Pulling an image manifest can be fetched using the following URL:

```
GET /v2/<name>/manifests/<reference>
```

Here is the `curl` command to get the image manifest details.

```
curl -i http://localhost:5000/v2/
hello-world/manifests/latestHTTP/1.1 200 OK
Content-Length: 2742
Content-Type: application/vnd.docker.distribution.
manifest.v1+prettyjws
Docker-Content-Digest:
sha256:f18d040ea7bf47c7ea8f7ff1a8682811cf375
51c747158e37b9c75f5450e6fac
Docker-Distribution-Api-Version: registry/2.0
Date: Mon, 21 Nov 2016 18:54:05 GMT
{
    "schemaVersion": 1,
    "name": "hello-world",
    "tag": "latest",
    "architecture": "amd64",
    "fsLayers": [
```

```
    {
        "blobSum":
        "sha256:a3ed95caeb02ffe68cdd9fd8440
        6680ae93d633cb16422d00e8a7c22955b46d4"
    },
    {
        "blobSum":
        "sha256:c04b14da8d1441880ed3fe6106fb2cc
        6fa1c9661846ac0266b8a5ec8edf37b7c"
    }
    ],
    "history": [
        }{
            "v1Compatibility": "----
        }
    ],
    "signatures":[
        {
            "----------------"
        }
    ]
}
```

- Pulling the layers of an image stored in blob:

  GET /v2/<name>/blobs/<digest>

  This will be an exercise for the reader to download the image using <digest> received in the preceding pulling manifest API.

A list of methods and URIs are covered in the following table:

Method	Path	Entity	Description
GET	/v2/	Base	Check that the endpoint implements the Docker Registry API V2
GET	/v2/<name>/tag/list	Tags	Fetch the tags under the repository identified by name

GET	`/v2/<name>/manifests/<reference>`	Manifest	Fetch the manifest identified by name and reference, where reference can be a tag or digest
PUT	`/v2/<name>/manifests/<reference>`	Manifest	Put the manifest identified by name and reference, where reference can be a tag or digest
Delete	`/v2/<name>/manifests/<reference>`	Manifest	Delete the manifest identified by name and reference, where reference can be a tag or digest
GET	`/v2/<name>/blobs/<digest>`	Blob	Retrieve the blob from the registry identified by a digest
DELETE	`/v2/<name>/blobs/<digest>`	Blob	Delete the blob from the registry identified by a digest
POST	`/v2/<name>/blobs/uploads`	Initiate blob upload	Initiate a resumable blob upload; if successful, an upload location will be provided to complete the upload
GET	`/v2/<name>/blobs/uploads/<uuid>`	Blob upload	Retrieve the status of upload identified by `uuid`
PATCH	`/v2/<name>/blobs/uploads/<uuid>`	Blob upload	Update a chunk of data for the specified upload
PUT	`/v2/<name>/blobs/uploads/<uuid>`	Blob upload	Complete the upload specified by `uuid`

DELETE	/v2/<name>/blobs/uploads/<uuid>	Blob upload	Cancel outstanding upload processes, releasing associated resources
GET	/v2/_catalog	Catalog	Retrieve a sorted JSON list of repositories from the registry

Summary

Docker Engine allows every value-adding software solution to be containerized, indexed, registered, and stocked. Docker is turning out to be a great tool for systematically developing, shipping, deploying, and running containers everywhere. While docker.io lets you upload your Docker creations to its registry for free, anything you upload there is publicly discoverable and accessible. Innovators and companies aren't keen on this and therefore insist on private Docker Hubs. In this chapter, we explained all the steps, syntaxes, and semantics for you in an easy-to-understand manner. We showed how to retrieve images to generate Docker containers, and described how to push our images to Docker Registry in a secure manner in order to be found and used by authenticated developers. The authentication and authorization mechanisms, a major part of the whole process, have been explained in detail. Precisely speaking, this chapter is conceived and concretized as a guide for setting up your own Docker Hubs. As world organizations are showing exemplary interest in having containerized clouds, private container hubs are becoming more essential.

At this point in time, we understand that distribution and management of Docker images is possible using Docker Hub, DTR, and the Docker open source registry. Both Docker Hub and DTR are commercial products that incorporate the open source registry capabilities into their respective solutions. Docker Hub is a multi-tenant service while DTR and the open source registry provide users with the option to host private registries behind their own firewall or a dedicated cloud environment.

In the next chapter, we will dive deep into containers, which is the natural progression from images. We will demonstrate the capability to run services, such as a web server in a Docker container and its interaction with the host machine and the outside world.

6
Running Services in a Container

We have come thus far by carefully explaining the various aspects of the Docker technology. The previous chapters definitely have laid down a stellar foundation for the overwhelmingly accepted Docker platform and the forthcoming chapters will be like the meticulously crafted buildings on that grandiose foundation.

We described the important building blocks (the highly usable and reusable Docker images) to bring forth powerful Docker containers. There are briefs about the various easy-to-learn-and-employ techniques and tips on how to store and share Docker images through a well-designed storage framework. Typically, images have to go through a series of verifications, validations, and refinements constantly in order to be right and relevant for the aspiring development community.

In this chapter, we are going to take our learning to the next level by detailing the key steps in creating a small web server, run the same inside a container, and enable outsiders to connect to the containerized web server through the Internet.

In this chapter, we will cover the following topics:

- Container networking
- **Container as a Service (CaaS)** – building, running, exposing, and connecting to container services
- Publishing and retrieving containers' port
- Binding a container to a specific IP address
- Autogenerating the Docker host port
- Port binding using the EXPOSE and –P options

A brief overview of container networking

Networking is a critical infrastructure component of enterprise and cloud IT. Especially, as computing becomes extremely distributed, networking becomes indispensable. Typically, a Docker host comprises multiple Docker containers and hence the networking has become a crucial component for realizing composite containerized applications. Docker containers also need to interact and collaborate with local as well as remote ones to come out with distributed applications. Precisely speaking, different and distributed containers need to be publicly found, network-accessible, and composable to bring forth business-centric and process-aware applications.

One of the key strengths of the Docker containerization paradigm is the ability to network seamlessly without much effort from the user. The earlier version of Docker supported just the bridge network; later, Docker acquired the SDN startup SocketPlane to add additional networking capabilities. Since then, Docker's networking capability has grown leaps and bounds and a separate set of subcommands, namely `docker network connect`, `docker network create`, `docker network disconnect`, `docker network inspect`, `docker network ls`, and `docker network rm`, were introduced to handle the nitty-gritty of the Docker networking. By default, during installation, the Docker Engine creates three networks for you, which you can list using the `docker network ls` subcommand, as shown here:

```
$ docker network ls
NETWORK ID          NAME                DRIVER              SCOPE
daa55dd5830a        bridge              bridge              local
3e99b1085979        host                host                local
9b06957b4a00        none                null                local
$
```

As you can see in the preceding screenshot, during the Docker setup, the Docker Engine creates the `bridge`, `host`, and `none` (`null`) networks. When Docker spins up a new container, by default, it creates a network stack for the container and attaches to the default `bridge` network. However, optionally, you could attach the container to the `host` or `none` network or the user-defined network using the `--net` option of the `docker run` subcommand. If you choose the `host` network, the container gets attached to the `host` network stack and shares the host's IP addresses and ports. The `none` network mode creates a network stack with just the Loopback (`lo`) interface. We can confirm this using the `docker run --rm --net=none busybox ip addr` command, as shown here:

```
$ docker run --rm --net=none busybox ip addr
1: lo: <LOOPBACK,UP,LOWER_UP> mtu 65536 qdisc noqueue
    link/loopback 00:00:00:00:00:00 brd 00:00:00:00:00:00
    inet 127.0.0.1/8 scope host lo
       valid_lft forever preferred_lft forever
    inet6 ::1/128 scope host
       valid_lft forever preferred_lft forever
$ █
```

Evidently, as you can see in the preceding screenshot, the container has got just a Loopback interface. Since this container has got just a Loopback interface, the container cannot communicate with other containers or the external world.

The `bridge` network is the default network interface that Docker Engine assigns to a container if the network is not configured using the `--net` option of the `docker run` subcommand. To have a better understanding of the `bridge` network, let's begin by inspecting it using the `docker network inspect` subcommand, as shown here:

```
$ docker network inspect bridge
[
    {
        "Name": "bridge",
        "Id": "daa55dd5830a4d5ad2cfa68085644baea2651a1a6ed8664ed8ef0a74b18f6bc5",
        "Scope": "local",
        "Driver": "bridge",
        "EnableIPv6": false,
        "IPAM": {
            "Driver": "default",
            "Options": null,
            "Config": [
                {
                    "Subnet": "172.17.0.0/16",          ⬅ 2
                    "Gateway": "172.17.0.1"             ⬅ 3
                }
            ]
        },
        "Internal": false,
        "Containers": {},
        "Options": {
            "com.docker.network.bridge.default_bridge": "true",
            "com.docker.network.bridge.enable_icc": "true",
            "com.docker.network.bridge.enable_ip_masquerade": "true",
            "com.docker.network.bridge.host_binding_ipv4": "0.0.0.0",
            "com.docker.network.bridge.name": "docker0",  ⬅ 1
            "com.docker.network.driver.mtu": "1500"
        },
        "Labels": {}
    }
]
$ █
```

Here, in the preceding screenshot, we have highlighted three paramount insights. You can find the relevant description of what happens during the Docker installation process:

- docker0: Docker creates an Ethernet bridge interface inside the Linux kernel with the docker0 name on the Docker host. This interface is used as a bridge to pass the Ethernet frames between containers and also between containers and an external network.
- Subnet: Docker also selects a private IP subnet from the address range of 172.17.0.0 to 172.17.255.255 and keeps it revered for its containers. In the preceding screenshot, Docker has selected the 172.17.0.0/16 subnet for the containers.
- Gateway: The docker0 interface is the gateway for the bridge network and Docker, from the IP subnet range selected earlier, assigns an IP address to docker0. Here, in the preceding example, 172.17.0.1 is assigned to the gateway.

We can cross-check the gateway address by listing the docker0 interface using the ip addr show Linux command:

```
$ ip addr show docker0
```

The third line of the output shows the assigned IP address and its network prefix:

```
inet 172.17.0.1/16 scope global docker0
```

Apparently, from the preceding text, 172.17.0.1 is the IP address assigned to docker0, the Ethernet bridge interface, which is also listed as the gateway address in the output of the docker network inspect bridge command.

Now that we have a clear understanding of the bridge creation and the subnet/gateway address selection process, let's explore the container networking in the bridge mode a bit more in detail. In the bridge network mode, the Docker Engine creates a network stack with a Loopback (lo) interface and an Ethernet (eth0) interface during the launch of the container. We can quickly examine this by running the docker run --rm busybox ip addr command:

```
$ docker run -it busybox ip addr
1: lo: <LOOPBACK,UP,LOWER_UP> mtu 65536 qdisc noqueue
    link/loopback 00:00:00:00:00:00 brd 00:00:00:00:00:00
    inet 127.0.0.1/8 scope host lo
       valid_lft forever preferred_lft forever
    inet6 ::1/128 scope host
       valid_lft forever preferred_lft forever
201: eth0: <NO-CARRIER,BROADCAST,MULTICAST,UP,LOWER_UP> mtu 1500 qdisc noqueue
    link/ether 02:42:ac:11:00:03 brd ff:ff:ff:ff:ff:ff
    inet 172.17.0.3/16 scope global eth0
       valid_lft forever preferred_lft forever
    inet6 fe80::42:acff:fe11:3/64 scope link tentative
       valid_lft forever preferred_lft forever
$
```

Evidently, the preceding output of the `ip addr` command shows that the Docker Engine
has created a network stack for the container with two network interfaces, which are as
follows:

- The first interface is the `lo` (Loopback) interface, for which the Docker Engine
  assigned the `127.0.0.1` Loopback address. The Loopback interface is used for
  local communication within a container.

- The second interface is an `eth0` (Ethernet) interface, for which the Docker Engine
  assigned the `172.17.0.3` IP address. Obviously, this address also falls within the
  same IP address range of the `docker0` Ethernet bridge interface. Besides, the
  address assigned to the `eth0` interface is used for intra-container communication
  and host-to-container communication.

> The `ip addr` and/or `ifconfig` commands are not supported by all
> Docker images, including `ubuntu:14.04` and `ubuntu:16.04`. The
> `docker inspect` subcommand is the reliable way to find the IP address
> of the container.

Earlier, we mentioned that docker0, the Ethernet bridge interface, acts as a conduit to pass the Ethernet frames between containers and also between containers and the external world. However, we have not yet clarified how the containers connect with the docker0 bridge. The following diagram unravels some of the mystery around this connection:

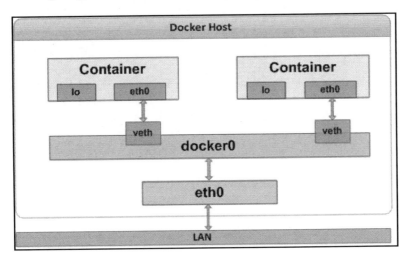

As depicted here, the container's eth0 interface is connected to the docker0 bridge using veth. The eth0 and veth interfaces belong to a special type of Linux network interface called a **Virtual Ethernet (veth)** Interface. The veth interface always comes in a pair, and they are like a water pipe wherein the data send from one veth interface will come out of the other interface and vice versa. The Docker Engine assigns one of the veth interfaces to the container with the eth0 name and assigns the container IP address to that interface. The other veth interface of the pair is bound to the docker0 bridge interface. This ensures the seamless flow of data between the Docker host and the containers.

Docker assigns private IP addresses to the container, which is not reachable from outside of the Docker host. However, the container IP address comes in handy for debugging within the Docker host. As we noted earlier, many Docker images do not support the ip addr or ifconfig commands, besides we may not directly have access to the container prompt to run any of these commands. Fortunately, Docker provides a docker inspect subcommand, which is as handy as a Swiss Army knife, to dive deep into the low-level details of the Docker container or image. The docker inspect subcommand reports quite a lot of details including the IP address and the gateway address. For the practical purpose, here you can either select a running container or temporarily launch a container, as follows:

```
$ sudo docker run -itd ubuntu:16.04
```

Here, let's assume the container ID is 4b0b567b6019 and run the docker inspect subcommand, as shown here:

```
$ sudo docker inspect 4b0b567b6019
```

This command generates quite a lot of information about the container. Here, we show some excerpts of the container's network configuration from the output of the docker inspect subcommand:

```
"Networks": {
    "bridge": {
        "IPAMConfig": null,
        "Links": null,
        "Aliases": null,
        "NetworkID": "ID removed for readability",
        "EndpointID": "ID removed for readability",
        "Gateway": "172.17.0.1",
        "IPAddress": "172.17.0.3",
        "IPPrefixLen": 16,
        "IPv6Gateway": "",
        "GlobalIPv6Address": "",
        "GlobalIPv6PrefixLen": 0,
        "MacAddress": "02:42:ac:11:00:03"
    }
}
```

Here are the details of some of the important fields in the network configuration:

- Gateway: This is the gateway address of the container, which is the address of the bridge interface as well
- IPAddress: This is the IP address assigned to the container
- IPPrefixLen: This is the IP prefix length, another way of representing the subnet mask

Without doubt, the docker inspect subcommand is quite convenient to find the minute details of a container or an image. However, it's a tiresome job to go through the intimidating details and to find the right information that we are keenly looking for. Perhaps, you can narrow it down to the right information, using the grep command. Alternatively, even better, the docker inspect subcommand helps you pick the right field from the JSON array using the --format option of the docker inspect subcommand.

Notably, in the following example, we use the `--format` option of the `docker inspect` subcommand to retrieve just the IP address of the container. The IP address is accessible through the `.NetworkSettings.IPAddress` field of the JSON array:

```
$ sudo docker inspect \
  --format='{{.NetworkSettings.IPAddress}}' 4b0b567b6019
172.17.0.3
```

In addition to the `none`, `host`, and `bridge` networking modes, Docker also supports the `overlay`, `macvlan`, and `ipvlan` network modes.

Envisaging container as a service

We laid a good foundation of the fundamentals of the Docker technology. In this section, we are going to focus on crafting an image with the HTTP service, launch the HTTP service inside the container using the crafted image, and then, demonstrate the connectivity to the HTTP service running inside the container.

Building an HTTP server image

In this section, we are going to craft a Docker image in order to install Apache2 on top of the Ubuntu 16.04 base image, and configure an Apache HTTP server to run as an executable, using the `ENTRYPOINT` instruction.

In *Chapter 3*, *Building Images*, we illustrated the concept of `Dockerfile` to craft an Apache2 image on top of the Ubuntu 16.04 base image. Here, in this example, we are going to extend this `Dockerfile` by setting the Apache log path and setting Apache2 as the default execution application, using the `ENTRYPOINT` instruction. The following is a detailed explanation of the content of `Dockerfile`.

We are going to build an image using `ubuntu:16.04` as the base image, using the `FROM` instruction, as shown in the `Dockerfile` snippet:

```
###########################################
# Dockerfile to build an apache2 image
###########################################
# Base image is Ubuntu
FROM ubuntu:16.04
```

Set the author's detail using the `MAINTAINER` instruction:

```
# Author: Dr. Peter
MAINTAINER Dr. Peter <peterindia@gmail.com>
```

Using one `RUN` instruction, we will synchronize the APT repository source list, install the apache2 package, and then clean the retrieved files:

```
# Install apache2 package
RUN apt-get update && \
    apt-get install -y apache2 && \
    apt-get clean
```

Set the Apache log directory path using the `ENV` instruction:

```
# Set the log directory PATH
ENV APACHE_LOG_DIR /var/log/apache2
```

Now, the final instruction is to launch the apache2 server using the `ENTRYPOINT` instruction:

```
# Launch apache2 server in the foreground
ENTRYPOINT ["/usr/sbin/apache2ctl", "-D", "FOREGROUND"]
```

In the preceding line, you might be surprised to see the `FOREGROUND` argument. This is one of the key differences between the traditional and the container paradigm. In the traditional paradigm, the server applications are usually launched in the background either as a service or a daemon because the host system is a general-purpose system. However, in the container paradigm, it is imperative to launch an application in the foreground because the images are crafted for a sole purpose.

Having prescribed the image building instruction in the `Dockerfile`, let's now move to the next logical step of building the image using the `docker build` subcommand by naming the image as apache2, as shown here:

```
$ sudo docker build -t apache2 .
```

Let's now do a quick verification of the images using the `docker images` subcommand:

```
$ sudo docker images
```

As we have seen in the previous chapters, the docker images command displays the details of all the images in the Docker host. However, in order to illustrate precisely the images created using the docker build subcommand, we highlight the details of apache2:latest (the target image) and ubuntu:16.04 (the base image) from the complete image list, as shown in the following output snippet:

```
       apache2              latest              1b34e47c273d         About a
minute ago    265.5 MB
       ubuntu               16.04               f753707788c5         3 weeks ago
127.2 MB
```

Having built the HTTP server image, let's now move on to the next session to learn how to run the HTTP service.

Running the HTTP server image as a service

In this section, we are going to launch a container using the Apache HTTP server image, we crafted in the previous section. Here, we launch the container in the detached mode (similar to the UNIX daemon process) using the -d option of the docker run subcommand:

```
$ sudo docker run -d apache2
9d4d3566e55c0b8829086e9be2040751017989a47b5411c9c4f170ab865afcef
```

Having launched the container, let's run the docker logs subcommand to see whether our Docker container generates any output on its stdin (standard input) or stderr (standard error):

```
$ sudo docker logs \
9d4d3566e55c0b8829086e9be2040751017989a47b5411c9c4f170ab865afcef
```

As we have not fully configured the Apache HTTP server, you will find the following warning, as the output of the docker logs subcommand:

```
AH00558: apache2: Could not reliably determine the server's fully qualified
domain name, using 172.17.0.13. Set the 'ServerName' directive globally to
suppress this message
```

From the preceding warning message, it is quite evident that the IP address assigned to this container is 172.17.0.13.

Connecting to the HTTP service

In the preceding section, indecently, from the warning message, we find out that the IP address of the container is 172.17.0.13. On a fully configured HTTP server container, no such warning is available, so let's still run the docker inspect subcommand to retrieve the IP address using the container ID:

```
$ sudo docker inspect \
--format='{{.NetworkSettings.IPAddress}}'
9d4d3566e55c0b8829086e9be2040751017989a47b5411c9c4f170ab865afcef
172.17.0.13
```

Having found the IP address of the container as 172.17.0.13, let's quickly run a web request on this IP address from the shell prompt of the Docker host, using the wget command. Here, we choose to run the wget command with –qO – in order to run in the quiet mode and also display the retrieved HTML file on the screen:

```
$ wget -qO - 172.17.0.13
```

Here, we are showcasing just the first five lines of the retrieved HTML file:

```
<!DOCTYPE html PUBLIC "-//W3C//DTD XHTML 1.0 Transitional//EN"
  "http://www.w3.org/TR/xhtml1/DTD/xhtml1-transitional.dtd">
<html xmlns="http://www.w3.org/1999/xhtml">
  <!--
    Modified from the Debian original for Ubuntu
    Last updated: 2014-03-19
```

Awesome, isn't it? We got our first service running in a container, and we are able to reach out to our service from our Docker host.

Furthermore, on a plain vanilla Docker installation, the service offered by one container is accessible by any other container within the Docker host. You can go ahead, launch a new Ubuntu container in the interactive mode, install the wget package using apt-get, and run the same wget -qO - 172.17.0.13 command, as we did in the Docker host. Of course, you will see the same output.

Exposing container services

So far, we successfully launched an HTTP service and accessed the service from the Docker host as well as another container within the same Docker host. Furthermore, as demonstrated in the *Building images from containers* section of Chapter 2, *Handling Docker Containers*, the container is able to successfully install the wget package by making a connection to the publicly available APT repository over the Internet. Nonetheless, the outside world cannot access the service offered by a container by default. At the outset, this might seem like a limitation in the Docker technology. However, the fact is, the containers are isolated from the outside world by design.

Docker achieves network isolation for the containers by the IP address assignment criteria, as enumerated here:

- Assigning a private IP address to the container, which is not reachable from an external network
- Assigning an IP address to the container outside the host's IP network

Consequently, the Docker container is not reachable even from the systems that are connected to the same IP network as the Docker host. This assignment scheme also provides protection from an IP address conflict that might otherwise arise.

Now, you might wonder how to make the services run inside a container that is accessible to the outside world, in other words, exposing container services. Well, Docker bridges this connectivity gap in a classy manner by leveraging the Linux iptables functionality under the hood.

At the frontend, Docker provides two different building blocks for bridging this connectivity gap for its users. One of the building blocks is to bind the container port using the -p (publish a container's port to the host interface) option of the docker run subcommand. Another alternative is to use the combination of the EXPOSE instruction of Dockerfile and the -P (publish all exposed ports to the host interfaces) option of the docker run subcommand.

Publishing a container's port – the -p option

Docker enables you to publish a service offered inside a container by binding the container's port to the host interface. The -p option of the docker run subcommand enables you to bind a container port to a user-specified or autogenerated port of the Docker host. Thus, any communication destined for the IP address and the port of the Docker host will be forwarded to the port of the container. The -p option, actually, supports the following four formats of arguments:

- <hostPort>:<containerPort>
- <containerPort>
- <ip>:<hostPort>:<containerPort>
- <ip>::<containerPort>

Here, <ip> is the IP address of the Docker host, <hostPort> is the Docker host port number, and <containerPort> is the port number of the container. Here, in this section, we present you with the -p <hostPort>:<containerPort> format and introduce other formats in the succeeding sections.

In order to understand the port binding process better, let's reuse the apache2 HTTP server image that we crafted previously and spin up a container using a -p option of the docker run subcommand. The 80 port is the published port of the HTTP service, and as the default behavior, our apache2 HTTP server is also available on port 80. Here, in order to demonstrate this capability, we are going to bind port 80 of the container to port 80 of the Docker host, using the -p <hostPort>:<containerPort> option of the docker run subcommand, as shown in the following command:

```
$ sudo docker run -d -p 80:80 apache2
baddba8afa98725ec85ad953557cd0614b4d0254f45436f9cb440f3f9eeae134
```

Now that we have successfully launched the container, we can connect to our HTTP server using any web browser from any external system (provided it has a network connectivity) to reach our Docker host.

So far, we have not added any web pages to our apache2 HTTP server image. Hence, when we connect from a web browser, we will get the following screen, which is nothing but the default page that comes along with the Ubuntu Apache2 package:

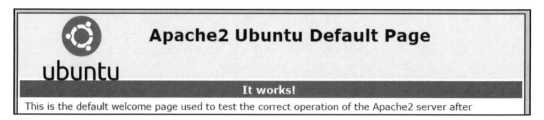

NAT for containers

In the previous section, we saw how a -p 80:80 option did the magic, didn't we? Well, in reality, under the hood, the Docker Engine achieves this seamless connectivity by automatically configuring the **Network Address Translation** (**NAT**) rule in the Linux iptables configuration files.

To illustrate the automatic configuration of the NAT rule in Linux iptables, let's query the Docker hosts iptables for its NAT entries, as follows:

```
$ sudo iptables -t nat -L -n
```

The ensuing text is an excerpt from the iptables NAT entry, which is automatically added by the Docker Engine:

```
Chain DOCKER (2 references)
target      prot opt source          destination
DNAT        tcp  --  0.0.0.0/0       0.0.0.0/0          tcp dpt:80
to:172.17.0.14:80
```

From the preceding excerpt, it is quite evident that the Docker Engine has effectively added a DNAT rule. The following are the details of the DNAT rule:

- The tcp keyword signifies that this DNAT rule applies only to the TCP transport protocol.
- The first 0.0.0.0/0 address is a meta IP address of the source address. This address indicates that the connection can originate from any IP address.

- The second `0.0.0.0/0` address is a meta IP address of the destination address on the Docker host. This address indicates that the connection can be made to any valid IP address in the Docker host.
- Finally, `dpt:80 to:172.17.0.14:80` is the forwarding instruction used to forward any TCP activity on port 80 of the Docker host to be forwarded to the `172.17.0.17` IP address, the IP address of our container and port 80.

 Therefore, any TCP packet that the Docker host receives on port 80 will be forwarded to port 80 of the container.

Retrieving the container port

The Docker Engine provides at least three different options to retrieve the container's port binding details. Here, let's first explore the options, and then, move on to dissect the retrieved information. The options are as follows:

- The `docker ps` subcommand always displays the port binding details of a container, as shown here:

```
$ sudo docker ps
CONTAINER ID        IMAGE              COMMAND
CREATED             STATUS             PORTS
NAMES
baddba8afa98        apache2:latest
"/usr/sbin/apache2ct
26 seconds ago      Up 25 seconds
0.0.0.0:80->80/tcp
furious_carson
```

- The `docker inspect` subcommand is another alternative; however, you have to skim through quite a lot of details. Run the following command:

```
$ sudo docker inspect baddba8afa98
```

- The `docker inspect` subcommand displays the port binding related information in three JSON objects, as shown here:

  - The `ExposedPorts` object enumerates all ports that are exposed through the `EXPOSE` instruction in `Dockerfile`, as well as the container ports that are mapped using the `-p` option in the `docker run` subcommand. Since we didn't add the `EXPOSE` instruction in our `Dockerfile`, what we have is just the container port that was mapped using `-p 80:80` as an argument to the `docker run` subcommand:

```
"ExposedPorts": {
        "80/tcp": {}
},
```

  - The `PortBindings` object is part of the `HostConfig` object, and this object lists out all the port binding done through the `-p` option in the `docker run` subcommand. This object will never list the ports exposed through the `EXPOSE` instruction in the `Dockerfile`:

```
"PortBindings": {
    "80/tcp": [
        {
            "HostIp": "",
            "HostPort": "80"
        }
    ]
},
```

  - The `Ports` object of the `NetworkSettings` object has the same level of details, as the preceding `PortBindings` object. However, this object encompasses all ports that are exposed through the `EXPOSE` instruction in `Dockerfile`, as well as the container ports that are mapped using the `-p` option in the `docker run` subcommand:

```
"NetworkSettings": {
    "Bridge": "",
    "SandboxID":"ID removed for readability",
    "HairpinMode": false,
    "LinkLocalIPv6Address": "",
    "LinkLocalIPv6PrefixLen": 0,
    "Ports": {
        "80/tcp": [
```

```
                        {
                            "HostIp": "0.0.0.0",
                            "HostPort": "80"
                        }
                    ]
                },
```

Of course, the specific port field can be filtered using the `--format` option of the `docker inspect` subcommand.

The `docker port` subcommand enables you to retrieve the port binding on the Docker host by specifying the container's port number:

```
$ sudo docker port baddba8afa98 80
0.0.0.0:80
```

Evidently, in all the preceding output excerpts, the information that stands out is the `0.0.0.0` IP address and the `80` port number. The `0.0.0.0` IP address is a meta address, which represents all the IP addresses configured on the Docker host. In effect, the `80` container's port is bound to all the valid IP addresses on the Docker host. Therefore, the HTTP service is accessible through any of the valid IP addresses configured on the Docker host.

Binding a container to a specific IP address

Until now, with the method that you learned, the containers always get bound to all the IP addresses configured on the Docker host. However, you may want to offer different services on different IP addresses. In other words, a specific IP address and port would be configured to offer a particular service. We can achieve this in Docker using the `-p` `<ip>:<hostPort>:<containerPort>` option of the `docker run` subcommand, as shown in the following example:

```
$ sudo docker run -d -p 198.51.100.73:80:80 apache2
92f107537bebd48e8917ea4f4788bf3f57064c8c996fc23ea0fd8ea49b4f3335
```

Here, the IP address must be a valid IP address on the Docker host. If the specified IP address is not a valid IP address on the Docker host, the container launch will fail with an error message, as follows:

```
2014/11/09 10:22:10 Error response from daemon: Cannot start container
99db8d30b284c0a0826d68044c42c370875d2c3cad0b87001b858ba78e9de53b:
Error starting user land proxy: listen tcp 10.110.73.34:49153: bind:cannot
assign requested address
```

Now, let's quickly review the port mapping as well the NAT entry for the preceding example:

- The following text is an excerpt from the output of the `docker ps` subcommand that shows the details of this container:

```
92f107537beb          apache2:latest          "/usr/sbin/apache2ct
About a minute ago   Up About a minute    198.51.100.73:80->80/tcp
boring_ptolemy
```

- The following text is an excerpt from the output of the `iptables -n nat -L -n` command that shows the DNAT entry created for this container:

```
DNAT     tcp -- 0.0.0.0/0          198.51.100.73      tcp dpt:80
to:172.17.0.15:80
```

After reviewing both the output of the `docker run` subcommand and the DNAT entry of `iptables`, you will realize how elegantly the Docker Engine has configured the service offered by the container on the `198.51.100.73` IP address and `80` port of the Docker host.

Autogenerating the Docker host port

The Docker containers are innately lightweight and due to their lightweight nature, you can run multiple containers with the same or different service on a single Docker host. Particularly, autoscaling of the same service across several containers based on the demand is the need of the IT infrastructure today. Here, in this section, you will be informed about the challenge in spinning up multiple containers with the same service and also the Docker's way of addressing this challenge.

Earlier in this chapter, we launched a container using Apache2 HTTP server by binding it to port `80` of the Docker host. Now, if we attempt to launch one more container with the same port `80` binding, the container would fail to start with an error message, as you can see in the following example:

```
$ sudo docker run -d -p 80:80 apache2
6f01f485ab3ce81d45dc6369316659aed17eb341e9ad0229f66060a8ba4a2d0e
2014/11/03 23:28:07 Error response from daemon: Cannot start container
6f01f485ab3ce81d45dc6369316659aed17eb341e9ad0229f66060a8ba4a2d0e:
Bind for 0.0.0.0:80 failed: port is already allocated
```

Obviously, in the preceding example, the container failed to start because the previous container is already mapped to `0.0.0.0` (all the IP addresses of the Docker host) and port `80`. In the TCP/IP communication model, the combination of the IP address, port, and the transport protocols (TCP, UDP, and so on) has to be unique.

We could have overcome this issue by manually choosing the Docker host port number (for instance, `-p 81:80` or `-p 8081:80`). Though this is an excellent solution, it does not scale well for autoscaling scenarios. Instead, if we give the control to Docker, it would autogenerate the port number on the Docker host. This port number generation is achieved by underspecifying the Docker host port number, using the `-p <containerPort>` option of the `docker run` subcommand, as shown in the following example:

```
$ sudo docker run -d -p 80 apache2
ea3e0d1b18cff40ffcddd2bf077647dc94bceffad967b86c1a343bd33187d7a8
```

Having successfully started the new container with the autogenerated port, let's review the port mapping as well the NAT entry for the preceding example:

- The following text is an excerpt from the output of the `docker ps` subcommand that shows the details of this container:

```
ea3e0d1b18cf          apache2:latest        "/usr/sbin/apache2ct
5 minutes ago         Up 5 minutes          0.0.0.0:49158->80/tcp
nostalgic_morse
```

- The following text is an excerpt from the output of the `iptables -n nat -L -n` command that shows the DNAT entry created for this container:

```
DNAT      tcp -- 0.0.0.0/0         0.0.0.0/0         tcp dpt:49158
to:172.17.0.18:80
```

After reviewing both the output of the `docker run` subcommand and the DNAT entry of `iptables`, what stands out is the `49158` port number. The `49158` port number is niftily autogenerated by the Docker Engine on the Docker host, with the help of the underlying operating system. Besides, the `0.0.0.0` meta IP address implies that the service offered by the container is accessible from outside, through any of the valid IP addresses configured on the Docker host.

You may have a use case where you want to autogenerate the port number. However, if you still want to restrict the service to a particular IP address of the Docker host, you can use the `-p <IP>::<containerPort>` option of the `docker run` subcommand, as shown in the following example:

```
$ sudo docker run -d -p 198.51.100.73::80 apache2
6b5de258b3b82da0290f29946436d7ae307c8b72f22239956e453356532ec2a7
```

In the preceding two scenarios, the Docker Engine autogenerated the port number on the Docker host and exposed it to the outside world. The general norm of network communication is to expose any service through a predefined port number so that anybody knows the IP address, and the port number can easily access the offered service. Whereas, here the port numbers are autogenerated and as a result, the outside world cannot directly reach the offered service. So, the primary purpose of this method of container creation is to achieve autoscaling, and the container created in this fashion would be interfaced with a proxy or load balance service on a predefined port.

Port binding using EXPOSE and -P option

So far, we have discussed the four distinct methods to publish a service running inside a container to the outside world. In all these four methods, the port binding decision is taken during the container launch, and the image has no information about the ports on which the service is being offered. It has worked well so far because the image is being built by us, and we are pretty much aware of the port in which the service is being offered.

However, in the case of third-party images, the port usage inside a container has to be published unambiguously. Besides, if we build images for third-party consumption or even for our own use, it is a good practice to explicitly state the ports in which the container offers its service. Perhaps, the image builders could ship a README document along with the image. However, it is even better to embed the port details in the image itself so that you can easily find the port details from the image both manually as well as through automated scripts.

The Docker technology allows us to embed the port information using the EXPOSE instruction in the `Dockerfile`, which we introduced in Chapter 3, *Building Images*. Here, let's edit the `Dockerfile` we used to build the apache2 HTTP server image earlier in this chapter, and add an EXPOSE instruction, as shown in the following code. The default port for the HTTP service is port 80, hence port 80 is exposed:

```
###########################################
# Dockerfile to build an apache2 image
###########################################
```

```
# Base image is Ubuntu
FROM ubuntu:16.04
# Author: Dr. Peter
MAINTAINER Dr. Peter <peterindia@gmail.com>
# Install apache2 package
RUN apt-get update &&
    apt-get install -y apache2 &&
    apt-get clean
# Set the log directory PATH
ENV APACHE_LOG_DIR /var/log/apache2
# Expose port 80
EXPOSE 80
# Launch apache2 server in the foreground
ENTRYPOINT ["/usr/sbin/apache2ctl", "-D", "FOREGROUND"]
```

Now that we have added the EXPOSE instruction to our Dockerfile, let's move to the next step of building the image using the docker build command. Here, let's reuse the apache2 image name, as shown here:

```
$ sudo docker build -t apache2 .
```

Having successfully built the image, let's inspect the image to verify the effects of the EXPOSE instruction to the image. As we learned earlier, we can resort to the docker inspect subcommand, as shown here:

```
$ sudo docker inspect apache2
```

On a close review of the output generated by the preceding command, you will realize that Docker stores the exposed port information in the ExposedPorts field of the Config object. The following is an excerpt to show how the exposed port information is being displayed:

```
"ExposedPorts": {
    "80/tcp": {}
},
```

Alternatively, you can apply the --format option to the docker inspect subcommand in order to narrow down the output to a very specific information. In this case, the ExposedPorts field of the Config object is shown in the following example:

```
$ sudo docker inspect --format='{{.Config.ExposedPorts}}'  apache2
map[80/tcp:map[]]
```

To resume our discussion on the EXPOSE instruction, we can now spin up containers using an apache2 image, we just crafted. Yet, the EXPOSE instruction by itself cannot create a port binding on the Docker host. In order to create a port binding for the port declared using the EXPOSE instruction, the Docker Engine provides a -P option in the docker run subcommand.

In the following example, a container is launched from the apache2 image, which was rebuilt earlier. Here, the -d option is used to launch the container in the detached mode, and the -P option is used to create the port binding on the Docker host for all the ports declared, using the EXPOSE instruction in the Dockerfile:

```
$ sudo docker run -d -P apache2
fdb1c8d68226c384ab4f84882714fec206a73fd8c12ab57981fbd874e3fa9074
```

Now that we have started the new container with the image that was created using the EXPOSE instruction, like the previous containers, let's review the port mapping as well the NAT entry for the preceding example:

- The following text is an excerpt from the output of the docker ps subcommand that shows the details of this container:

```
ea3e0d1b18cf        apache2:latest       "/usr/sbin/apache2ct
5 minutes ago       Up 5 minutes         0.0.0.0:49159->80/tcp
nostalgic_morse
```

- The following text is an excerpt from the output of the iptables -t nat -L -n command that shows the DNAT entry created for this container:

```
DNAT    tcp -- 0.0.0.0/0       0.0.0.0/0
tcp dpt:49159 to:172.17.0.19:80
```

The -P option of the docker run subcommand does not take any additional arguments, such as an IP address or a port number; consequently, fine-tuning of the port binding is not possible, such as the -p option of the docker run subcommand. You can always resort to the -p option of the docker run subcommand if fine-tuning of port binding is critical to you.

Summary

Containers do not deliver anything substantial in an isolated or solo way. They need to be systematically built and provided with a network interface along with a port number. These lead to the standardized exposition of containers to the outside world, facilitating other hosts or containers to find, bind, and leverage their unique capabilities on any network. Thus, the network accessibility is paramount for containers to get noticed across and be utilized in innumerable ways. This chapter was dedicated to showcase how containers are being designed and deployed as a service, and how the aspect of container networking comes in handy in precisely and profusely empowering the peculiar world of container services as the days unfold. In the forthcoming chapters, we will deal and dwell at length on the various capabilities of Docker containers in the software-intensive IT environments.

7
Sharing Data with Containers

"Do one thing at a time and do it well," has been one of the successful mantras in the **Information Technology (IT)** sector for quite a long time now. This widely used tenet fits nicely to build and expose Docker containers too, and it is being prescribed as one of the best practices to avail the originally envisaged benefits of the Docker-inspired containerization paradigm. This means that, we must inscribe a single application along with its direct dependencies and libraries inside a Docker container in order to ensure the container's independence, self-sufficiency, horizontal scalability, and maneuverability. Let's see why containers are that important:

- **The temporal nature of containers**: The container typically lives as long as the application lives and vice versa. However, this has some negative implications for the application data. Applications naturally go through a variety of changes in order to accommodate both business as well as technical changes, even in their production environments. There are other causes, such as application malfunctions, version changes, and application maintenance, for software applications to be consistently and constantly updated and upgraded. In the case of a general-purpose computing model, even when an application dies for any reason, the persistent data associated with this application can be preserved in the filesystem. However, in the case of the container paradigm, the application upgrades are usually performed by systematically crafting a new container with the newer version of the application by simply discarding the old one. Similarly, when an application malfunctions, a new container needs to be launched and the old one has to be discarded. To sum it up, containers are typically temporal in nature.

- **The need for a business continuity**: In the container landscape, the complete execution environment, including its data files, is usually bundled and encapsulated inside the container. For any reason, when a container gets discarded, the application data files also perish along with the container. However, in order to provide software applications without any interruption and disruption of service, these application data files must be preserved outside the container and passed on to the container on a need basis in order to ensure business continuity. This means that the resiliency and reliability of containers need to be guaranteed. Besides, some application data files, such as the log files, needs to be collected and accessed outside the container for various posterior analyses. The Docker technology addresses this file persistence issue very innovatively through a new building block called data volume.

The Docker technology has three different ways of providing persistent storage:

- The first and recommended approach is to use volumes that are created using Docker's volume management.
- The second method is to mount a directory from the Docker host to a specified location inside the container.
- The other alternative is to use a data-only container. The data-only container is a specially crafted container that is used to share data with one or more containers.

In this chapter, we will cover the following topics:

- Data volume
- Sharing host data
- Sharing data between containers
- The avoidable common pitfalls

Data volume

Data volume is the fundamental building block of data sharing in the Docker environment. Before getting into the details of data sharing, it is imperative to get a good understanding of the data volume concept. Until now, all the files that we create in an image or a container is part and parcel of the union filesystem. The container's union filesystem perishes along with the container. In other words, when the container is removed, its filesystem is also automatically removed. However, the enterprise-grade applications must persist data and the container's filesystem will not render itself for such a requirement.

The Docker ecosystem, however, elegantly addresses this issue with the data volume concept. Data volume is essentially a part of the Docker host filesystem and it simply gets mounted inside the container. Optionally, you can use other advanced filesystems such as Flocker and GlusterFS as data volumes through pluggable volume drivers. Since data volume is not a part of the container's filesystem, it has a life cycle independent of the container.

A data volume can be inscribed in a Docker image using the VOLUME instruction of the Dockerfile. Also, it can be prescribed during the launch of a container using the −v option of the docker run subcommand. Here, in the following example, the implication of the VOLUME instruction in the Dockerfile is illustrated in detail in the following steps:

1. Create a very simple Dockerfile with the instruction of the base image (ubuntu:16.04) and the data volume (/MountPointDemo):

```
FROM ubuntu:16.04
VOLUME /MountPointDemo
```

2. Build the image with the mount-point-demo name using the docker build subcommand:

```
$ sudo docker build -t mount-point-demo .
```

3. Having built the image, let's quickly inspect the image for our data volume using the docker inspect subcommand:

```
$ sudo docker inspect mount-point-demo
[
    {
        "Id": "sha256:<64 bit hex id>",
        "RepoTags": [
            "mount-point-demo:latest"
        ],
... TRUNCATED OUTPUT ...
        "Volumes": {
            "/MountPointDemo": {}
        },
... TRUNCATED OUTPUT ...
```

Evidently, in the preceding output, data volume is inscribed in the image itself.

4. Now, let's launch an interactive container using the `docker run` subcommand from the earlier crafted image, as shown in the following command:

```
$ sudo docker run --rm -it mount-point-demo
```

From the container's prompt, let's check the presence of data volume using the `ls -ld` command:

```
root@8d22f73b5b46:/# ls -ld /MountPointDemo
drwxr-xr-x 2 root root 4096 Nov 18 19:22
/MountPointDemo
```

As mentioned earlier, data volume is part of the Docker host filesystem and it gets mounted, as shown in the following command:

```
root@8d22f73b5b46:/# mount | grep MountPointDemo
/dev/xvda2 on /MountPointDemo type ext3
(rw,noatime,nobarrier,errors=remount-ro,data=ordered)
```

5. In this section, we inspected the image to find out about the data volume declaration in the image. Now that we have launched the container, let's inspect the container's data volume using the `docker inspect` subcommand with the container ID as its argument in a different Terminal. We created a few containers previously and for this purpose, let's take the 8d22f73b5b46 container ID directly from the container's prompt:

```
$ sudo docker inspect -f
'{{json .Mounts}}' 8d22f73b5b46
    [
        {
            "Propagation": "",
            "RW": true,
            "Mode": "",
            "Driver": "local",
            "Destination": "/MountPointDemo",
            "Source":
"/var/lib/docker/volumes/720e2a2478e70a7cb49ab7385b8be627d4b6ec52e6bb33063e
4144355d59592a/_data",
"Name": "720e2a2478e70a7cb49ab7385b8be627d4b6ec52e6bb33063e4144355d59592a"
        }
    ]
```

Apparently, here, data volume is mapped to a directory in the Docker host, and the directory is mounted in the read-write mode. This directory, also called as volume, is created by the Docker Engine automatically during the launch of the container. Since version 1.9 of Docker, the volumes are managed through a top-level volume management command, which we will dive and dig further down into tell all in the next section.

So far, we have seen the implication of the VOLUME instruction in the `Dockerfile`, and how Docker manages data volume. Like the VOLUME instruction of the `Dockerfile`, we can use the `-v <container mount point path>` option of the `docker run` subcommand, as shown in the following command:

```
$ sudo docker run -v /MountPointDemo -it ubuntu:16.04
```

Having launched the container, we encourage you to try the `ls -ld /MountPointDemo` and `mount` commands in the newly launched container, and then also, inspect the container, as shown in the preceding step 5.

In both the scenarios described here, the Docker Engine automatically creates the volume under the `/var/lib/docker/volumes/` directory and mounts it to the container. When a container is removed using the `docker rm` subcommand, the Docker Engine does not remove the volume that was automatically created during the launch of the container. This behavior is innately designed to preserve the state of the container's application that was stored in the volume filesystem. If you want to remove the volume that was automatically created by the Docker Engine, you can do so while removing the container by providing a `-v` option to the `docker rm` subcommand, on an already stopped container:

```
$ sudo docker rm -v 8d22f73b5b46
```

If the container is still running, then you can remove the container as well as the autogenerated directory by adding a `-f` option to the previous command:

```
$ sudo docker rm -fv 8d22f73b5b46
```

We have taken you through the techniques and tips to autogenerate a directory in the Docker host and mount it to the data volume in the container. However, with the `-v` option of the `docker run` subcommand, a user-defined directory can be mounted to the data volume. In such cases, the Docker Engine will not autogenerate any directory.

 The system generation of a directory has a caveat of directory leak. In other words, if you forget to delete the system-generated directories, you may face some unwanted issues. For further information, read the *Avoiding common pitfalls* section in this chapter.

The volume management command

Docker has introduced a top-level volume management command from version 1.9 in order to manage the persistent filesystem effectively. The volume management command is capable of managing data volumes that are part of the Docker host. In addition to that, it also helps us to extend the Docker persistent capability using pluggable volume drivers (Flocker, GlusterFS, and so on). You can find the list of supported plugins at `https://docs.docker.com/engine/extend/legacy_plugins/`.

The `docker volume` command supports four subcommands as listed here:

- `create`: This creates a new volume
- `inspect`: This displays detailed information about one or more volumes
- `ls`: This lists the volumes in the Docker host
- `rm`: This removes a volume

Let's quickly explore the volume management command through a few examples. You can create a volume using the `docker volume create` subcommand, as shown here:

```
$ sudo docker volume create
50957995c7304e7d398429585d36213bb87781c53550b72a6a27c755c7a99639
```

The preceding command will create a volume by autogenerating a 64-hex digit string as the volume name. However, it is more effective to name the volume with a meaningful name for easy identification. You can name a volume using the `--name` option of the `docker volume create` subcommand:

```
$ sudo docker volume create --name example
example
```

Now, that we have created two volumes with and without a volume name, let's use the `docker volume ls` subcommand to display them:

```
$ sudo docker volume ls
DRIVER              VOLUME NAME
local
50957995c7304e7d398429585d36213bb87781c53550b72a6a27c755c7a99639
local               example
```

Having listed out the volumes, let's run the `docker volume inspect` subcommand into the details of the volumes we have created earlier:

```
$ sudo docker volume inspect example
[
    {
        "Name": "example",
        "Driver": "local",
        "Mountpoint":
        "/var/lib/docker/volumes/example/_data",
        "Labels": {},
        "Scope": "local"
    }
]
```

The `docker volume rm` subcommand enables you to remove the volumes you don't need anymore:

```
$ sudo docker volume rm example
example
```

Now that we are familiar with Docker volume management, let's dive deep into data sharing in the ensuing sections.

Sharing host data

Earlier, we described the steps to create a data volume in a Docker image using the VOLUME instruction in the `Dockerfile`. However, Docker does not provide any mechanism to mount the host directory or file during the build time in order to ensure the Docker images to be portable. The only provision Docker provides is to mount the host directory or file to a container's data volume during the container's launch. Docker exposes the host directory or file mounting facility through the -v option of the `docker run` subcommand. The -v option has five different formats, enumerated as follows:

- -v <container mount path>
- -v <host path>:<container mount path>
- -v <host path>:<container mount path>:<read write mode>
- -v <volume name>:<container mount path>
- -v <volume name>:<container mount path>:<read write mode>

The `<host path>` format is an absolute path in the Docker host, `<container mount path>` is an absolute path in the container filesystem, `<volume name>` is the name of the volume created using the `docker volume create` subcommand, and `<read write mode>` can be either the read-only (`ro`) or read-write (`rw`) mode. The first `-v <container mount path>` format has already been explained in the *Data volume* section in this chapter, as a method to create a mount point during the launch of the container launch. The second and third formats enable us to mount a file or directory from the Docker host to the container mount point. The fourth and fifth formats allow us to mount volumes created using the `docker volume create` subcommand.

We would like to dig deeper to gain a better understanding of the host's data sharing through a couple of examples. In the first example, we will demonstrate how to share a directory between the Docker host and the container, and in the second example, we will demonstrate file sharing.

Here, in the first example, we mount a directory from the Docker host to a container, perform a few basic file operations on the container, and verify these operations from the Docker host, as detailed in the following steps:

1. First, let's launch an interactive container with the `-v` option of the `docker run` subcommand to mount `/tmp/hostdir` of the Docker host directory to `/MountPoint` of the container:

   ```
   $ sudo docker run -v /tmp/hostdir:/MountPoint \
     -it ubuntu:16.04
   ```

    If `/tmp/hostdir` is not found on the Docker host, the Docker Engine will create the directory per se. However, the problem is that the system-generated directory cannot be deleted using the `-v` option of the `docker rm` subcommand.

2. Having successfully launched the container, we can check the presence of `/MountPoint` using the `ls` command:

   ```
   root@4a018d99c133:/# ls -ld /MountPoint
   drwxr-xr-x 2 root root 4096 Nov 23 18:28
   /MountPoint
   ```

3. Now, we can proceed to check the mount details using the `mount` command:

   ```
   root@4a018d99c133:/# mount | grep MountPoint
   /dev/xvda2 on /MountPoint type ext3
   (rw,noatime,nobarrier,errors=
   remount-ro,data=ordered)
   ```

4. Here, we are going to validate /MountPoint, change to the /MountPoint directory using the cd command, create a few files using the touch command, and list the files using the ls command, as shown in the following script:

```
root@4a018d99c133:/# cd /MountPoint/
root@4a018d99c133:/MountPoint# touch {a,b,c}
root@4a018d99c133:/MountPoint# ls -l
total 0
-rw-r--r-- 1 root root 0 Nov 23 18:39 a
-rw-r--r-- 1 root root 0 Nov 23 18:39 b
-rw-r--r-- 1 root root 0 Nov 23 18:39 c
```

5. It might be worth the effort to verify the files in the /tmp/hostdir Docker host directory using the ls command on a new Terminal, as our container is running in an interactive mode on the existing Terminal:

```
$ sudo  ls -l /tmp/hostdir/
total 0
-rw-r--r-- 1 root root 0 Nov 23 12:39 a
-rw-r--r-- 1 root root 0 Nov 23 12:39 b
-rw-r--r-- 1 root root 0 Nov 23 12:39 c
```

Here, we can see the same set of files, as we saw in step 4. However, you might have noticed the difference in the timestamp of the files. This time difference is due to the time zone difference between the Docker host and the container.

6. Finally, let's run the docker inspect subcommand with the 4a018d99c133 container ID as an argument to see whether the directory mapping is set up between the Docker host and the container mount point, as shown in the following command:

```
$ sudo docker inspect \
            --format='{{json .Mounts}}' 4a018d99c133
[{"Source":"/tmp/hostdir",
"Destination":"/MountPoint","Mode":"",
"RW":true,"Propagation":"rprivate"}]
```

Apparently, in the preceding output of the docker inspect subcommand, the /tmp/hostdir directory of the Docker host is mounted on the /MountPoint mount point of the container.

For the second example, we will mount a file from the Docker host to a container, update the file from the container, and verify those operations from the Docker host, as detailed in the following steps:

1. In order to mount a file from the Docker host to the container, the file must preexist in the Docker host. Otherwise, the Docker Engine will create a new directory with the specified name and mount it as a directory. We can start by creating a file on the Docker host using the `touch` command:

   ```
   $ touch /tmp/hostfile.txt
   ```

2. Launch an interactive container with the `-v` option of the `docker run` subcommand to mount the `/tmp/hostfile.txt` Docker host file to the container as `/tmp/mntfile.txt`:

   ```
   $ sudo docker run -v /tmp/hostfile.txt:/mntfile.txt \
               -it ubuntu:16.04
   ```

3. Having successfully launched the container, now let's check the presence of `/mntfile.txt` using the `ls` command:

   ```
   root@d23a15527eeb:/# ls -l /mntfile.txt
   -rw-rw-r-- 1 1000 1000 0 Nov 23 19:33 /mntfile.txt
   ```

4. Then, proceed to check the mount details using the `mount` command:

   ```
   root@d23a15527eeb:/# mount | grep mntfile
   /dev/xvda2 on /mntfile.txt type ext3
   (rw,noatime,nobarrier,errors=remount-ro,data=ordered)
   ```

5. Then, update some text to `/mntfile.txt` using the `echo` command:

   ```
   root@d23a15527eeb:/# echo "Writing from Container"
            > mntfile.txt
   ```

6. Meanwhile, switch to a different Terminal in the Docker host, and print the `/tmp/hostfile.txt` Docker host file using the `cat` command:

   ```
   $ cat /tmp/hostfile.txt
   Writing from Container
   ```

7. Finally, run the `docker inspect` subcommand with the d23a15527eeb container ID as it's argument to see the file mapping between the Docker host and the container mount point:

```
$ sudo docker inspect \
               --format='{{json .Mounts}}' d23a15527eeb
[{"Source":"/tmp/hostfile.txt",
"Destination":"/mntfile.txt",
"Mode":"","RW":true,"Propagation":"rprivate"}]
```

From the preceding output, it is evident that the `/tmp/hostfile.txt` file from the Docker host is mounted as `/mntfile.txt` inside the container.

For the last example, we will create a Docker volume and mount a named data volume to a container. In this example, we are not going to run the verification steps as we did in the previous two examples. However, you are encouraged to run the verification steps we laid out in the first example.

1. Create a named data volume using the `docker volume create` subcommand, as shown here:

```
$ docker volume create --name namedvol
```

2. Now, launch an interactive container with the `-v` option of the `docker run` subcommand to mount `namedvol` a named data value to `/MountPoint` of the container:

```
$ sudo docker run -v namedvol:/MountPoint \
          -it ubuntu:16.04
```

 During the launch of the container, Docker Engine creates `namedvol` if it is not created already.

3. Having successfully launched the container, you can repeat the verification steps 2 to 6 of the first example and you will find the same output pattern in this example as well.

The practicality of host data sharing

In the previous chapter, we launched an HTTP service in a Docker container. However, if you remember correctly, the log file for the HTTP service is still inside the container, and it cannot be accessed directly from the Docker host. Here, in this section, we elucidate the procedure of accessing the log files from the Docker host in a step-by-step manner:

1. Let's begin with launching an Apache2 HTTP service container by mounting the /var/log/myhttpd directory of the Docker host to the /var/log/apache2 directory of the container, using the -v option of the docker run subcommand. In this example, we are leveraging the apache2 image, which we had built in the previous chapter, by invoking the following command:

   ```
   $ sudo docker run -d -p 80:80 \
      -v /var/log/myhttpd:/var/log/apache2 apache2
   9c2f0c0b126f21887efaa35a1432ba7092b69e0c6d523ffd50684e27eeab37ac
   ```

   If you recall the Dockerfile in Chapter 6, *Running Services in a Container*, the APACHE_LOG_DIR environment variable is set to the /var/log/apache2 directory, using the ENV instruction. This will make the Apache2 HTTP service to route all log messages to the /var/log/apache2 data volume.

2. Once the container is launched, we can change the directory to /var/log/myhttpd on the Docker host:

   ```
   $ cd /var/log/myhttpd
   ```

3. Perhaps, a quick check of the files present in the /var/log/myhttpd directory is appropriate here:

   ```
   $ ls -1
   access.log
   error.log
   other_vhosts_access.log
   ```

   Here, the access.log file contains all the access requests handled by the Apache2 HTTP server. The error.log file is a very important log file, where our HTTP server records the errors it encounters while processing any HTTP requests. The other_vhosts_access.log file is the virtual host log, which will always be empty in our case.

4. We can display the content of all the log files in the `/var/log/myhttpd` directory using the `tail` command with the `-f` option:

```
$ tail -f *.log
==> access.log <==

==> error.log <==
AH00558: apache2: Could not reliably determine the
server's fully qualified domain name, using 172.17.0.17.
Set the 'ServerName' directive globally to suppress this
message
[Thu Nov 20 17:45:35.619648 2014] [mpm_event:notice]
[pid 16:tid 140572055459712] AH00489: Apache/2.4.7
(Ubuntu) configured -- resuming normal operations
[Thu Nov 20 17:45:35.619877 2014] [core:notice]
[pid 16:tid 140572055459712] AH00094: Command line:
'/usr/sbin/apache2 -D FOREGROUND'
==> other_vhosts_access.log <==
```

The `tail -f` command will run continuously and display the content of the files, as soon as they get updated. Here, both `access.log` and `other_vhosts_access.log` are empty, and there are a few error messages on the `error.log` file. Apparently, these error logs are generated by the HTTP service running inside the container. The logs are then stocked in the Docker host directory, which is mounted during the launch of the container.

5. As we continue to run `tail -f *`, let's connect to the HTTP service from a web browser running inside the container, and observe the log files:

```
==> access.log <==
111.111.172.18 - - [20/Nov/2014:17:53:38 +0000] "GET /
HTTP/1.1" 200 3594 "-" "Mozilla/5.0 (Windows NT 6.1;
WOW64)
AppleWebKit/537.36 (KHTML, like Gecko) Chrome/39.0.2171.65
Safari/537.36"
111.111.172.18 - - [20/Nov/2014:17:53:39 +0000] "GET
/icons/ubuntu-logo.png HTTP/1.1" 200 3688
"http://111.71.123.110/" "Mozilla/5.0 (Windows NT 6.1;
WOW64)
AppleWebKit/537.36 (KHTML, like Gecko) Chrome/39.0.2171.65
Safari/537.36"
111.111.172.18 - - [20/Nov/2014:17:54:21 +0000] "GET
/favicon.ico HTTP/1.1" 404 504 "-" "Mozilla/5.0 (Windows
NT 6.1; WOW64) AppleWebKit/537.36 (KHTML, like Gecko)
Chrome/39.0.2171.65 Safari/537.36"
```

The HTTP service updates the `access.log` file, which we can manipulate from the host directory mounted through the `-v` option of the `docker run` subcommand.

Sharing data between containers

In the previous section, you learned how seamlessly the Docker Engine enables data sharing between the Docker host and the container. Although it is a very effective solution for most of the use cases, there are use cases wherein you will have to share data between one or more containers. The Docker's prescription to address this use case is to mount the data volume of one container to other containers using the `--volume-from` option of the `docker run` subcommand.

Data-only containers

Before Docker introduced the top-level volume management feature, the data-only container was the recommended approach to achieve data persistency. It is worth understanding data-only containers because you will find many implementations that are based on data-only containers. The prime responsibility of a data-only container is to preserve the data. Creating a data-only container is very similar to the method illustrated in the *Data volume* section. In addition, the containers are named explicitly for other containers to mount the data volume using the container's name. Besides, the container's data volumes are accessible from other containers even when the data-only containers are in the stopped state. The data-only containers can be created in two ways, as follows:

- During the launch of the container by configuring the data volume and the container's name
- Data volume can also be inscribed with `Dockerfile` during image-building, and later, the container can be named during the container's launch

In the following example, we are launching a data-only container by configuring the container launch with the `-v` and `--name` options of the `docker run` subcommand, as shown here:

```
$ sudo docker run --name datavol \
                  -v /DataMount \
                  busybox:latest /bin/true
```

Here, the container is launched from the `busybox` image, which is widely used for its smaller footprint. Here, we choose to execute the `/bin/true` command because we don't intend to do any operations on the container. Therefore, we named the container `datavol` using the `--name` option and created a new `/DataMount` data volume using the `-v` option of the `docker run` subcommand. The `/bin/true` command exits immediately with the `0` exit status, which in turn will stop the container and continue to be in the stopped state.

Mounting data volume from other containers

The Docker Engine provides a nifty interface to mount (share) the data volume from one container to another. Docker makes this interface available through the `--volumes-from` option of the `docker run` subcommand. The `--volumes-from` option takes a container name or container ID as its input and automatically mounts all the data volumes available on the specified container. Docker allows you to mount multiple containers with data volume using the `--volumes-from` option multiple times.

Here is a practical example that demonstrates how to mount data volume from another container and showcases the data volume mount step by step:

1. We begin with launching an interactive Ubuntu container by mounting the data volume from the data-only container (`datavol`), which we launched in the previous section:

```
$ sudo docker run -it \
            --volumes-from datavol \
            ubuntu:latest /bin/bash
```

2. Now from the container's prompt, let's verify the data volume mounts using the `mount` command:

```
root@e09979cacec8:/# mount | grep DataMount
/dev/xvda2 on /DataMount type ext3
(rw,noatime,nobarrier,errors=remount-ro,data=ordered)
```

Here, we successfully mounted the data volume from the `datavol` data-only container.

3. Next, we need to inspect the data volume of this container from another Terminal using the `docker inspect` subcommand:

```
$ sudo docker inspect --format='{{json .Mounts}}'
e09979cacec8
[{"Name":
"7907245e5962ac07b31c6661a4dd9b283722d3e7d0b0fb40a90
43b2f28365021","Source":
"/var/lib/docker/volumes
/7907245e5962ac07b31c6661a4dd9b283722d3e7d0b0fb40a9043b
2f28365021/_data","Destination":"
/DataMount","Driver":"local","Mode":"",
"RW":true,"Propagation":""}]
```

Evidently, the data volume from the `datavol` data-only container is mounted as if they were mounted directly on to this container.

We can mount a data volume from another container and also showcase the mount points. We can make the mounted data volume to work by sharing data between containers using the data volume, as demonstrated here:

1. Let's reuse the container that we launched in the previous example and create a `/DataMount/testfile` file in the `/DataMount` data volume by writing some text to the file, as shown here:

```
root@e09979cacec8:/# echo \
    "Data Sharing between Container" > \
    /DataMount/testfile
```

2. Just spin off a container to display the text that we wrote in the previous step, using the `cat` command:

```
$ sudo docker run --rm \
            --volumes-from datavol \
            busybox:latest cat /DataMount/testfile
```

The following is the typical output of the preceding command:

```
Data Sharing between Container
```

Evidently, the preceding `Data Sharing between Container` output of our newly containerized `cat` command is the text that we have written in `/DataMount/testfile` of the `datavol` container in step 1.

Cool, isn't it? You can share data seamlessly between containers by sharing the data volumes. Here, in this example, we used data-only containers as the base container for data sharing. However, Docker allows us to share any type of data volumes and to mount data volumes one after another, as depicted here:

```
$ sudo docker run --name vol1 --volumes-from datavol \
        busybox:latest /bin/true
$ sudo docker run --name vol2 --volumes-from vol1 \
        busybox:latest /bin/true
```

Here, in the `vol1` container, we mounted the data volume from the `datavol` container. Then, in the `vol2` container, we mounted the data volume from the `vol1` container, which is eventually from the `datavol` container.

The practicality of data sharing between containers

Earlier in this chapter, you learned the mechanism of accessing the log files of the Apache2 HTTP service from the Docker host. Although it was fairly convenient to share data by mounting the Docker host directory to a container, later we came to know that data can be shared between containers by just using data volumes. So here, we are bringing in a twist to the method of the Apache2 HTTP service log handling by sharing data between containers. To share log files between containers, we will spin off the following containers as enlisted in the following steps:

1. First, a data-only container that will expose the data volume to other containers.
2. Then, an Apache2 HTTP service container leveraging the data volume of the data-only container.
3. A container to view the log files generated by our Apache2 HTTP service.

 If you are running any HTTP service on the 80 port number of your Docker host machine, pick any other unused port number for the following example. If not, first stop the HTTP service, then proceed with the example in order to avoid any port conflict.

Now, we'll meticulously walk you through the steps to craft the respective images and launch the containers to view the log files:

1. Here, we begin with crafting a `Dockerfile` with the `/var/log/apache2` data volume using the VOLUME instruction. The `/var/log/apache2` data volume is a direct mapping to APACHE_LOG_DIR, the environment variable set in the `Dockerfile` in Chapter 6, *Running Services in a Container*, using the ENV instruction:

```
##########################################################
# Dockerfile to build a LOG Volume for Apache2 Service
##########################################################
# Base image is BusyBox
FROM busybox:latest
# Author: Dr. Peter
MAINTAINER Dr. Peter <peterindia@gmail.com>
# Create a data volume at /var/log/apache2, which is
# same as the log directory PATH set for the apache image
VOLUME /var/log/apache2
# Execute command true
CMD ["/bin/true"]
```

Since this `Dockerfile` is crafted to launch data-only containers, the default execution command is set to `/bin/true`.

2. We will continue to build a Docker image with the `apache2log` name from the preceding `Dockerfile` using `docker build`, as presented here:

```
$ sudo docker build -t apache2log .
Sending build context to Docker daemon 2.56 kB
Sending build context to Docker daemon
Step 0 : FROM busybox:latest
... TRUNCATED OUTPUT ...
```

3. Launch a data-only container from the `apache2log` image using the `docker run` subcommand and name the resulting container `log_vol`, using the `--name` option:

```
$ sudo docker run --name log_vol apache2log
```

Acting on the preceding command, the container will create a data volume in `/var/log/apache2` and move it to a stop state.

4. Meanwhile, you can run the `docker ps` subcommand with the `-a` option to verify the container's state:

```
$ sudo docker ps -a
CONTAINER ID          IMAGE              COMMAND
CREATED               STATUS             PORTS
NAMES
40332e5fa0ae          apache2log:latest  "/bin/true"
2 minutes ago         Exited (0) 2 minutes ago
log_vol
```

As per the output, the container exits with the 0 exit value.

5. Launch the Apache2 HTTP service using the `docker run` subcommand. Here, we are reusing the `apache2` image we crafted in `Chapter 6`, *Running Services in a Container*. Besides, in this container, we will mount the `/var/log/apache2` data volume from `log_vol`, the data-only container that we launched in step 3, using the `--volumes-from` option:

```
$ sudo docker run -d -p 80:80 \
          --volumes-from log_vol \
          apache2
7dfbf87e341c320a12c1baae14bff2840e64afcd082dda3094e7cb0a0023cf42
```

With the successful launch of the Apache2 HTTP service with the `/var/log/apache2` data volume mounted from `log_vol`, we can access the log files using transient containers.

6. Here, we are listing the files stored by the Apache2 HTTP service, using a transient container. This transient container is spun off by mounting the `/var/log/apache2` data volume from `log_vol`, and the files in `/var/log/apache2` are listed using the `ls` command. Further, the `--rm` option of the `docker run` subcommand is used to remove the container once it is done executing the `ls` command:

```
$ sudo docker run --rm \
          --volumes-from log_vol \
          busybox:latest ls -l /var/log/apache2
total 4
-rw-r--r--    1    root    root      0 Dec 5 15:27
access.log
-rw-r--r--    1    root    root    461 Dec 5 15:27
error.log
```

```
-rw-r--r--    1    root    root    0 Dec 5 15:27
other_vhosts_access.log
```

7. Finally, the error log produced by the Apache2 HTTP service is accessed using the `tail` command, as highlighted in the following command:

```
$ sudo docker run --rm \
                  --volumes-from log_vol \
                  ubuntu:16.04 \
                  tail /var/log/apache2/error.log
AH00558: apache2: Could not reliably determine the
server's fully qualified domain name, using 172.17.0.24.
Set the 'ServerName' directive globally to suppress this
message
[Fri Dec 05 17:28:12.358034 2014] [mpm_event:notice]
[pid 18:tid 140689145714560] AH00489: Apache/2.4.7
(Ubuntu) configured -- resuming normal operations
[Fri Dec 05 17:28:12.358306 2014] [core:notice]
[pid 18:tid 140689145714560] AH00094: Command line:
'/usr/sbin/apache2 -D FOREGROUND'
```

Avoiding common pitfalls

Until now, we have discussed how effectively data volumes can be used to share data between the Docker host and the containers as well as between containers. Data sharing using data volumes is turning out to be a very powerful and essential tool in the Docker paradigm. However, it does carry a few pitfalls that are to be carefully identified and eliminated. In this section, we make an attempt to list out a few common issues associated with data sharing and the ways and means to overcome them.

Directory leaks

Earlier in the *Data volume* section, you learned that the Docker Engine automatically creates directories based on the VOLUME instruction in the `Dockerfile` as well as the -v option of the `docker run` subcommand. We also understood that the Docker Engine does not automatically delete these autogenerated directories in order to preserve the state of the application(s) run inside the container. We can force Docker to remove these directories using the -v option of the `docker rm` subcommand. This process of manual deletion poses two major challenges enumerated as follows:

- **Undeleted directories:** There can be scenarios where you may intentionally or unintentionally choose not to remove the generated directory while removing the container.
- **Third-party images:** Quite often, we leverage third-party Docker images that could have been built with the VOLUME instruction. Likewise, we might also have our own Docker images with VOLUME inscribed in it. When we launch containers using such Docker images, the Docker Engine will autogenerate the prescribed directories. Since we are not aware of the data volume creation, we may not call the docker rm subcommand with the -v option to delete the autogenerated directory.

In the previously mentioned scenarios, once the associated container is removed, there is no direct way to identify the directories whose containers were removed. Here are a few recommendations on how to avoid this pitfall:

- Always inspect the Docker images using the docker inspect subcommand and check whether any data volume is inscribed in the image or not.
- Always run the docker rm subcommand with the -v option to remove any data volume (directory) created for the container. Even if the data volume is shared by multiple containers, it is still safe to run the docker rm subcommand with the -v option because the directory associated with the data volume will be deleted only when the last container sharing that data volume is removed.
- For any reason, if you choose to preserve the autogenerated directory, you must keep a clear record so that you can remove them at a later point.
- Implement an audit framework that will audit and find out the directories that do not have any container association.

The undesirable effect of data volume

As mentioned earlier, Docker enables access for us to each data volume in a Docker image using the VOLUME instruction during the build time. Nevertheless, data volumes should never be used to store any data during the build time, otherwise it will result in an unwanted effect.

In this section, we will demonstrate the undesirable effect of using data volume during the build by crafting a Dockerfile, and then showcase the implication by building this Dockerfile.

The following are the details of `Dockerfile`:

1. Build the image using Ubuntu 16.04 as the base image:

    ```
    # Use Ubuntu as the base image
    FROM ubuntu:16.04
    ```

2. Create a `/MountPointDemo` data volume using the VOLUME instruction:

    ```
    VOLUME /MountPointDemo
    ```

3. Create a file in the `/MountPointDemo` data volume using the RUN instruction:

    ```
    RUN date > /MountPointDemo/date.txt
    ```

4. Display the file in the `/MountPointDemo` data volume using the RUN instruction:

    ```
    RUN cat /MountPointDemo/date.txt
    ```

5. Proceed to build an image from this `Dockerfile` using the `docker build` subcommand, as shown here:

    ```
    $ sudo docker build -t testvol .
    Sending build context to Docker daemon 2.56 kB
    Sending build context to Docker daemon
    Step 0 : FROM ubuntu:16.04
    ---> 9bd07e480c5b
    Step 1 : VOLUME /MountPointDemo
    ---> Using cache
    ---> e8b1799d4969
    Step 2 : RUN date > /MountPointDemo/date.txt
    ---> Using cache
    ---> 8267e251a984
    Step 3 : RUN cat /MountPointDemo/date.txt
    ---> Running in a3e40444de2e
    cat: /MountPointDemo/date.txt: No such file or directory
    2014/12/07 11:32:36 The command [/bin/sh -c cat
    /MountPointDemo/date.txt] returned a non-zero code: 1
    ```

In the preceding output of the `docker build` subcommand, you would have noticed that the build fails in step 3 because it could not find the file created in step 2. Apparently, the file that was created in step 2 vanishes when it reaches step 3. This undesirable effect is due to the approach Docker uses to build its images. An understanding of the Docker image-building process will unravel the mystery.

In the build process, for every instruction in a `Dockerfile`, the following steps are followed:

1. Create a new container by translating the `Dockerfile` instruction to an equivalent `docker run` subcommand.
2. Commit the newly-created container to an image.
3. Repeat steps 1 and 2 by treating the newly-created image as the base image for step 1.

When a container is committed, it saves the filesystem of the container and deliberately does not save the filesystem of the data volumes. Therefore, any data stored in the data volume will be lost in this process. So, never use a data volume as a storage during the build process.

Summary

For enterprise-scale distributed applications to be distinct in their operations and outputs, data is the most important instrument and ingredient. With IT containerization, the journey takes off in a brisk and bright fashion. IT as well as business software solutions are intelligently containerized through the smart leverage of the Docker Engine. However, the original instigation is the need for a faster and flawless realization of application-aware Docker containers, and hence, the data is tightly coupled with the application within the container. However, this closeness brings in some real risks. If the application collapses, then the data is also gone. Also, multiple applications might depend on the same data and hence, data has to be shared across.

In this chapter, we discussed the capabilities of the Docker Engine in facilitating the seamless data sharing between the Docker host and container as well as between containers. The data volume is being prescribed as the foundational building block for enabling data sharing among the constituents of the growing Docker ecosystem. In the next chapter, we will explain the concept behind the container orchestration, and see how this complicated aspect gets simplified through a few automated tools. Orchestration is indispensable for realizing composite containers.

8

Orchestrating Containers

In the earlier chapters, we laid down a strong foundation on the need for container networking, how to run a service inside a Docker container, and how to expose this service to the outside world by opening up network ports and other prerequisites. However, recently, there are advanced mechanisms being made available and a few third-party orchestration platforms hitting the market for sagaciously establishing dynamic and decisive linkages between distributed and differently-enabled containers in order to compose powerful containers for comprehensively, yet compactly containing process-centric, multi-tiered, and enterprise-class distributed applications. In the extremely diversified yet connected world, the concept of orchestration cannot be kept away from the deserved prominence for long. This chapter is precisely allocated for explaining the nitty-gritty of container orchestration, and its direct role is in picking up discrete containers to systematically compose sophisticated containers that are more directly aligned with the varying business expectations and expediencies.

In this chapter, we will discuss the following topics in detail:

- Linking containers
- Orchestrating containers
- Orchestrating containers using the `docker-compose` tool

As mission-critical applications are overwhelmingly being built through loosely coupled, yet highly cohesive components/services destined to run on geographically-distributed IT infrastructures and platforms, the concept of composition is getting a lot of attention and attraction. For sustaining the well-begun containerization journey, the orchestration of containers is being prescribed as one of the most critical and crucial requirements in the ensuing, instant-on, adaptive, and smart IT era. There are a few proven and promising methods and standards-compliant tools for enabling the enigmatic orchestration goals.

Docker inbuilt service discovery

The Docker platform inherently supports the service discovery for the containers that are attached to any user-defined network using an embedded **Domain Name Service** (**DNS**). This functionality has been added to Docker since the version 1.10. The embedded DNS feature enables the Docker containers to discover each other using their names or aliases within the user-defined network. In other words, the name resolution request from the container is first sent to the embedded DNS. The user-defined network then uses a special 127.0.0.11 IP address for the embedded DNS, which is also listed in /etc/resolv.conf.

The following example will help to gain a better understanding of Docker's built-in service discovery capability:

1. Let's begin by creating a user-defined bridge network, mybridge, using the following command:

```
$ sudo docker network create mybridge
```

2. Inspect the newly created network to understand the subnet range and gateway IP:

```
$ sudo docker network inspect mybridge
[
    {
        "Name": "mybridge",
        "Id":
"36e5e088543895f6d335eb92299ee8e118cd0610e0d023f7c42e6e603b935e17",
        "Created":
        "2017-02-12T14:56:48.553408611Z",
        "Scope": "local",
        "Driver": "bridge",
        "EnableIPv6": false,
        "IPAM": {
            "Driver": "default",
            "Options": {},
            "Config": [
                {
                    "Subnet": "172.18.0.0/16",
                    "Gateway": "172.18.0.1"
                }
            ]
        },
        "Internal": false,
        "Attachable": false,
```

```
        "Containers": {},
        "Options": {},
        "Labels": {}
    }
]
```

Here, the subnet assigned to the `mybridge` network is `172.18.0.0/16` and the gateway is `172.18.0.1`.

3. Now, let's create a container by attaching it to the `mybridge` network, as shown here:

```
$ sudo docker container run \
-itd --net mybridge --name testdns ubuntu
```

4. Continue to list the IP address assigned to the container, as illustrated here:

```
$ sudo docker container inspect --format \
'{{.NetworkSettings.Networks.mybridge.IPAddress}}' \
testdns
172.18.0.2
```

Evidently, the `testdns` container is assigned a `172.18.0.2` IP address. The `172.18.0.2` IP address is from the subnet of the `mybridge` network (that is, `172.18.0.0/16`).

5. Having got the IP address of the container, let's look into the content of the `/etc/resolv.conf` file of the container using the `docker container exec` subcommand, as shown here:

```
$ sudo docker container exec testdns \
cat /etc/resolv.conf
nameserver 127.0.0.11
options ndots:0
```

Here the `nameserver` is configured as `127.0.0.11`, which is the IP address of the embedded DNS.

6. As a final step, let's ping the `testdns` container using the `busybox` image. We picked the `busybox` image here because the `ubuntu` image is shipped without the `ping` command:

```
$ sudo docker container run --rm --net mybridge \
                    busybox ping -c 2 testdns
PING testdns (172.18.0.2): 56 data bytes
64 bytes from 172.18.0.2: seq=0 ttl=64
time=0.085 ms
64 bytes from 172.18.0.2: seq=1 ttl=64
time=0.133 ms

--- testdns ping statistics ---
2 packets transmitted, 2 packets received,
0% packet loss
round-trip min/avg/max = 0.085/0.109/0.133 ms
```

Awesome, isn't it! The folks behind Docker have made it so simple that with no effort we are able to discover the containers in the same network.

Linking containers

Before the introduction of the concept of the user-defined network, container linking was predominantly used for inter-container discovery and communication. That is, cooperating containers can be linked together to offer complex and business-aware services. The linked containers have a kind of source-recipient relationship, wherein the source container gets linked to the recipient container, and the recipient securely receives a variety of information from the source container. However, the source container will know nothing about the recipients to which it is linked. Another noteworthy feature of linking containers in a secured setup is that the linked containers can communicate using secure tunnels without exposing the ports used for the setup to the external world. Though you will find lots of deployments that use container-linking techniques, they are cumbersome and time-consuming to configure. Also, they are error-prone. So the new method of embedded DNS is highly preferred over the traditional container-linking techniques.

The Docker Engine provides the `--link` option in the `docker run` subcommand to link a source container to a recipient container.

The format of the `--link` option is as follows:

```
--link <container>:<alias>
```

Here, `<container>` is the name of the source container and `<alias>` is the name seen by the recipient container. The name of the container must be unique in a Docker host, whereas alias is very specific and local to the recipient container, and hence, the alias need not be unique in the Docker host. This gives a lot of flexibility to implement and incorporate functionalities with a fixed source alias name inside the recipient container.

When two containers are linked together, the Docker Engine automatically exports a few environment variables to the recipient container. These environment variables have a well-defined naming convention, where the variables are always prefixed with the capitalized form of the alias name. For instance, if `src` is the alias name given to the source container, then the exported environment variables will begin with `SRC_`. Docker exports three categories of environment variables, as enumerated here:

- NAME: This is the first category of environment variables. These variables take the form of `<ALIAS>_NAME`, and they carry the recipient container's hierarchical name as their value. For instance, if the source container's alias is `src` and the recipient container's name is `rec`, then the environment variable and its value will be `SRC_NAME=/rec/src`.
- ENV: This is the second category of environment variables used to export the environment variables configured in the source container by the `-e` option of the `docker run` subcommand or the ENV instruction of the `Dockerfile`. This type of an environment variable takes the form of `<ALIAS>_ENV_<VAR_NAME>`. For instance, if the source container's alias is `src` and the variable name is `SAMPLE`, then the environment variable will be `SRC_ENV_SAMPLE`.
- PORT: This is the final and third category of environment variables that is used to export the connectivity details of the source container to the recipient. Docker creates a bunch of variables for each port exposed by the source container through the `-p` option of the `docker run` subcommand or the EXPOSE instruction of the `Dockerfile`.

  These variables take the `<ALIAS>_PORT_<port>_<protocol>` form. This form is used to share the source's IP address, port, and protocol as a URL. For example, if the source container's alias is `src`, the exposed port is `8080`, the protocol is `tcp`, and the IP address is `172.17.0.2`, then the environment variable and its value will be `SRC_PORT_8080_TCP=tcp://172.17.0.2:8080`. This URL further splits into the following three environment variables:

  - `<ALIAS>_PORT_<port>_<protocol>_ADDR`: This form carries the IP address part of the URL (for example, `SRC_PORT_8080_TCP_ADDR= 172.17.0.2`)

- `<ALIAS>_PORT_<port>_<protocol>_PORT`: This form carries the port part of the URL (for example, `SRC_PORT_8080_TCP_PORT=8080`)
- `<ALIAS>_PORT_<port>_<protocol>_PROTO`: This form carries the protocol part of the URL (for example, `SRC_PORT_8080_TCP_PROTO=tcp`)

In addition to the preceding environment variables, the Docker Engine exports one more variable in this category, that is, of the `<ALIAS>_PORT` form, and its value will be the URL of the lowest number of all the exposed ports of the source container. For instance, if the source container's alias is `src`, the exposed port numbers are `7070`, `8080`, and `80`, the protocol is `tcp`, and the IP address is `172.17.0.2`, then the environment variable and its value will be `SRC_PORT=tcp://172.17.0.2:80`.

Docker exports these autogenerated environment variables in a well-structured format so that they can be easily discovered programmatically. Thus, it becomes very easy for the recipient container to discover the information about the source container. In addition, Docker automatically updates the source IP address and its alias as an entry in the `/etc/hosts` file of the recipient.

In this chapter, we will dive deep into the mentioned features provided by the Docker Engine for container linkage through a bevy of pragmatic examples.

To start with, let's choose a simple container linking example. Here, we will show you how to establish a linkage between two containers, and transfer some basic information from the source container to the recipient container, as illustrated in the following steps:

1. We begin with launching an interactive container that can be used as a source container for linking, using the following command:

   ```
   $ sudo docker run --rm --name example -it \
   busybox:latest
   ```

   The container is named `example` using the `--name` option. In addition, the `--rm` option is used to clean up the container as soon as you exit from the container.

2. Display the `/etc/hosts` entry of the source container using the `cat` command:

   ```
   / # cat /etc/hosts
   172.17.0.3       a02895551686
   127.0.0.1        localhost
   ::1        localhost ip6-localhost ip6-loopback
   fe00::0  ip6-localnet
   ff00::0  ip6-mcastprefix
   ```

```
ff02::1  ip6-allnodes
ff02::2  ip6-allrouters
```

Here, the first entry in the /etc/hosts file is the source container's IP address (172.17.0.3) and its hostname (a02895551686).

3. We will continue to display the environment variables of the source container using the env command:

```
/ # env
HOSTNAME=a02895551686
SHLVL=1
HOME=/root
TERM=xterm
PATH=
/usr/local/sbin:/usr/local/bin:/usr/sbin:/usr/bin:/sbin:/bin
PWD=/
```

4. We have now launched the source container. From another Terminal of the same Docker host, let's launch the interactive recipient container by linking it to our source container using the --link option of the docker run subcommand, as shown here:

```
$ sudo docker run --rm --link example:ex \
-it busybox:latest
```

Here, the source container named example is linked to the recipient container with ex as its alias.

5. Let's display the content of the /etc/hosts file of the recipient container using the cat command:

```
/ # cat /etc/hosts
172.17.0.4       a17e5578b98e
127.0.0.1        localhost
::1       localhost ip6-localhost ip6-loopback
fe00::0  ip6-localnet
ff00::0  ip6-mcastprefix
ff02::1  ip6-allnodes
ff02::2  ip6-allrouters
72.17.0.3        ex
```

Of course, as always, the first entry in the /etc/hosts file is the IP address of the container and its hostname. However, the noteworthy entry in the /etc/hosts file is the last entry, where the IP address (172.17.0.3) of the source container and its alias (ex) are added automatically.

6. We will continue to display the recipient container's environment variable using the env command:

```
/ # env
HOSTNAME=a17e5578b98e
SHLVL=1
HOME=/root
EX_NAME=/berserk_mcclintock/ex
TERM=xterm
PATH=/usr/local/sbin:/usr/local/bin:/usr/sbin:/usr/bin:/sbin:/bin
PWD=/
```

Apparently, a new EX_NAME environment variable is added automatically to /berserk_mcclintock/ex, as its value. Here EX is the capitalized form of the alias ex and berserk_mcclintock is the autogenerated name of the recipient container.

7. As a final step, ping the source container using the widely used ping command for two counts and use the alias name as the ping address:

```
/ # ping -c 2 ex
PING ex (172.17.0.3): 56 data bytes
64 bytes from 172.17.0.3: seq=0 ttl=64
time=0.108 ms
64 bytes from 172.17.0.3: seq=1 ttl=64
time=0.079 ms

--- ex ping statistics ---
2 packets transmitted, 2 packets received,
0% packet loss
round-trip min/avg/max = 0.079/0.093/0.108 ms
```

Evidently, the alias ex of the source container is resolved to the 172.17.0.3 IP address, and the recipient container is able to successfully reach the source. In the case of secured container communication, pinging between containers is not allowed. We will see more details on the aspect of securing containers in Chapter 11, *Securing Docker Containers*.

In the preceding example, we can link two containers together, and also, observe how elegantly networking is enabled between the containers by updating the IP address of the source container in the /etc/hosts file of the recipient container.

The next example is to demonstrate how container linking exports the environment variables of the source container, which are configured using the –e option of the docker run subcommand or the ENV instruction of Dockerfile, to the recipient container. For this purpose, we are going to craft a file named Dockerfile with the ENV instruction, build an image, launch a source container using this image, and then launch a recipient container by linking it to the source container:

1. We begin with composing a Dockerfile with the ENV instruction, as shown here:

```
FROM busybox:latest
ENV BOOK="Learning Docker"  \
    CHAPTER="Orchestrating Containers"
```

Here, we are setting up two environment variables, BOOK and CHAPTER.

2. Proceed to build a Docker image envex using the docker build subcommand from the preceding Dockerfile:

```
$ sudo docker build -t envex .
```

3. Now, let's launch an interactive source container with the example name using the envex image we just built:

```
$ sudo docker run -it --rm \
              --name example envex
```

4. From the source container prompt, display all the environment variables by invoking the env command:

```
/ # env
HOSTNAME=b53bc036725c
SHLVL=1
HOME=/root
TERM=xterm
PATH=/usr/local/sbin:/usr/local/bin:/usr/sbin:/usr/bin:/sbin:/bin
BOOK=Learning Docker
CHAPTER=Orchestrating Containers
PWD=/
```

In all the preceding environment variables, both the BOOK and the CHAPTER variables are configured with the ENV instruction of the Dockerfile.

5. As a final step, to illustrate the `ENV` category of environment variables, launch the recipient container with the `env` command, as shown here:

```
$ sudo docker run --rm --link example:ex \
                  busybox:latest env
PATH=/usr/local/sbin:/usr/local/bin:/usr/sbin:/usr/bin:/sbin:/bin
HOSTNAME=a5e0c07fd643
TERM=xterm
EX_NAME=/stoic_hawking/ex
EX_ENV_BOOK=Learning Docker
EX_ENV_CHAPTER=Orchestrating Containers
HOME=/root
```

 This example is also available on GitHub at `https://github.com/thedocker/learning-docker/blob/master/chap08/Dockerfile-Env`.

Strikingly, in the preceding output, the variables that are prefixed with `EX_` are the outcome of container linking. The environment variables of our interest are `EX_ENV_BOOK` and `EX_ENV_CHAPTER`, which were originally set through the `Dockerfile` as `BOOK` and `CHAPTER` but modified to `EX_ENV_BOOK` and `EX_ENV_CHAPTER`, as an effect of container linking. Though the environment variable names get translated, the values stored in these environment variables are preserved as is. We already discussed the `EX_NAME` variable name in the previous example.

In the preceding example, we experienced how elegantly and effortlessly Docker exports the `ENV` category variables from the source container to the recipient container. These environment variables are completely decoupled from the source and the recipient, thus a change in the value of these environment variables in one container does not impact the other. To be even more precise, the values the recipient container receives are the values set during the launch of the source container. Any changes made to the value of these environment variables in the source container after its launch have no effect on the recipient container. It does not matter when the recipient container is launched because the values are being read from the JSON file.

In our final illustration of linking containers, we are going to show you how to take advantage of the Docker feature to share the connectivity details between two containers. In order to share the connectivity details between containers, Docker uses the `PORT` category of environment variables. The following are the steps used to craft two containers and share the connectivity details between them:

1. Craft a `Dockerfile` to expose port `80` and `8080` using the `EXPOSE` instruction, as shown here:

```
FROM busybox:latest
EXPOSE 8080 80
```

2. Proceed to build a `portex` Docker image using the `docker build` subcommand from the `Dockerfile`, we created just now, by running the following command:

```
$ sudo docker build -t portex .
```

3. Now, let's launch an interactive source container with the `example` name using the earlier built `portex` image:

```
$ sudo docker run -it --rm --name example portex
```

4. Now that we have launched the source container, let's continue to create a recipient container on another Terminal by linking it to the source container, and invoke the `env` command to display all the environment variables, as shown here:

```
$ sudo docker run --rm --link example:ex \
                busybox:latest env
PATH=/usr/local/sbin:/usr/local/bin:/usr/sbin:/usr/bin:/sbin:/bin
HOSTNAME=c378bb55e69c
TERM=xterm
EX_PORT=tcp://172.17.0.4:80
EX_PORT_80_TCP=tcp://172.17.0.4:80
EX_PORT_80_TCP_ADDR=172.17.0.4
EX_PORT_80_TCP_PORT=80
EX_PORT_80_TCP_PROTO=tcp
EX_PORT_8080_TCP=tcp://172.17.0.4:8080
EX_PORT_8080_TCP_ADDR=172.17.0.4
EX_PORT_8080_TCP_PORT=8080
EX_PORT_8080_TCP_PROTO=tcp
EX_NAME=/prickly_rosalind/ex
HOME=/root
```

This example is also available on GitHub at
`https://github.com/thedocker/learning-docker/blob/master/chap08/`
`Dockerfile-Expose`.

From the preceding output of the `env` command, it is quite evident that the Docker Engine exported a bunch of four `PORT` category environment variables for each port that was exposed using the `EXPOSE` instruction in the `Dockerfile`. In addition, Docker also exported another `PORT` category variable `EX_PORT`.

Orchestration of containers

The pioneering concept of orchestration in the IT domain has been there for a long time now. For instance, in the **Service Computing (SC)** arena, the idea of service orchestration has been thriving in an unprecedented manner in order to produce and sustain highly robust and resilient services. Discrete or atomic services do not serve any substantial purpose unless they are composed together in a particular sequence to derive process-aware composite services. As orchestrated services are more strategically advantageous for businesses in expressing and exposing their unique capabilities in the form of identifiable/discoverable, interoperable, usable, and composable services to the outside world, corporates are showing exemplary interest in having an easily searchable repository of services (atomic as well as composite). This repository, in turn, enables businesses in realizing large-scale data as well as process-intensive applications. It is clear that the multiplicity of services is very pivotal for organizations to grow and glow. This increasingly mandated requirement gets solved using the proven and promising orchestration capabilities cognitively.

Now, as we are fast tending toward containerized IT environments, application and data containers ought to be smartly composed to realize a host of new generation software services.

However, for producing highly competent orchestrated containers, both purpose-specific as well as agnostic containers need to be meticulously selected and launched in the right sequence in order to create orchestrated containers. The sequence can come from the process (control as well as data) flow diagrams. Doing this complicated and daunting activity manually evokes a series of cynicisms and criticisms. Fortunately, there are orchestration tools in the Docker space that come in handy to build, run, and manage multiple containers to build enterprise-class services. The Docker firm, which has been in charge of producing and promoting the generation and assembly of Docker-inspired containers, has come out with a standardized and simplified orchestration tool (named as `docker-compose`) in order to reduce the workloads of developers as well as system administrators.

The proven composition technique of the SC paradigm is being replicated here in the raging containerization paradigm in order to reap the originally envisaged benefits of containerization, especially in building powerful application-aware containers.

The **Microservice Architecture (MSA)** is an architectural concept that aims to decouple a software solution by decomposing its functionality in a pool of discrete services. This is done by applying an architectural level to many of the principles. The MSA is slowly emerging as a championed way to design and build large-scale IT and business systems. It not only facilitates loose and light coupling and software modularity but it is also a boon to continuous integration and deployment for the agile world. Any changes being made to one part of the application mandates massive changes that are made to the application as a whole. This has been a bane and barrier to the aspect of continuous deployment. Microservices aim to resolve this situation, and hence, the MSA needs light-weight mechanisms, small, independently deployable services, and to ensure scalability and portability. These requirements can be met using Docker-sponsored containers.

Microservices are being built around business capabilities and can be independently deployed by fully automated deployment machinery. Each microservice can be deployed without interrupting the other microservices, and containers provide an ideal deployment and execution environment for services along with other noteworthy facilities, such as the reduced time to deployment, isolation management, and a simple life cycle. It is easy to quickly deploy new versions of services inside containers. All of these factors led to the explosion of microservices using the features that Docker had to offer.

As explained, Docker is being positioned as the next-generation containerization technology, which provides a proven and potentially sound mechanism to distribute applications in a highly efficient and distributed fashion. The beauty is that developers can tweak the application pieces within the container while maintaining the overall integrity of the container. This has a bigger impact as the brewing trend is that instead of large monolithic applications distributed on a single physical or virtual server, companies are building smaller, self-defined and contained, easily manageable, and discrete services to be contained inside standardized and automated containers. In short, the raging containerization technology from Docker has come as a boon for the ensuing era of microservices.

Docker was built and sustained to fulfill the elusive goal of *run it once and run it everywhere*. Docker containers are generally isolated at the process level, portable across IT environments, and easily repeatable. A single physical host can host multiple containers, and hence, every IT environment is generally stuffed with a variety of Docker containers. The unprecedented growth of containers is to spell out troubles for effective container management. The multiplicity and the associated heterogeneity of containers are used to sharply increase the management complexities of containers. Hence, the technique of orchestration and the flourishing orchestration tools have come as a strategic solace for accelerating the containerization journey in safe waters.

Orchestrating applications that span multiple containers containing microservices has become a major part of the Docker world, via projects, such as Google's Kubernetes or Flocker. Decking is another option used to facilitate the orchestration of Docker containers. Docker's new offering in this area is a set of three orchestration services designed to cover all aspects of the dynamic life cycle of distributed applications from application development to deployment and maintenance. Helios is another Docker orchestration platform used to deploy and manage containers across an entire fleet. In the beginning, `fig` was the most preferred tool for container orchestration. However, in the recent past, the company at the forefront of elevating the Docker technology has come out with an advanced container orchestration tool (`docker-compose`) to make life easier for developers working with Docker containers as they move through the container life cycle.

Having realized the significance of having the capability of container orchestration for the next generation, business-critical, and containerized workloads, the Docker company purchased the company that originally conceived and concretized the `fig` tool. Then, the Docker company appropriately renamed the tool as `docker-compose` and brought in a good number of enhancements to make the tool more tuned to the varying expectations of the containers' developers and operation teams.

Here is a gist of `docker-compose`, which is being positioned as a futuristic and flexible tool used for defining and running complex applications with Docker. With `docker-compose`, you define your application's components (their containers, configuration, links, volumes, and so on) in a single file, and then, you can spin everything up with a single command, which does everything to get it up and running.

This tool simplifies container management by providing a set of built-in tools to do a number of jobs that are being performed manually at this point in time. In this section, we supplied all the details of using `docker-compose` to perform orchestration of containers in order to have a stream of next-generation distributed applications.

Orchestrating containers using docker-compose

In this section, we will discuss the widely used container orchestration tool `docker-compose`. The `docker-compose` tool is a very simple, yet power tool and has been conceived and concretized to facilitate the running of a group of Docker containers. In other words, `docker-compose` is an orchestration framework that lets you define and control a multi-container service. It enables you to create a fast and isolated development environment as well as orchestrating multiple Docker containers in production. The `docker-compose` tool internally leverages the Docker Engine for pulling images, building the images, starting the containers in the correct sequence, and making the right connectivity/linking among the containers/services based on the definition given in the `docker-compose.yml` file.

Installing docker-compose

At the time of writing this book, the latest release of `docker-compose` is 1.11.2, and it is recommended that you use it with the Docker release 1.9.1 or above. You can find the latest official release of `docker-compose` at the GitHub location (`https://github.com/docker/compose/releases/latest`).

We have automated the installation process of `docker-compose` and also made it available for public consumption at `http://sjeeva.github.io/getcompose`. These automated scripts precisely identify the latest version of `docker-compose`, download it, and install it at `/usr/local/bin/docker-compose`:

- Use the `wget` tool like this:

```
$ wget -qO- http://sjeeva.github.io/getcompose \
| sudo sh
```

- Use the `curl` tool like this:

```
$ curl -sSL http://sjeeva.github.io/getcompose \
| sudo sh
```

Alternatively, you may choose to install a particular version of docker-compose directly from the GitHub software repository. Here, you can find the ways and means of downloading and installing the docker-compose version 1.11.2:

Use the wget tool like this:

```
sudo sh -c 'wget -qO- \
    https://github.com/docker/compose/releases/tag/1.11.2/ \
    docker-compose-`uname -s`-`uname -m` > \
    /usr/local/bin/docker-compose; \
    chmod +x /usr/local/bin/docker-compose'
```

Use the curl tool like this:

```
curl -L
https://github.com/docker/compose/releases/download/1.11.2/docker-compose-`
uname -s`-`uname -m` > /usr/local/bin/docker-compose
chmod +x /usr/local/bin/docker-compose
```

The docker-compose tool is also available as a Python package, which you can install using the pip installer, as shown here:

```
$ sudo pip install -U docker-compose
```

If pip is not installed on the system, install the pip package before the docker-compose installation.

Having successfully installed docker-compose, you can now check the docker-compose version:

```
$ docker-compose --version
docker-compose version 1.11.2, build dfed245
```

The docker-compose file

The `docker-compose` tool orchestrates containers using **YAML**, which is a **Yet Another Markup Language** called the `docker-compose` file. YAML is a human-friendly data serialization format. Docker began its journey as a container enablement tool, and it is growing by leaps and bounds as an ecosystem to automate and accelerate most of the tasks such as container provisioning, networking, storage, management, orchestration, security, governance, and persistence. Consequently, the `docker-compose` file format and its version are revised multiple times to keep up with the Docker platform. At the time of writing this edition, the latest version of the `docker-compose` file is version 3. The following table lists the `docker-compose` file and the Docker Engine version compatibility matrix:

Docker Compose file format	Docker Engine	Remarks
3, 3.1	1.13.0+	Provides support for `docker stack deploy` and `docker secrets`
2.1	1.12.0+	Introduced a few new parameters
2	1.10.0+	Introduced support for named volumes and networks
1	1.9.0+	Will be deprecated in the future compose releases

The `docker-compose` tool by default uses a file named as `docker-compose.yml` or `docker-compose.yaml` to orchestrate containers. This default file can be modified using the `-f` option of the `docker-compose` tool. The following is the format of the `docker-compose` file:

```
version: "<version>"
services:
  <service>:
    <key>: <value>
    <key>:
       - <value>
       - <value>
networks:
  <network>:
    <key>: <value>

volumes:
  <volume>:
    <key>: <value>
```

Here, the options used are as follows:

- `<version>`: This is the version of the `docker-compose` file. Refer to the preceding version table.
- `<service>`: This is the name of the service. You can have more than one service definition in a single `docker-compose` file. The service name should be followed by one or more keys. However, all the services must either have an `image` or a `build` key, followed by any number of optional keys. Except for the `image` and `build` keys, the rest of the keys can be directly mapped to the options in the `docker run` subcommand. The value can be either a single value or multiple values. All the `<service>` definitions must be grouped under the top-level `services` key.
- `<network>`: This is the name of the networks that are used by the services. All the `<network>` definitions must be grouped under the top-level `networks` key.
- `<volume>`: This is the name of the volume that is used by the services. All the `<volume>` definitions must be grouped under the top-level `volume` key.

Here, we are listing a few keys supported in the `docker-compose` file version 3. Refer to `https://docs.docker.com/compose/compose-file` for all the keys supported by `docker-compose`.

- `image`: This is the tag or image ID.
- `build`: This is the path to a directory containing a `Dockerfile`.
- `command`: This key overrides the default command.
- `deploy`: This key has many subkeys and is used to specify deployment configuration. This is used only in the `docker swarm` mode.
- `depends_on`: This is used to specify the dependencies between services. It can be further extended to chain services based on their conditions.
- `cap_add`: This adds a capability to the container.
- `cap_drop`: This drops a capability of the container.
- `dns`: This sets custom DNS servers.
- `dns_search`: This sets custom DNS search servers.
- `entrypoint`: This key overrides the default entrypoint.
- `env_file`: This key lets you add environment variables through files.
- `environment`: This adds environment variables and uses either an array or a dictionary.
- `expose`: This key exposes ports without publishing them to the host machine.

- `extends`: This extends another service defined in the same or a different configuration file.
- `extra_hosts`: This enables you to add additional hosts to `/etc/hosts` inside the container.
- `healthcheck`: This allows us to configure the service health check.
- `labels`: This key lets you add metadata to your container.
- `links`: This key links to containers in another service. Usage of links is strongly discouraged.
- `logging`: This is used to configure the logging for the service.
- `network`: This is used to join the service to the network defined in the top-level `networks` key.
- `pid`: This enables the PID space sharing between the host and the containers.
- `ports`: This key exposes ports and specifies both the `HOST_port:CONTAINER_port` ports.
- `volumes`: This key mounts path or named volumes. The named volumes need to be defined in the top-level `volumes` key.

The docker-compose command

The `docker-compose` tool provides sophisticated orchestration functionality with a handful of commands. In this section, we will list out the `docker-compose` options and commands:

```
docker-compose [<options>] <command> [<args>...]
```

The `docker-compose` tool supports the following options:

- `-f, --file <file>`: This specifies an alternate file for `docker-compose` (default is the `docker-compose.yml` file)
- `-p, --project-name <name>`: This specifies an alternate project name (default is the directory name)
- `--verbose`: This shows more output
- `-v, --version`: This prints the version and exits
- `-H, --host <host>`: This is to specify the daemon socket to connect to
- `-tls, --tlscacert, --tlskey`, and `--skip-hostname-check`: The `docker-compose` tool also supports these flags for **Transport Layer Security (TLS)**

The `docker-compose` tool supports the following commands:

- `build`: This command builds or rebuilds services.
- `bundle`: This is used to create a Docker bundle from the compose file, this is still an experimental feature on Docker 1.13.
- `config`: This is a command to validate and display the compose file.
- `create`: This creates the services defined in the compose file.
- `down`: This command is used to stop and remove containers and networks.
- `events`: This can be used to view the real-time container life cycle events.
- `exec`: This enables you to run a command in a running container. It is used predominantly for debugging purposes.
- `kill`: This command kills running containers.
- `logs`: This displays the output from the containers.
- `pause`: This command is used to pause services.
- `port`: This prints the public port for a port binding.
- `ps`: This lists the containers.
- `pull`: This command pulls the images from the repository.
- `push`: This command pushes the images to the repository.
- `restart`: This is used to restart the services defined in the compose file.
- `rm`: This removes the stopped containers.
- `run`: This runs a one-off command.
- `scale`: This sets a number of containers for a service.
- `start`: This command starts services defined in the compose file.
- `stop`: This stops services.
- `unpause`: This command is used to unpause services.
- `up`: This creates and starts containers.
- `version`: This prints the version of Docker Compose.

Common usage

In this section, we are going to experience the power of the orchestration feature provided by the Docker Compose framework with the help of an example. For this purpose, we are going to build a two-tiered web application that will receive your inputs through a URL and respond with the associated response text. This application is built using the following two services, as enumerated here:

- **Redis**: This is a key-value database used to store a key and its associated value
- **Node.js**: This is a JavaScript runtime environment used to implement the web server functionality as well the application logic

Each of these services is packed inside two different containers that are stitched together using the `docker-compose` tool. The following is the architectural representation of the services:

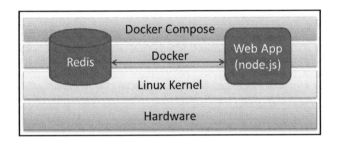

Here, in this example, we begin with implementing the `example.js` module, a Node.js file to realize the web server, and the key lookup functionality. Further, we will craft the `Dockerfile` on the same directory as `example.js` to package the Node.js runtime environment, and then, define the service orchestration using a `docker-compose.yml` file in the same directory as `example.js`.

The following is the `example.js` file, which is a Node.js implementation of the simple request/response web application. For demonstration, in this sample code, we restrict the request and response for just two `docker-compose` commands (`build` and `kill`). For the code to be self-explanatory, we added comments in the code:

```
// A Simple Request/Response web application

// Load all required libraries
var http = require('http');
var url = require('url');
var redis = require('redis');

// Connect to redis server running
// createClient API is called with
//  -- 6379, a well-known port to which the
//           redis server listens to
//  -- redis, is the name of the service (container)
//           that runs redis server
var client = redis.createClient(6379, 'redis');

// Set the key value pair in the redis server
```

```
// Here all the keys proceeds with "/", because
// URL parser always have "/" as its first character
client.set("/", "Welcome to Docker-Compose helpernEnter the docker-compose
command in the URL for helpn", redis.print);
client.set("/build", "Build or rebuild services", redis.print);
client.set("/kill", "Kill containers", redis.print);

var server = http.createServer(function (request, response) {
  var href = url.parse(request.url, true).href;
  response.writeHead(200, {"Content-Type": "text/plain"});

  // Pull the response (value) string using the URL
  client.get(href, function (err, reply) {
    if ( reply == null ) response.write("Command: " +
    href.slice(1) + " not supportedn");
    else response.write(reply + "n");
    response.end();
  });
});

console.log("Listening on port 80");
server.listen(80);
```

This example is also available at
`https://github.com/thedocker/learning-docker/tree/master/chap08/`
`orchestrate-using-compose`.

The following text is the content of `Dockerfile` that packs the Node.js image, the `redis` driver for Node.js, and the `example.js` file, as defined earlier:

```
###############################################
# Dockerfile to build a sample web application
###############################################

# Base image is node.js
FROM node:latest

# Author: Dr. Peter
MAINTAINER Dr. Peter <peterindia@gmail.com>

# Install redis driver for node.js
RUN npm install redis

# Copy the source code to the Docker image
ADD example.js /myapp/example.js
```

This code is also available at
`https://github.com/thedocker/learning-docker/tree/master/chap08/`
`orchestrate-using-compose`.

The following text is from the `docker-compose.yml` file that defines the services that the
Docker Compose tool orchestrates:

```
version: "3.1"
services:
  web:
    build: .
    command: node /myapp/example.js
    depends_on:
       - redis
    ports:
    - 8080:80
  redis:
    image: redis:latest
```

This example is also available at
`https://github.com/thedocker/learning-docker/tree/master/chap08/`
`orchestrate-using-compose`.

We defined two services in this `docker-compose.yml` file, wherein these services serve the
following purposes:

- The service named `web` is built using the `Dockerfile` in the current directory.
  Also, it is instructed that you launch the container by running the `node` (the
  Node.js runtime) with `/myapp/example.js` (web application implementation),
  as its argument. Since this Node.js application uses the `redis` database, the `web`
  service is forced to start after the `redis` service using the `depends_on`
  instruction. Besides, the `80` container port is mapped to the `8080` Docker host's
  port.
- The service named `redis` is instructed to launch a container with the
  `redis:latest` image. If the image is not present in the Docker host, the Docker
  Engine will pull it from the central repository or the private repository.

Now, let's continue with our example by building the Docker images using the `docker-compose build` command, launch the containers using the `docker-compose up` command, and connect with a browser to verify the request/response functionality, as explained step by step here:

1. The `docker-compose` commands must be executed from the directory in which the `docker-compose.yml` file is stored. Besides, `docker-compose` considers each `docker-compose.yml` file as a project, and it assumes the project name from the `docker-compose.yml` file's directory. Of course, this can be overridden using the `-p` option. So, as a first step, let's change the directory, wherein the `docker-compose.yml` file is stored:

    ```
    $ cd ~/example
    ```

2. Build the services using the `docker-compose build` command:

    ```
    $ sudo docker-compose build
    ```

3. Pull the images from the repository using the `docker-compose pull` command:

    ```
    $ sudo docker-compose pull
    ```

4. Proceed to bring up the services as indicated in the `docker-compose.yml` file using the `docker-compose up` command:

    ```
    $ sudo docker-compose up
    Creating network "example_default" with the default
    driver
    Creating example_redis_1
    Creating example_web_1
    Attaching to example_redis_1, example_web_1
    redis_1  | 1:C 03 Feb 18:09:40.743 # Warning: no
    config file specified, using the default config.
    In order to specify a config file use redis-server
    /path/to/redis.conf
    . . . TRUNCATED OUTPUT . . .
    redis_1  | 1:M 03 Feb 18:03:47.438 * The server
    is now ready to accept connections on port 6379
    web_1    | Listening on port 80
    web_1    | Reply: OK
    web_1    | Reply: OK
    web_1    | Reply: OK
    ```

Since the directory name is `example`, the `docker-compose` tool has assumed that the project name is `example`. If you pay attention to the first line of the output, you will notice the `example_default` network being created. The Docker Compose tool creates this bridge network by default and this network is used by the service for IP address resolution. Thus the services can reach the other services by just using the service names defined in the compose file.

5. Having successfully orchestrated the services using the `docker-compose` tool, let's invoke the `docker-compose ps` command from a different Terminal to list the containers associated with the example `docker-compose` project:

```
$ sudo docker-compose ps
      Name                        Command
State                       Ports
---------------------------------------------------------
-------------------------------
      example_redis_1             /entrypoint.sh redis-server
Up                            6379/tcp
      example_web_1 node          /myapp/example.js
Up                            0.0.0.0:8080->80/tcp
```

Evidently, the two `example_redis_1` and `example_web_1` containers are up and running. The container name is prefixed with `example_`, which is the `docker-compose` project name.

6. Explore the functionality of our own request/response web application on a different Terminal of the Docker host, as illustrated here:

```
$ curl http://localhost:8080
Welcome to Docker-Compose helper
Enter the docker-compose command in the URL for help
$ curl http://localhost:8080/build
Build or rebuild services
$ curl http://localhost:8080/something
Command: something not supported
```

 Here, we are directly connecting to the web service using `http://localhost:8080` because the web service is bound to the Docker host on port `8080`. You can also access the service externally using the Docker host IP address and port `8080` (`https://<docker host ip>:8080`), provided the IP address and the port is reachable from the external system.

Cool, isn't it? With very minimal effort and with the help of the `docker-compose.yml` file, we are able to compose two different services together and offer a composite service.

Summary

This chapter was incorporated into this book in order to provide you with all the probing and prescribing details on seamlessly orchestrating multiple containers. We extensively discussed the need for container orchestration and the enabling tools to simplify and streamline the increasingly complicated process of container orchestration. In order to substantiate how orchestration is handy and helpful in crafting enterprise-class containers and to illustrate the orchestration process, we took the widely followed way of explaining the whole gamut through a simple example. We developed a web application and contained it within a standard container. Similarly, we took a database container, which is a backend for the frontend web application. The database gets executed inside another container. We saw how to make the web application container aware of the database, using different technologies through the container-linkage feature of the Docker Engine. We used an open-source tool (`docker-compose`) for this purpose.

In the next chapter, we will discuss how Docker facilitates software testing, especially integration testing with a few pragmatic examples.

9
Testing with Docker

Undoubtedly, the trait of testing has been at the forefront of the software engineering discipline. The deep and decisive presence of software in every kind of tangible object in our daily environments these days in order to have plenty of smart, connected, and digitized assets is widely accepted. Also, with an increased focus on distributed and synchronized software, the complexity of the software design, development, testing and debugging, deployment, and delivery are continuously on the rise. Various means and mechanisms are unearthed to simplify and streamline the much-needed automation of software building and the authentication of software reliability, resiliency, and sustainability. Docker is emerging as an extremely flexible tool to test a wide variety of software applications. In this chapter, we will discuss how to effectively leverage the noteworthy advancements of Docker for software testing and its unique advantages in accelerating and augmenting testing automation.

The following topics are discussed in this chapter:

- A brief overview of TDD
- Testing your code inside Docker
- Integrating the Docker testing process into Jenkins

Docker containers are currently being leveraged to create development and testing environments that are the exact replicas of the production environment. Containers require less overhead when compared with virtual machines, which have been the primary environments for development, staging, and deployment environments. Let's start with an overview of **Test-driven Development (TDD)** of the next generation software and how Docker-inspired containerization becomes handy in simplifying the TDD process.

A brief overview of TDD

The long and arduous journey of software development has taken many twists and turns in the past decades, and one of the prominent software engineering technique is nonetheless TDD.

For more details and documents on TDD refer to `http://agiledata.org/essays/tdd.html`.

In a nutshell, TDD is a software development practice in which the development cycle begins with writing a test case that will fail, then writes the actual software to make the test pass, and continues to refactor and repeat the cycle till the software reaches the acceptable level. This process is depicted in the following diagram:

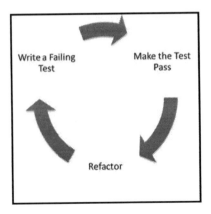

Testing your code inside Docker

In this section, we will take you through a journey in which we will show you how TDD is done using stubs and how Docker can come in handy when developing software in the deployment equivalent system. For this purpose, we take a web application use case that has a feature to track the visit count of each of its users. For this example, we use Python as the implementation language and `redis` as the key-value pair database to store the users hit count. Besides, to showcase the testing capability of Docker, we limit our implementation to just two functions—`hit` and `getHit`.

All the examples in this chapter use Python 3 as the runtime environment. The Ubuntu 16.04 installation comes with Python 3 by default. If you don't have Python 3 installed on your system, refer to the respective manual to install Python 3.

As per the TDD practice, we start by adding unit test cases for the `hit` and `getHit` functions, as depicted in the following code snippet. Here, the test file is named `test_hitcount.py`:

```
import unittest
import hitcount

class HitCountTest (unittest.TestCase):
    def testOneHit(self):
        # increase the hit count for user user1
        hitcount.hit("user1")
        # ensure that the hit count for user1 is just 1
        self.assertEqual(b'1', hitcount.getHit("user1"))

if __name__ == '__main__':
    unittest.main()
```

This example is also available at
`https://github.com/thedocker/testing/tree/master/src`.

Here, in the first line, we are importing the `unittest` Python module that provides the necessary framework and functionality to run the unit test and generate a detailed report on the test execution. In the second line, we are importing the `hitcount` Python module, where we are going to implement the hit count functionality. Then, we will continue to add the test code that will test the `hitcount` module's functionality.

Now, run the test suite using the unit test framework of Python, as follows:

```
$ python3 -m unittest
```

The following is the output generated by the unit test framework:

```
E
======================================================================
ERROR: test_hitcount (unittest.loader.ModuleImportFailure)
----------------------------------------------------------------------
Traceback (most recent call last):
...OUTPUT TRUNCATED ...
ImportError: No module named 'hitcount'


----------------------------------------------------------------------
```

```
Ran 1 test in 0.001s
```

```
FAILED (errors=1)
```

As expected, the test failed with the `ImportError: No module named 'hitcount'` error message because we had not even created the file and hence, it could not import the `hitcount` module.

Now, create a file with the `hitcount.py` name in the same directory as `test_hitcount.py`:

```
$ touch hitcount.py
```

Continue to run the unit test suite:

```
$ python3 -m unittest
```

The following is the output generated by the unit test framework:

```
E
======================================================================
ERROR: testOneHit (test_hitcount.HitCountTest)
----------------------------------------------------------------------
Traceback (most recent call last):
  File "/home/user/test_hitcount.py", line 10, in testOneHit
    hitcount.hit("peter")
AttributeError: 'module' object has no attribute 'hit'


----------------------------------------------------------------------
```

```
Ran 1 test in 0.001s
```

```
FAILED (errors=1)
```

Again, the test suite failed like earlier, but with a different error message `AttributeError: 'module' object has no attribute 'hit'`. We are getting this error because we have not implemented the `hit` function yet.

Let's proceed to implement the `hit` and `getHit` functions in `hitcount.py`, as shown here:

```
import redis
# connect to redis server
r = redis.StrictRedis(host='0.0.0.0', port=6379, db=0)

# increase the hit count for the usr
def hit(usr):
    r.incr(usr)
```

```
# get the hit count for the usr
def getHit(usr):
    return (r.get(usr))
```

This example is also available on GitHub
at https://github.com/thedocker/testing/tree/master/src.

To continue with this example, you must have the Python 3 compatible
version of package installer (pip3).

The following command is used to install pip3:

```
$ wget -qO- https://bootstrap.pypa.io/get-pip.py | sudo python3 -
```

In the first line of the preceding program, we are importing the redis driver, which is the
connectivity driver of the redis database. In the following line, we are connecting to the
redis database, and then we will continue to implement the hit and getHit function.

The redis driver is an optional Python module, so let's proceed to install the redis driver
using the pip installer, which is illustrated as follows:

```
$ sudo pip3 install redis
```

Our unittest module will still fail even after installing the redis driver because we are
not running a redis database server yet. So, we can either run a redis database server to
successfully complete our unit testing or take the traditional TDD approach of mocking the
redis driver. Mocking is a testing approach wherein complex behavior is substituted by
predefined or simulated behavior. In our example, to mock the redis driver, we are going
to leverage a third-party Python package called mockredis. This mock package is available
at https://github.com/locationlabs/mockredis and the pip installer name is
mockredispy. Let's install this mock using the pip installer:

```
$ sudo pip3 install mockredispy
```

Having installed `mockredispy`, the `redis` mock, let's refactor our test code `test_hitcount.py` (which we had written earlier) to use the simulated `redis` functionality provided by the `mockredis` module. This is accomplished by the `patch` method provided by the `unittest.mock` mocking framework, as shown in the following code:

```
import unittest
from unittest.mock import patch

# Mock for redis
import mockredis
import hitcount

class HitCountTest(unittest.TestCase):


    @patch('hitcount.r',
        mockredis.mock_strict_redis_client(host='0.0.0.0',
        port=6379,  db=0))
    def testOneHit(self):
        # increase the hit count for user user1
        hitcount.hit("user1")
        # ensure that the hit count for user1 is just 1
        self.assertEqual(b'1', hitcount.getHit("user1"))

if __name__ == '__main__':
    unittest.main()
```

This example is also available on GitHub at `https://github.com/thedocker/testing/tree/master/src`.

Now, run the test suite again:

```
$ python3 -m unittest
.
----------------------------------------------------------------------
Ran 1 test in 0.000s

OK
```

Finally, as we can see in the preceding output, we successfully implemented our visitors count functionality through the test, code, and refactor cycle.

Running the test inside a container

In the previous section, we walked you through the complete cycle of TDD, in which we installed additional Python packages to complete our development. However, in the real world, one might work on multiple projects that might have conflicting libraries and hence, there is a need for the isolation of runtime environments. Before the advent of Docker technology, the Python community used to leverage the Virtualenv tool to isolate the Python runtime environment. Docker takes this isolation a step further by packaging the OS, the Python toolchain, and the runtime environment. This type of isolation gives a lot of flexibility to the development community to use appropriate software versions and libraries as per the project needs.

Here is the step-by-step procedure to package the test and visitor count implementation of the previous section to a Docker container and perform the test inside the container:

1. Craft a `Dockerfile` to build an image with the `python3` runtime, the `redis` and `mockredispy` packages, and both the `test_hitcount.py` test file and the visitors count implementation `hitcount.py`, and finally, launch the unit test:

```
#############################################
# Dockerfile to build the unittest container
#############################################

# Base image is python
FROM python:latest

# Author: Dr. Peter
MAINTAINER Dr. Peter <peterindia@gmail.com>

# Install redis driver for python and the redis mock
RUN pip install redis && pip install mockredispy

# Copy the test and source to the Docker image
ADD src/ /src/

# Change the working directory to /src/
WORKDIR /src/

# Make unittest as the default execution
ENTRYPOINT python3 -m unittest
```

This example is also available on GitHub at `https://github.com/thedocker/testing/tree/master/src`.

2. Now create a directory called `src`, where we crafted our `Dockerfile`. Move the `test_hitcount.py` and `hitcount.py` files to the newly created `src` directory.

3. Build the `hit_unittest` Docker image using the `docker build` subcommand:

```
$ sudo docker build -t hit_unittest .
Sending build context to Docker daemon 11.78 kB
Sending build context to Docker daemon
Step 0 : FROM python:latest
---> 32b9d937b993
Step 1 : MAINTAINER Dr. Peter <peterindia@gmail.com>
---> Using cache
---> bf40ee5f5563
Step 2 : RUN pip install redis && pip install mockredispy
---> Using cache
---> a55f3bdb62b3
Step 3 : ADD src/ /src/
---> 526e13dbf4c3
Removing intermediate container a6d89cbce053
Step 4 : WORKDIR /src/
---> Running in 5c180e180a93
---> 53d3f4e68f6b
Removing intermediate container 5c180e180a93
Step 5 : ENTRYPOINT python3 -m unittest
---> Running in 74d81f4fe817
---> 063bfe92eae0
Removing intermediate container 74d81f4fe817
Successfully built 063bfe92eae0
```

4. Now that we have successfully built the image, let's launch our container with the unit testing bundle using the `docker run` subcommand, as illustrated here:

```
$ sudo docker run --rm -it hit_unittest .
----------------------------------------------------------------
-------
Ran 1 test in 0.001s

OK
```

Apparently, the unit test ran successfully with no errors because we already packaged the tested code.

In this approach, for every change, the Docker image is built and then the container is launched to complete the test.

Using a Docker container as a runtime environment

In the previous section, we built a Docker image to perform the testing. Particularly, in the TDD practice, the unit test cases and the code go through multiple changes. Consequently, the Docker image needs to be built over and over again, which is a daunting task. In this section, we will see an alternative approach in which the Docker container is built with a runtime environment, the development directory is mounted as a volume, and the test is performed inside the container.

During this TDD cycle, if an additional library or update to the existing library is required, then the container will be updated with the required libraries and the updated container will be committed as a new image. This approach gives the isolation and flexibility that any developer would dream of because the runtime and its dependency live within the container, and any misconfigured runtime environment can be discarded and a new runtime environment can be built from a previously working image. This also helps to preserve the sanity of the Docker host from the installation and uninstallation of libraries.

The following example is a step-by-step instruction on how to use the Docker container as a non-polluting yet very powerful runtime environment:

1. We begin with launching the Python runtime interactive container, using the `docker run` subcommand:

```
$ sudo docker run -it \
    -v /home/peter/src/hitcount:/src \
    python:latest /bin/bash
```

Here, in this example, the `/home/peter/src/hitcount` Docker host directory is earmarked as the placeholder for the source code and test files. This directory is mounted in the container as `/src`.

2. Now, on another Terminal of the Docker host, copy both the `test_hitcount.py` test file and the `hitcount.py` visitors count implementation to the `/home/peter/src/hitcount` directory.

3. Switch to the Python runtime interactive container Terminal, change the current working directory to `/src`, and run the unit test:

```
root@a8219ac7ed8e:~# cd /src
root@a8219ac7ed8e:/src# python3 -m unittest
E
=====================================================
===================
ERROR: test_hitcount
(unittest.loader.ModuleImportFailure)
```

```
. . . TRUNCATED OUTPUT . . .
  File "/src/test_hitcount.py", line 4, in <module>
    import mockredis
ImportError: No module named 'mockredis'
---------------------------------------------------------

Ran 1 test in 0.001s

FAILED (errors=1)
```

Evidently, the test failed because it could not find the mockredis Python library.

4. Proceed to install the mockredispy pip package because the previous step failed as it could not find the mockredis library in the runtime environment:

```
root@a8219ac7ed8e:/src# pip install mockredispy
```

5. Rerun the Python unit test:

```
root@a8219ac7ed8e:/src# python3 -m unittest
E
=======================================================
============
ERROR: test_hitcount
(unittest.loader.ModuleImportFailure)
. . . TRUNCATED OUTPUT . . .
  File "/src/hitcount.py", line 1, in <module>
    import redis
ImportError: No module named 'redis'

Ran 1 test in 0.001s

FAILED (errors=1)
```

Again, the test failed because the redis driver is not yet installed.

6. Continue to install the redis driver using the pip installer, as shown here:

```
root@a8219ac7ed8e:/src# pip install redis
```

7. Having successfully installed the redis driver, let's once again run the unit test:

```
root@a8219ac7ed8e:/src# python3 -m unittest
.
---------------------------------------------------------
--
```

```
Ran 1 test in 0.000s

OK
```

Apparently, this time the unit test passed with no warnings or error messages.

8. Now we have a runtime environment that is good enough to run our test cases. It is better to commit these changes to a Docker image for reuse, using the `docker commit` subcommand:

```
$ sudo docker commit a8219ac7ed8e \
python_rediswithmock
fcf27247ff5bb240a935ec4ba1bddbd8c90cd79cba66e52b21e1b48f984c7db2
```

9. From now on, we can use the `python_rediswithmock` image to launch new containers for our TDD.

In this section, we vividly illustrated the approach on how to use the Docker container as a testing environment, and also at the same time, preserve the sanity and sanctity of the Docker host by isolating and limiting the runtime dependency within the container.

Integrating Docker testing into Jenkins

In the previous section, we laid out a stimulating foundation on software testing, how to leverage the Docker technology for the software testing, and the unique benefits of the container technology during the testing phase. In this section, we will introduce you to the steps required to prepare the Jenkins environment for testing with Docker, and then, demonstrate how Jenkins can be extended to integrate and automate testing with Docker, using the well-known hit count use case.

Preparing the Jenkins environment

In this section, we will take you through the steps to install Jenkins, the GitHub plugin for Jenkins and `git`, and the revision control tool. The steps are as follows:

1. We begin with adding the Jenkins' trusted PGP public key:

```
$ wget -q -O - \
https://jenkins-ci.org/debian/jenkins-ci.org.key | \
sudo apt-key add -
```

Here, we are using `wget` to download the PGP public key, and then we add it to the list of trusted keys using the `apt-key` tool. Since Ubuntu and Debian share the same software packaging, Jenkins provides a single common package for both Ubuntu and Debian.

2. Add the Debian package location to the `apt` package source list, as follows:

```
$ sudo sh -c \
'echo deb http://pkg.jenkins-ci.org/debian binary/ > \
/etc/apt/sources.list.d/jenkins.list'
```

3. After adding the package source, continue to run the `apt-get` command `update` option to resynchronize the package index from the sources:

```
$ sudo apt-get update
```

4. Now, install Jenkins using the `apt-get` command `install` option, as demonstrated here:

```
$ sudo apt-get install jenkins
```

5. Finally, activate the Jenkins service using the `service` command:

```
$ sudo service jenkins start
```

The Jenkins service can be accessed through any web browser by specifying the IP address (`54.86.87.243`) of the system in which Jenkins is installed. The default port number for Jenkins is `8080`. The latest Jenkins 2.62 is already installed. The following screenshot is the entry page or dashboard of Jenkins:

Getting Started

Unlock Jenkins

To ensure Jenkins is securely set up by the administrator, a password has been written to the log (not sure where to find it?) and this file on the server:

/var/lib/jenkins/secrets/initialAdminPassword

Please copy the password from either location and paste it below.

Administrator password

6. Provide the password from the file and login. This user is the admin:

```
$ sudo cat \
/var/lib/jenkins/secrets/initialAdminPassword
b7ed7cfbde1443819455ab1502a19de2
```

7. This will take you to the **Customize Jenkins** page, as shown in the following screenshot:

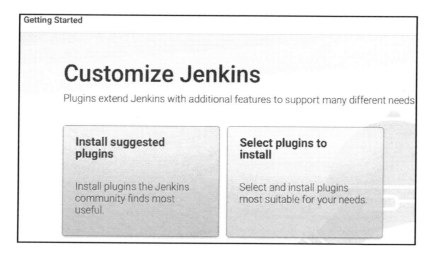

8. Select **Install suggested plugins** on the left-hand side of the screen, which will take us to the installation page.

9. On the **Create First Admin User** page, select **Continue as admin**:

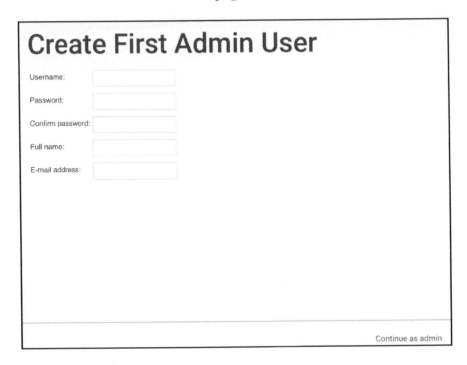

This will take us to the **Jenkins is ready!** page, as shown in the following screenshot:

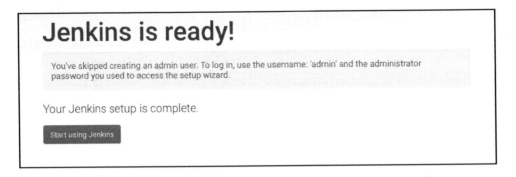

10. Now, clicking on the **Start using Jenkins** button will take you to the **Welcome to Jenkins!** page:

11. Ensure that the git package is installed, otherwise install the git package using the apt-get command:

```
$ sudo apt-get install git
```

12. So far, we have been running the Docker client using the sudo command, but unfortunately, we could not invoke sudo inside Jenkins because sometimes it prompts for a password. To overcome the sudo password prompt issue, we can make use of the Docker group, wherein any user who is part of the Docker group can invoke the Docker client without using the sudo command. Jenkins installation always sets up a user and group called jenkins and runs the Jenkins server using that user and group. So, we just need to add the jenkins user to the Docker group to get the Docker client working without the sudo command:

```
$ sudo gpasswd -a jenkins docker
Adding user jenkins to group docker
```

13. Restart the Jenkins service for the group change to take effect using the following command:

```
$ sudo service jenkins restart
 * Restarting Jenkins Continuous Integration Server
jenkins                  [ OK ]
```

We have set up a Jenkins environment that is now capable of automatically pulling the latest source code from the `http://github.com` repository, packaging it as a Docker image, and executing the prescribed test scenarios.

You are also encouraged to run Jenkins as a Docker container from the official Jenkins Docker image at `https://github.com/jenkinsci/docker`. This will be very good exercise also to validate your Docker container concepts from previous chapters.

Automating the Docker testing process

In this section, we will explore how to automate testing using Jenkins and Docker. As mentioned earlier, we are going to use GitHub as our repository. We have already uploaded the `Dockerfile`, `test_hitcount.py`, and `hitcount.py` files of our previous example to GitHub at `https://github.com/thedocker/testing`, which we are to use in the ensuing example. However, we strongly encourage you to set up your own repository at `http://github.com`, using the fork option that you can find at `https://github.com/thedocker/testing`, and substitute this address wherever applicable in the ensuing example.

The following are the detailed steps to automate Docker testing:

Configure Jenkins to trigger a build when a file is modified in the GitHub repository, which is illustrated in the following substeps:

1. Connect to the Jenkins server again.
2. Select **create new jobs**.

3. As shown in the following screenshot, give a name to the project (for example, `Docker-Testing`), and select **Freestyle project**:

4. As shown in the next screenshot, select the **Git** radio button under **Source Code Management**, and specify the GitHub repository URL in the **Repository URL** text field:

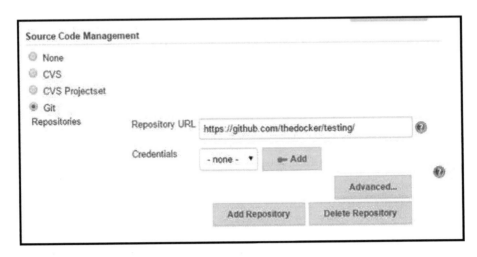

5. Select **Poll SCM** under **Build Triggers** to schedule GitHub polling for every 15-minute interval. Type the following line of code H/15 * * * * in the **Schedule** textbox, as shown in the following screenshot. For testing purposes, you can reduce the polling interval:

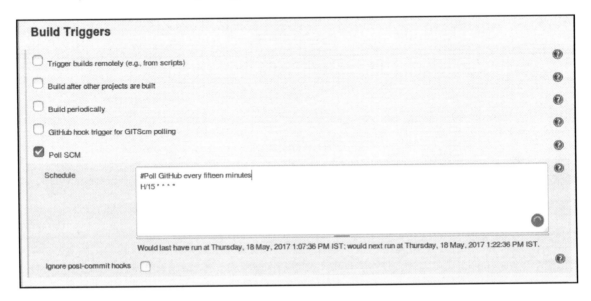

6. Scroll down the screen a little further and click on the **Add build step** button under **Build**. In the drop-down list, select **Execute shell** and type in the text, as shown in the following screenshot:

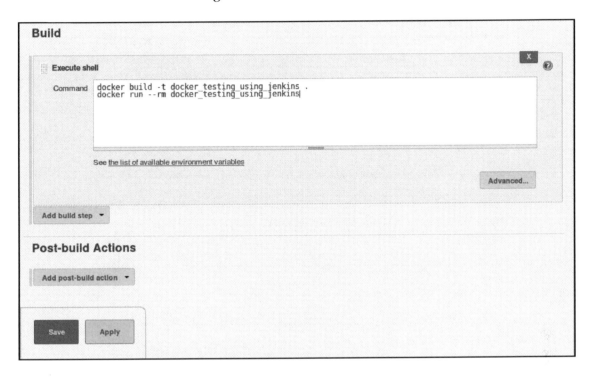

7. Finally, save the configuration by clicking on the **Save** button.
8. Go back to the Jenkins dashboard, and you can find your test listed on the dashboard:

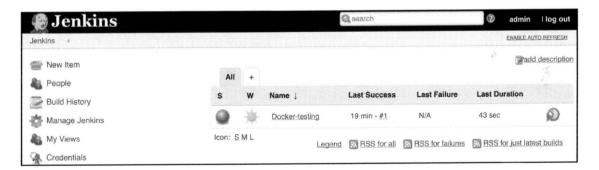

9. You can either wait for the Jenkins schedule to kick-start the build or you can click on the clock icon on the right-hand side of the screen to kick-start the build immediately. As soon as the build is done, the dashboard is updated with the build status as a success or failure and the build number:

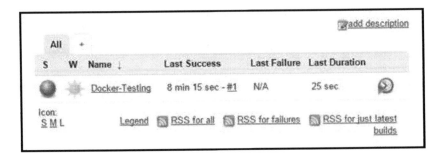

10. If you hover the mouse closer to the build number, you will get a drop-down button with options, such as **Changes** and **Console Output**, as shown in the following screenshot:

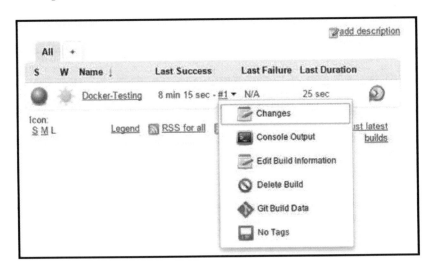

11. The **Console Output** option will show the details highlighted for the build, as follows:

```
Started by user Vinod Singh
Building in workspace
  /var/lib/jenkins/workspace/Docker-testing
Cloning the remote Git repository
Cloning repository
```

```
    https://github.com/thedocker/testing
> git init \
  /var/lib/jenkins/workspace/Docker-testing \
  # timeout=10
Fetching upstream changes from
https://github.com/thedocker/testing
> git --version # timeout=10
Removing intermediate container 76a53284f1e3
Successfully built d9e22d1d52c6
+ docker run --rm docker_testing_using_jenkins
.
_____
_____
Ran 1 test in 0.000s

OK
Finished: SUCCESS
```

12. Now, let's test the failed case because of the wrong module name, `error_hitcount`, which we deliberately introduced. Now, let's experiment a negative scenario by deliberately introducing a bug in `test_hitcount.py` and observe the effect on the Jenkins build. As we have configured Jenkins, it faithfully polls the GitHub and kick-starts the build.

   Apparently, the build failed as we expected:

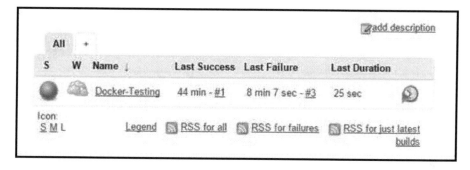

13. As a final step, open **Console Output** of the failed build:

```
Started by an SCM change
Building in workspace
/var/lib/jenkins/jobs/Docker-Testing/workspace
. . . OUTPUT TRUNCATED . . .
ImportError: No module named 'error_hitcount'
```

```
-----------------------------------------------
-------------------------------
Ran 1 test in 0.001s

FAILED (errors=1)
Build step 'Execute shell' marked build as failure
Finished: FAILURE
```

Evidently, the test failed because of the wrong module name, `error_hitcount`, which we deliberately introduced.

Cool, isn't it? We automated our testing using Jenkins and Docker. Besides, we are able to experience the power of testing automation using Jenkins and Docker. In a large-scale project, Jenkins and Docker can be combined together to automate the complete unit testing needs, and thus, to automatically capture any defects and deficiencies introduced by any developers.

Summary

The potential benefits of containerization are being discovered across the breadth and the length of software engineering. Previously, testing sophisticated software systems involved a number of expensive and hard-to-manage server modules and clusters. Considering the costs and complexities involved, most of the software testing is accomplished using mocking procedures and stubs. All of this is going to end for good with the maturity of the Docker technology. The openness and flexibility of Docker enable it to work seamlessly with other technologies to substantially reduce the testing time and complexity.

For a long time, the leading ways of testing software systems included mocking, dependency, injection, and so on. Usually, these mandate creating many sophisticated abstractions in the code. The current practice for developing and running test cases against an application is actually done on stubs rather than on the full application. This means that, with a containerized workflow, it is very much possible to test against real application containers with all the dependencies. The contributions of the Docker paradigm, especially for the testing phenomenon and phase are therefore being carefully expounded and recorded in the recent past. Precisely speaking, the field of software engineering is moving towards smarter and sunnier days with all the innovations in the Docker space.

In this chapter, we clearly expounded and explained a powerful testing framework for integrated applications using the Docker-inspired containerization paradigm. Increasingly, for the agile world, the proven and potential TDD method is being insisted as an efficient software building and sustenance methodology. This chapter has utilized the Python unit test framework to illustrate how the TDD methodology is a pioneering tool for software engineering. The unit test framework is tweaked to be efficiently and elegantly containerized, and the Docker container is seamlessly integrated with Jenkins, which is a modern day deployment tool for continuous delivery, and is part and parcel of the agile programming world, as described in this chapter. The Docker container source code is pre-checked before it enters into the GitHub code repository. The Jenkins tool downloads the code from GitHub and runs the test inside a container. In the next chapter, we will dive deep into and describe the theoretical aspects of the process isolation through the container technology and various debugging tools and techniques.

10
Debugging Containers

Debugging has been an artistic component in the field of software engineering. All kinds of software building blocks individually, as well as collectively, need to go through a stream of deeper and decisive investigations by software development and testing professionals to ensure the security and safety of the resulting software applications. As Docker containers are said to be key runtime environments for next generation mission-critical software workloads, it is pertinent and paramount for containers, crafters, and composers to embark on a systematic and sagacious verification and validation of containers.

This chapter has been dedicatedly written to enable technical guys who have all the accurate and relevant information to meticulously debug both the applications running inside containers and the containers themselves. In this chapter, we will also look at the theoretical aspects of process isolation for processes running as containers. A Docker container runs at a user-level process on host machines and typically has the same isolation level as provided by the operating system. With the latest Docker releases, many debugging tools are available which can be efficiently used to debug your applications. We will also cover the primary Docker debugging tools, such as `docker exec`, `stats`, `ps`, `top`, `events`, and `logs`. The current version of Docker is written in Go and it takes advantage of several features of the Linux kernel to deliver its functionality.

The list of topics that will be covered in this chapter is as follows:

- Process-level isolation for Docker containers
- Debugging a `Dockerfile`
- Debugging a containerized application

 All the commands in this chapter are tested on an Ubuntu environment and if you are running them on a local Mac environment, the results would differ.

After installing the Docker Engine on your host machine, the Docker daemon can be started with the −D debug option:

```
$ docker -D login
Login with your Docker ID to push and pull images from Docker Hub. If you
don't have a Docker ID, head over to https://hub.docker.com to create one.
Username (vinoddandy):
```

This −D debug flag can be enabled to the Docker configuration file (/etc/default/docker) also in the debug mode:

```
DOCKER_OPTS="-D"
```

After saving and closing the configuration file, restart the Docker daemon.

Process-level isolation for Docker containers

In the virtualization paradigm, the hypervisor emulates computing resources and provides a virtualized environment called a VM to install the operating system and applications on top of it. Whereas, in the case of the container paradigm, a single system (bare metal or VM) is effectively partitioned to run multiple services simultaneously without interfering with each other. These services must be isolated from each other in order to prevent them from stepping on each other's resources or dependency conflict (also known as dependency hell). The Docker container technology essentially achieves process-level isolation by leveraging the Linux kernel constructs, such as namespaces and cgroups, particularly, the namespaces. The Linux kernel provides the following five powerful namespace levers for isolating the global system resources from each other. These are the **Interprocess Communication** (**IPC**) namespaces used to isolate the IPC resources:

- **network**: This namespace is used to isolate networking resources such as the network devices, network stack, and port number
- **mount**: This namespace isolates the filesystem mount points
- **PID**: This namespace isolates the process identification number
- **user**: This namespace is used to isolate the user ID and group ID
- **UTS**: This namespace is used to isolate the hostname and the NIS domain name

These namespaces add an additional level of complexity when we have to debug the services running inside the containers, which you will learn more about in detail in the next section.

In this section, we will discuss how the Docker Engine provides process-level isolation by leveraging the Linux namespaces through a series of practical examples, and one of them is listed here:

1. Start by launching an Ubuntu container in an interactive mode using the `docker run` subcommand, as shown here:

```
$ sudo docker run -it --rm ubuntu /bin/bash
root@93f5d72c2f21:/#
```

2. Proceed to find the process ID of the preceding `93f5d72c2f21` container, using the `docker inspect` subcommand in a different Terminal:

```
$ sudo docker inspect \
        --format "{{ .State.Pid }}" 93f5d72c2f21
2543
```

Apparently, from the preceding output, the process ID of the container `93f5d72c2f21` is `2543`.

3. Having got the process ID of the container, let's continue to see how the process associated with the container looks in the Docker host, using the `ps` command:

```
$ ps -fp 2543
UID          PID  PPID  C STIME TTY          TIME
CMD
root        2543  6810  0 13:46 pts/7  00:00:00
/bin/bash
```

Amazing, isn't it? We launched a container with `/bin/bash` as its command, and we have the `/bin/bash` process in the Docker host as well.

4. Let's go one step further and display the `/proc/2543/environ` file in the Docker host using the `cat` command:

```
$ sudo cat -v /proc/2543/environ
PATH=/usr/local/sbin:/usr/local/bin:/usr/sbin:/usr/bin:/sbin
/bin^@HOSTNAME=93f5d72c2f21^@TERM=xterm^@HOME=/root^@$
```

In the preceding output, `HOSTNAME=93f5d72c2f21` stands out from the other environment variables because `93f5d72c2f21` is the container ID, as well as the hostname of the container, which we launched previously.

5. Now, let's get back to the Terminal, where we are running our interactive container `93f5d72c2f21`, and list all the processes running inside this container using the `ps` command:

```
root@93f5d72c2f21:/# ps -ef
UID     PID PPID C STIME TTY      TIME CMD
root      1   0  0 18:46 ?    00:00:00 /bin/bash
root     15   1  0 19:30 ?    00:00:00 ps -ef
```

Surprising, isn't it? Inside the container, the process ID of the `/bin/bash` process is 1, whereas outside the container, in the Docker host, the process ID is 2543. Besides, the **Parent Process ID (PPID)** is 0 (zero).

In the Linux world, every system has just one `root` process with the PID 1 and PPID 0, which is the root of the complete process tree of that system. The Docker framework cleverly leverages the Linux PID namespace to spin a completely new process tree; thus, the processes running inside a container have no access to the parent process of the Docker host. However, the Docker host has a complete view of the child PID namespace spun by the Docker Engine.

The network namespace ensures that all containers have independent network interfaces on the host machine. Also, each container has its own Loopback interface. Each container talks to the outside world using its own network interface. You will be surprised to know that the namespace not only has its own routing table, but also has its own iptables, chains, and rules. The author of this chapter is running three containers on his host machine. Here, it is natural to expect three network interfaces for each container. Let's run the `docker ps` command:

```
$ sudo docker ps
41668be6e513        docker-apache2:latest    "/bin/sh -c 'apachec
069e73d4f63c        nginx:latest             "nginx -g '
871da6a6cf43        ubuntu             "/bin/bash"
```

So, there are three interfaces, one for each container. Let's get their details by running the following command:

```
$ ifconfig
veth2d99bd3 Link encap:EthernetHWaddr 42:b2:cc:a5:d8:f3
inet6addr: fe80::40b2:ccff:fea5:d8f3/64 Scope:Link
      UP BROADCAST RUNNING  MTU:9001  Metric:1
veth422c684 Link encap:EthernetHWaddr 02:84:ab:68:42:bf
inet6addr: fe80::84:abff:fe68:42bf/64 Scope:Link
      UP BROADCAST RUNNING  MTU:9001  Metric:1
vethc359aec Link encap:EthernetHWaddr 06:be:35:47:0a:c4
```

```
inet6addr: fe80::4be:35ff:fe47:ac4/64 Scope:Link
          UP BROADCAST RUNNING  MTU:9001  Metric:1
```

The mount namespace ensures that the mounted filesystem is accessible only to the processes within the same namespace. The container A cannot see the mount points of the container B. If you want to check your mount points, you need to first log in to your container using the `exec` command (described in the next section), and then go to `/proc/mounts`:

```
root@871da6a6cf43:/# cat /proc/mounts
rootfs / rootfsrw 0 0/dev/mapper/docker-202:1-149807
871da6a6cf4320f625d5c96cc24f657b7b231fe89774e09fc771b3684bf405fb / ext4
rw,relatime,discard,stripe=16,data=ordered 0 0 proc /procproc
rw,nosuid,nodev,noexec,relatime 0 0
```

Let's run a container with a mount point that runs as the **Storage Area Network (SAN)** or **Network Attached Storage (NAS)** device and access it by logging in to the container. This is given to you as an exercise. I have implemented this in one of my projects at work.

There are other namespaces that these containers/processes can be isolated into, namely, user, IPC, and UTS. The user namespace allows you to have root privileges within the namespace without giving that particular access to processes outside the namespace. Isolating a process with the IPC namespace gives it its own IPC resources, for example, System V IPC and POSIX messages. The UTS namespace isolates the hostname of the system.

Docker has implemented this namespace using the `clone` system call. On the host machine, you can inspect the namespace created by Docker for the container (with PID 3728):

```
$ sudo ls /proc/3728/ns/
cgroup ipc mnt  netpid  user  uts
```

In most industrial deployments of Docker, people are extensively using patched Linux kernels to provide specific needs. Also, a few companies have patched their kernels to attach arbitrary processes to the existing namespaces because they feel that this is the most convenient and reliable way to deploy, control, and orchestrate containers.

Control groups

Linux containers rely on **Control groups** (**cgroups**), which not only track groups of processes, but also expose metrics of the CPU, memory, and block I/O usage. You can access these metrics and obtain network usage metrics as well. Cgroups are another important component of Linux containers. Cgroups have been around for a while and were initially merged into the Linux kernel code 2.6.24. They ensure that each Docker container will get a fixed amount of memory, CPU, and disk I/O, so that any container will not able to bring the host machine down at any point of time under any circumstances. Cgroups do not play a role in preventing one container from being accessed, but they are essential to fend off some **Denial of Service** (**DoS**) attacks.

On Ubuntu 16.04, a cgroup is implemented in the `/sys/fs/cgroup` path. The memory information of Docker is available at the `/sys/fs/cgroup/memory/docker/` path.

Similarly, the CPU details are made available in the `/sys/fs/cgroup/cpu/docker/` path.

Let's find out the maximum limit of memory that can be consumed by the container (`41668be6e513e845150abd2dd95dd574591912a7fda947f6744a0bfdb5cd9a85`).

For this, you can go to the cgroup memory path and check for the `memory.max_usage_in_bytes` file:

```
/sys/fs/cgroup/memory/docker/41668be6e513e845150abd2dd95dd574591912a7fda947
f6744a0bfdb5cd9a85
```

Execute the following command to see the contents:

```
$ cat memory.max_usage_in_bytes
13824000
```

So, by default, any container can use up to 13.18 MB memory only. Similarly, CPU parameters can be found in the following path:

```
/sys/fs/cgroup/cpu/docker/41668be6e513e845150abd2dd95dd574591912a7fda947f67
44a0bfdb5cd9a85
```

Traditionally, Docker runs only one process inside the containers. So typically, you have seen people running three containers each for PHP, NGINX, and MySQL. However, this is a myth. You can run all your three processes inside a single container also.

Docker isolates many aspects of the underlying host from an application running in a container without the root privileges. However, this separation is not as strong as that of virtual machines, which run independent OS instances on top of a hypervisor without sharing the kernel with the underlying OS. It's not a good idea to run applications with different security profiles as containers on the same host, but there are security benefits to encapsulate different applications into containerized applications that would otherwise run directly on the same host.

Debugging a containerized application

Computer programs (software) sometimes fail to behave as expected. This is due to faulty code or due to the environmental changes between the development, testing, and deployment systems. Docker container technology eliminates the environmental issues between development, testing, and deployment as much as possible by containerizing all the application dependencies. Nonetheless, there could be still anomalies due to faulty code or variations in the kernel behavior, which needs debugging. Debugging is one of the most complex processes in the software engineering world and it becomes much more complex in the container paradigm because of the isolation techniques. In this section, we are going to learn a few tips and tricks to debug a containerized application using the tools native to Docker, as well as the tools provided by external sources.

Initially, many people in the Docker community individually developed their own debugging tools, but later Docker started supporting native tools, such as `exec`, `top`, `logs`, and `events`. In this section, we will dive deep into the following Docker tools:

- `exec`
- `ps`
- `top`
- `stats`
- `events`
- `logs`
- `attach`

We shall also consider debugging a `Dockerfile`.

The docker exec command

The `docker exec` command provides the much-needed help to users, who are deploying their own web servers or have other applications running in the background. Now, it is not necessary to log in to run the SSH daemon in the container.

1. First, create a Docker container:

```
$ sudo docker run --name trainingapp \
training/webapp:latest
Unable to find image
'training/webapp:latest' locally
latest: Pulling from training/webapp
9dd97ef58ce9: Pull complete
a4c1b0cb7af7: Pull complete
Digest:
sha256:06e9c1983bd6d5db5fba376ccd63bfa529e8d02f23d5079b8f74a616308fb11d
Status: Downloaded newer image for
training/webapp:latest
```

2. Next, run the `docker ps -a` command to get the container ID:

```
$ sudo docker ps -a
a245253db38b          training/webapp:latest
"python app.py"
```

3. Then, run the `docker exec` command to log in to the container:

```
$ sudo docker exec -it a245253db38b bash
root@a245253db38b:/opt/webapp#
```

4. Note that the `docker exec` command can only access the running containers, so if the container stops functioning, then you need to restart the stopped container in order to proceed. The `docker exec` command spawns a new process in the target container using the Docker API and CLI. So if you run the `ps -aef` command inside the target container, it looks like this:

```
# ps -aef
UID          PID  PPID  C STIME  TTY      TIME
CMD
root           1     0  0 Nov 26  ?    00:00:53
python app.py
root          45     0  0  18:11  ?    00:00:00
bash
root          53    45  0  18:11  ?    00:00:00
ps -aef
```

Here, `python app.y` is the application that is already running in the target container, and the `docker exec` command has added the `bash` process inside the container. If you run `kill -9 pid(45)`, you will be automatically logged out of the container.

If you are an enthusiastic developer, and you want to enhance the `exec` functionality, you can refer to `https://github.com/chris-rock/docker-exec`.

Using the `docker exec` command only for monitoring and diagnostic purposes is recommended, and I personally believe in the concept of one process per container, which is one of the best practices widely accentuated.

The docker ps command

The `docker ps` command, which is available inside the container, is used to see the status of the process. This is similar to the standard `ps` command in the Linux environment and is *not* a `docker ps` command that we run on the Docker host machine.

This command runs inside the Docker container:

```
root@5562f2f29417:/# ps -s
UID    PID    PENDING    BLOCKED    IGNORED    CAUGHT STAT TTY         TIME
COMMAND
0      1      00000000   00010000   00380004   4b817efb Ss
?                0:00 /bin/bash
0      33     00000000   00000000   00000000   73d3fef9 R+    ?              0:00 ps -s
root@5562f2f29417:/# ps -l
F S    UID    PID   PPID  C PRI  NI ADDR SZ WCHAN    TTY            TIME CMD
4 S      0     1      0   0  80   0 -   4541 wait     ?          00:00:00  bash
root@5562f2f29417:/# ps -t
PID TTY        STAT    TIME COMMAND
  1 ?          Ss      0:00 /bin/bash
 35 ?          R+      0:00 ps -t
root@5562f2f29417:/# ps -m
PID TTY            TIME CMD
  1 ?          00:00:00 bash
  - -          00:00:00 -
 36 ?          00:00:00 ps
  - -          00:00:00 -
root@5562f2f29417:/# ps -a
PID TTY            TIME CMD
 37 ?          00:00:00 ps
```

Use `ps --help <simple|list|output|threads|misc|all>` or `ps --help <s|l|o|t|m|a>` for additional help text.

The docker top command

You can run the `top` command from the Docker host machine using the following command:

```
docker top [OPTIONS] CONTAINER [ps OPTIONS]
```

This gives a list of the running processes of a container without logging in to the container, as follows:

```
$ sudo docker top  a245253db38b
UID             PID             PPID            C
STIME           TTY             TIME            CMD
root            5232            3585            0
Mar22           ?               00:00:53        python  app.py
$ sudo docker top  a245253db38b  -aef
UID             PID             PPID            C
STIME           TTY             TIME            CMD
root            5232            3585            0
Mar22           ?               00:00:53        python  app.py
```

The Docker `top` command provides information about the CPU, memory, and swap usage if you run it inside a Docker container:

```
root@a245253db38b:/opt/webapp# top
top - 19:35:03 up 25 days, 15:50,  0 users,  load average: 0.00,  0.01,
0.05
Tasks:   3 total,   1 running,   2 sleeping,   0 stopped,   0 zombie
%Cpu(s):  0.0%us,  0.0%sy,  0.0%ni, 99.9%id,  0.0%wa,  0.0%hi,  0.0%si,
0.0%st
Mem:   1016292k total,    789812k used,    226480k free,     83280k  buffers
Swap:        0k total,        0k used,        0k free,    521972k  cached
PID USER      PR  NI  VIRT  RES  SHR S %CPU %MEM
TIME+  COMMAND
   1 root      20   0 44780  10m 1280 S  0.0  1.1   0:53.69 python
  62 root      20   0 18040 1944 1492 S  0.0  0.2   0:00.01 bash
  77 root      20   0 17208 1164  948 R  0.0  0.1   0:00.00 top
```

In case you get the `error - TERM environment variable not set` error while running the `top` command inside the container, perform the following steps to resolve it:

Run the `echo $TERM` command. You will get the result as `dumb`. Then, run the following command:

```
$ export TERM=dumb
```

This will resolve the error.

The docker stats command

The `docker stats` command provides you with the capability to view the memory, CPU, and the network usage of a container from a Docker host machine, as illustrated here:

```
$ sudo docker stats a245253db38b
CONTAINER           CPU %           MEM USAGE/LIMIT        MEM %    NET I/O
a245253db38b        0.02%           16.37 MiB/992.5 MiB    1.65%
3.818   KiB/2.43 KiB
```

You can run the `stats` command to also view the usage for multiple containers:

```
$ sudo docker stats a245253db38b f71b26cee2f1
```

Docker provides access to container statistics *read only* parameters. This streamlines the CPU, memory, network IO, and block IO of containers. This helps you choose the resource limits and also in profiling. The Docker `stats` utility provides you with these resource usage details only for running containers.

The Docker events command

Docker containers will report the following real-time events: `create`, `destroy`, `die`, `export`, `kill`, `omm`, `pause`, `restart`, `start`, `stop`, and `unpause`. The following are a few examples that illustrate how to use these commands:

```
$ sudo docker pause   a245253db38b
a245253db38b

$ sudo docker ps -a
a245253db38b    training/webapp:latest     "python app.py"
4 days ago      Up 4 days (Paused)         0.0.0.0:5000->5000/tcp sad_sammet

$ sudo docker unpause   a245253db38b
a245253db38b

$ sudo docker ps -a
a245253db38b        training/webapp:latest      "python app.py"
4 days ago      Up 4 days        0.0.0.0:5000->5000/tcpsad_sammet
```

The Docker image will also report the untag and delete events.

The usage of multiple filters will be handled as an AND operation; for example,

`--filter container= a245253db38b --filter event=start` will display events for the container `a245253db38b` and the event type is `start`.

Currently, the supported filters are container, event, and image.

The docker logs command

This command fetches the log of a container without logging in to the container. It batch-retrieves logs present at the time of execution. These logs are the output of stdout and stderr. The general usage is shown in `docker logs [OPTIONS] CONTAINER`.

The `-follow` option will continue to provide the output till the end, `-t` will provide the timestamp, and `--tail= <number of lines>` will show the number of lines of the log messages of your container:

```
$ sudo docker logs a245253db38b
* Running on http://0.0.0.0:5000/
172.17.42.1 - - [22/Mar/2015 06:04:23] "GET / HTTP/1.1" 200 -
172.17.42.1 - - [24/Mar/2015 13:43:32] "GET / HTTP/1.1" 200 -

$ sudo docker logs -t a245253db38b
2015-03-22T05:03:16.866547111Z  * Running on http://0.0.0.0:5000/
2015-03-22T06:04:23.349691099Z 172.17.42.1 - - [22/Mar/2015 06:04:23]   "GET
/ HTTP/1.1" 200 -
2015-03-24T13:43:32.754295010Z 172.17.42.1 - - [24/Mar/2015 13:43:32]   "GET
/ HTTP/1.1" 200 -
```

We also used the `docker logs` utility in Chapter 2, *Handling Docker Containers* and Chapter 6, *Running Services in a Container*, to view the logs of our containers.

The docker attach command

The `docker attach` command attaches the running container and it is very helpful when you want to see what is written in stdout in real time:

```
$ sudo docker run -d --name=newtest alpine /bin/sh -c "while true; do sleep
2; df -h; done"
Unable to find image 'alpine:latest' locally
latest: Pulling from library/alpine
3690ec4760f9: Pull complete
```

```
Digest:
sha256:1354db23ff5478120c980eca1611a51c9f2b88b61f24283ee8200bf9a54f2e5c
1825927d488bef7328a26556cfd72a54adeb3dd7deafb35e317de31e60c25d67
$ sudo docker attach newtest
Filesystem              Size       Used Available Use% Mounted on
none                    7.7G       3.2G      4.1G  44% /
tmpfs                 496.2M          0    496.2M   0% /dev
tmpfs                 496.2M          0    496.2M   0% /sys/fs/cgroup
/dev/xvda1              7.7G       3.2G      4.1G  44% /etc/resolv.conf
/dev/xvda1              7.7G       3.2G      4.1G  44% /etc/hostname
/dev/xvda1              7.7G       3.2G      4.1G  44% /etc/hosts
shm                    64.0M          0     64.0M   0% /dev/shm
tmpfs                 496.2M          0    496.2M   0% /proc/sched_debug
Filesystem              Size       Used Available Use% Mounted on
none                    7.7G       3.2G      4.1G  44% /
tmpfs                 496.2M          0    496.2M   0% /dev
```

By default, this command attaches stdin and proxies signals to the remote process. Options are available to control both of these behaviors. To detach from the process, use the default *Ctrl + C* sequence.

Debugging a Dockerfile

Sometimes creating a `Dockerfile` may not start with everything working. A `Dockerfile` does not always build images and sometimes it does, but starting a container would crash on startup.

Every instruction we set in the `Dockerfile` is going to be built as a separate, temporary image for the other instruction to build itself on top of the previous instruction. The following example explains this:

1. Create a `Dockerfile` using your favorite editor:

   ```
   FROM busybox
   RUN ls -lh
   CMD echo Hello world
   ```

2. Now, build the image by executing the following command:

   ```
   $ docker build .
   Sending build context to Docker daemon 2.048 kB
   Step 1 : FROM busybox
   latest: Pulling from library/busybox
   56bec22e3559: Pull complete
   Digest:
   ```

```
sha256:29f5d56d12684887bdfa50dcd29fc31eea4aaf4ad3bec43daf19026a7ce69912
      Status: Downloaded newer image for busybox:latest
      ---> e02e811dd08f
      Step 2 : RUN ls -lh
      ---> Running in 7b47d3c46cfa
      total 36
      drwxr-xr-x    2 root       root          12.0K Oct   7 18:18 bin
      dr-xr-xr-x  130 root       root              0 Nov  27 01:36 proc
      drwxr-xr-x    2 root       root           4.0K Oct   7 18:18 root
      dr-xr-xr-x   13 root       root              0 Nov  27 01:36 sys
      drwxrwxrwt    2 root       root           4.0K Oct   7 18:18 tmp
      ---> ca5bea5887d6
      Removing intermediate container 7b47d3c46cfa
      Step 3 : CMD echo Hello world
      ---> Running in 490ecc3d10a9
      ---> 490d1c3eb782
      Removing intermediate container 490ecc3d10a9
      Successfully built 490d1c3eb782

   $
```

Notice the `---> Running in 7b47d3c46cfa` line. `7b47d3c46cfa` is a valid image and can be used to retry the failed instruction and see what's happening

To debug this image, we need to create a container and then log in to analyze the error. Debugging is a process of analyzing what's going on and it's different for every situation, but usually, the way we start debugging is by trying to manually make the instruction that fails work manually and understand the error. When I get the instruction to work, I usually exit the container, update my `Dockerfile`, and repeat the process until I have something working.

Summary

In this chapter, you have seen the isolation of containers using the Linux container technology, such as LXC and now Libcontainer. Libcontainer is Docker's own implementation in the Go programming language to access the kernel namespace and cgroups. This namespace is used for process-level isolation, while cgroups are used for restricting the resource usage of running containers. Since the containers run as independent processes directly over the Linux kernel, the **Generally Available (GA)** debugging tools are not fit enough to work inside the containers to debug the containerized processes. Docker now provides you with a rich set of tools to effectively debug the container as well as processes inside the container itself. The `docker exec` command will allow you to log in to the container without running an SSH daemon in the container. You have seen the details of each debugging tool in this chapter.

The `docker stats` command provides information about the container's memory and CPU usage. The `docker events` command reports the events, such as create, destroy, and kill. Similarly, the `docker logs` command fetches the logs from the container without logging in to the container.

As a next step, you can try the latest Microsoft Visual Studio Tools for Docker. It provides a consistent way to develop and validate your application in the Linux Docker container. For details, you can refer to `https://docs.microsoft.com/en-us/azure/vs-azure-tools-docker-edit-and-refresh`.

Also, if you would like to debug the Node.js application live running in IDE (Visual Studio Code), try this blog: `https://blog.docker.com/2016/07/live-debugging-docker/`.

The next chapter expounds the plausible security threats of Docker containers and how they can be subdued with a variety of security approaches, automated tools, best practices, key guidelines, and metrics. We will discuss the security of containers versus virtual machines with Docker's adaptability of third-party security tools and practices.

11
Securing Docker Containers

So far, we have talked a lot about the fast-evolving Docker technology in this book. It is not a nice and neat finish if the Docker-specific security issues and solution approaches are not articulated in detail to you. Hence, this chapter is specially crafted and incorporated into this book in order to explain all about the security challenges of Docker-inspired containerization. We also wanted to throw more light on how the lingering security concerns are being addressed through a host of pioneering technologies, high-quality algorithms, enabling tools, and best practices. In this chapter, we will deal with the following crucial topics in detail:

- Are the Docker containers secure?
- The security features of containers
- The emerging security-enabling approaches
- The best practices for ensuring container security

The security scenario in the containerization domain

Ensuring unbreakable and impenetrable security for any IT systems and business services has been one of the prime needs and the predominant challenges in the IT field for decades now. Brilliant minds can identify and exploit all kinds of security holes and flaws (some of them are being carelessly and unknowingly introduced at the system conceptualization and concretization stages). This loophole ultimately brings innumerable breaches and chaos during IT service delivery. Sometimes, systems are even becoming unavailable for consumers and clients.

Security experts and engineers, on the other hand, try out every kind of trick and technique at their disposal in order to stop hackers in their evil journey. However, it has not been an outright victory so far. Here and there, there are some noteworthy intrusions from unknown sources resulting in highly disconcerting IT slowdowns and sometimes breakdowns. Organizations and governments across the globe are, therefore, investing heavily their talents, time, and treasures in security research endeavors in order to completely decimate all the security and safety-related incidents and accidents. There are many security-specific product vendors and managed security service providers aiming to minimize the irreparable and indescribable consequences of security threats and vulnerabilities on IT systems. Precisely speaking, for any existing and emerging technology, security has been the most crucial and critical aspect. The point to be noted here is that enterprise and cloud IT teams can't be carefree and complacent in fulfilling the security needs.

Docker-enabled containerization represents the next logical step on the memorable and indomitable journey from physical, underutilized, closed, monolithic, and single-tenanted IT resources to supple, open, affordable, automated, shared, service-oriented, optimally utilized, and virtual IT resources. Precisely speaking, we are tending toward software-defined and containerized cloud environments in order to reap a bunch of widely articulated business, technical, and user benefits. As accentuated several times in this book, Docker containers typically comprise a filesystem, network stack, process space, and everything else needed to run an application anywhere. This means that each Docker container includes the designated application and all its dependencies to be shipped, hosted, and executed in an independent manner. This widely celebrated abstraction, however, is prone to fresh and advanced security attacks, vulnerabilities, and holes. Systems can be made inaccessible, datasets can be breached, services can be stopped, and so on.

Precisely speaking, the raging Docker technology promises to drastically transform the way worldwide enterprises develop, deploy, and manage critical software applications. However, containers are no panacea. The same challenges we face while deploying and delivering an application on hybrid IT environments get replicated in containers. This chapter pinpoints the proven approaches for mitigating the containerization-induced and inspired security issues. As cloud environments are extensively containerized, the unbreakable and impenetrable containers ultimately vouch for safe, secure, and smart cloud centers. The long-term goal is to have many robust, resilient, and rewarding containers in publicly discoverable locations. There are undoubtedly pioneering tools and platforms to compose better and bigger containers out of those customizable, configurable, and compact containers through commingling and collaboration.

The security ramifications of Docker containers

The surging popularity of Docker technology is primarily due to the fact that Docker Inc., in collaboration with other interested parties, has introduced an open and industry-strength image format for efficiently packaging, distribution, and running of software applications. However, stuffing many applications into a system opens up definite worries and vulnerabilities:

- **Exploiting host kernels**: Containers share the same host kernel and this sharing may turn out to be a single point of failure for the containerization paradigm. A flaw in the host kernel could allow a process within a container to break out to bring down the host machine. Thus the domain of Docker security is about exploring various options toward limiting and controlling the attack surface on the kernel. Security administrators and architects have to meticulously leverage the security features of the host operating system to secure the kernel.
- **Denial-of-service (DoS) attacks**: All containers ought to share kernel resources. If one container can monopolize access to certain resources including memory and processing, other containers on the host are bound to starve for computing, storage, and networking resources. Ultimately, the enigma of DoS creeps in and legitimate users would struggle for accessing the services.
- **Container breakouts**: An attacker who gains access to a container should not be able to gain access to other containers or the host. By default, users are not namespaced and hence any process that breaks out of the container will have the same privileges on the host as it has in the container. That is, if a process has the root privilege, then it has the root privilege on the host machine also. This means that a user can gain the elevated and even root privileges through a bug in an application code. Then the result is simply irreparable damages. That is, we need to adhere to the least privilege: each process and container should run with the minimum set of access rights and resources.
- **Poisoned images**: Docker images also can be compromised and tampered resulting in bad containers and hosts. We wrote about the methods for thoroughly cleansing and curating Docker images while depositing in image repositories. Similarly, strong access control mechanisms are in place for mitigating the poisoning of images.

Thus, Docker images, containers, clusters, hosts, and clouds are bound to be impeded with a litany of viruses, malware, and other crucial threats. Thus, the domain of Docker security has become the most challenging area for both researchers and practitioners lately and we can expect a number of game-changing and security-enhancing algorithms, approaches, and articulations in the days ahead.

The security facets – virtual machines versus Docker containers

Docker security is being given prime importance, considering the fact that the adoption and adaptation of Docker containers are consistently on the rise. Undoubtedly, there are a lot of works for ensuring utmost security for Docker containers and the latest releases of the Docker platform have a number of security-enabling features embedded.

In this section, we are going to describe where the Docker containers stand as far as the security imbroglio is concerned. As containers are being closely examined in synchronization with **Virtual Machines** (**VMs**), we will start with a few security-related points of VMs and containers. Let's start with understanding how VMs differ from containers. Typically, VMs are heavyweight and hence bloating, whereas containers are lightweight and hence, slim and sleek. The following table captures the renowned qualities of VMs and containers:

Virtual Machines	Containers
A few VMs run together on a single physical machine (low density).	Tens of containers can run on a single physical machine or VM (high density).
This ensures complete isolation of VMs for security.	This enables the isolation at the process level and provides additional isolation using features, such as namespaces and cgroups.
Each VM has its own OS and the physical resources managed by an underlying hypervisor.	Containers share the same kernel with their Docker host.
For networking, VMs can be linked to virtual or physical switches. Hypervisors have a buffer for I/O performance improvement, NIC bonding, and so on.	Containers leverage standard IPC mechanisms, such as signals, pipes, sockets, and so on, for networking. Each container gets its own network stack.

The following diagram illustrates how hypervisor-based virtualization enables the realization of VMs out of a physical machine:

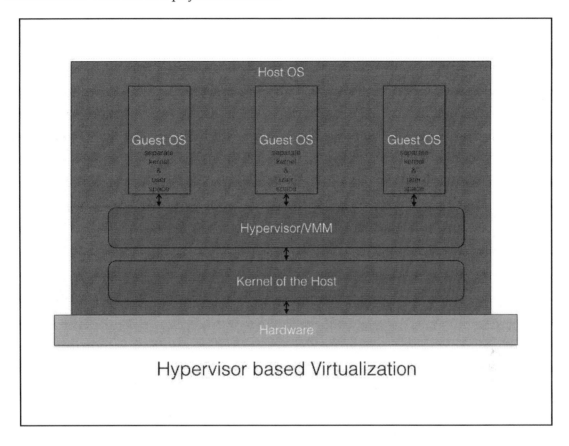

The following diagram vividly conveys how containerization is distinguishably deviating from hypervisor-based virtualization:

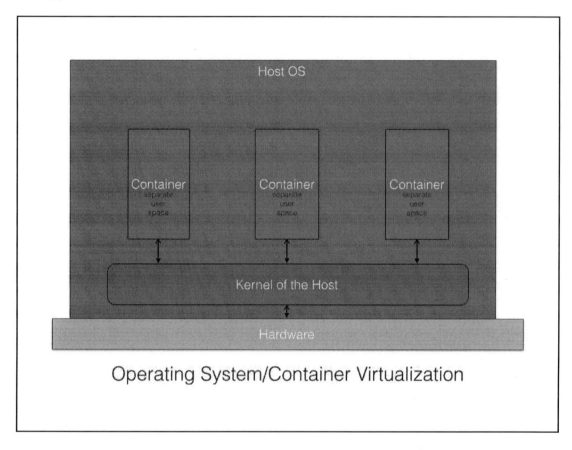

The debate on the security side of VMs and containers is heating up. There are arguments and counter arguments in favor of one or the other. In the case of the virtualization paradigm, the hypervisors are the centralized and core controllers for the VMs. Any kind of access of freshly provisioned VMs needs to go through this hypervisor solution, which stands as a solid wall for any kind of unauthenticated, unauthorized, and unethical purposes. Therefore, the attack surface of a VM is smaller when compared to containers. The hypervisor has to be hacked or broken into in order to impact other VMs. This means that an attacker has to route an attack through both the VM kernel and the hypervisor before being able to touch the host kernel.

In contrast to the virtualization paradigm, the containers are placed directly on top of the kernel of the host system. This lean and mean architecture gives a very much higher efficiency because it completely eliminates the emulation layer of a hypervisor and also offers a much higher container density. However, unlike the VM paradigm, the container paradigm does not have many layers, so one can easily gain access to the host and other containers if any of the containers is compromised. Therefore, the attack surface of a container is larger when compared to VMs.

However, the designers of the Docker platform have given a due consideration to this security risk and designed the system to thwart most of the security risks. In the ensuing sections, we will discuss the security that is innately designed in the system, the solutions being prescribed to substantially enhance the container security, and the best practices and guidelines.

The prominent security-fulfilment features of containers

Linux containers, especially Docker containers, have a few interesting security-fulfilling features innately.

As discussed, Docker uses a host of security barricades to stop breaking out. That is, if one security mechanism gets broken, other mechanisms quickly come in the way of containers being hacked. There are a few mainline zones that are to be examined when evaluating the security implications of Docker containers. As emphasized previously, Docker brings a variety of isolation capabilities to containerized applications to sharply increase their security. Most of them are made available out of the box. The policy addition, annulment, and amendment capabilities at granular level take care of the security requirements of containerization. The Docker platform allows you to do the following:

- Isolate applications from each other
- Isolate applications from the host
- Improve the security of your application by restricting its capabilities
- Encourage adoption of the principle of least privilege

This open-source platform is inherently able to provide these isolations for all kinds of applications on different runtime environments such as VMs, bare metal servers, and traditional IT.

Immutable infrastructure

When you deploy an update to your application, you should create new instances (servers and/or containers) and destroy the old ones, instead of trying to upgrade them in place. Once your application is running, *you don't touch it!* The benefits come in the form of repeatability, reduced management overhead, easier rollbacks, and so on. An **immutable image** is an image that contains everything it needs to run the application, so it comprises the source code. One of the principles of Docker containers is that an image is immutable. That is, once built, it is unchangeable, and if you want to make changes, you'll get a new image as a result.

Docker containers are self-sufficient and hence we just have to run the container without any hassle about anything else, such as mounting volumes. This means that we can share our application with our users or partners in a more easy and transparent way. The direct consequence is that we can easily scale our system in an automated manner with tools, such as Kubernetes, that allows us to run a set of containers on a set of machines, that is, a **cluster**.

Finally, the immutable containers are bound to collapse if someone tries to play with them and hence any kind of manipulation toward malfunctioning is nullified at the initial stage itself.

Resource isolation

As we all know, containers are being positioned for the era of the **Microservices Architecture (MSA)**. That is, in a single system, there can be multiple generic as well as purpose-specific services that dynamically collaborate with one another for realizing easy-to-sustain distributed applications. With the multiplicity and heterogeneity of services in a physical system on the climb, it is natural that the security complexity is bound to shoot up. Therefore, resources need to be clearly demarcated and isolated in order to escape from any kind of perilous security breaches. The widely accepted security approach is to leverage the kernel features including namespaces. The following is the explanation of namespaces and cgroups:

- **Namespaces**: A Linux namespace wraps a set of system resources and presents them to processes within the namespace, making it look as if they are dedicated to the processes. In short, the namespace is a resource management tool that helps in isolating system resources for processes. Kernel namespaces provide the first and foremost form of isolation. Processes running in a container don't affect processes running in another container or in the host system. The network namespace ensures that each container gets its own network stack, thus restricting the access to the interfaces of other containers.

- **Cgroups**: This is a Linux kernel concept that governs the isolation and usage of system resources, such as CPU and memory, for a group of processes. For example, if you have an application that is taking up a lot of CPU cycles and memory, such as a scientific computing application, you can put the application in a cgroup to limit its CPU and memory usage. It ensures that each container gets its fair share of memory, CPU, and disk I/O, and more importantly, that a single container cannot bring the system down by exhausting one of those resources.

Resource accounting and control

Containers consume different physical resources in order to deliver their unique capabilities. However, the resource consumption has to be disciplined, orderly and hence, critically regulated. When there is a deviation, there is a greater possibility of invalidating the containers from performing their assigned tasks in time. For example, the DoS results if the resource usage is not systematically synchronized.

The Linux containers leverage cgroups to implement resource accounting and auditing to run applications in a frictionless manner. As we all know, there are multiple resources that contribute to run the containers successfully. They provide many useful metrics and ensure that each container gets its fair share of memory, CPU, and disk I/O. Further, they guarantee that a single container cannot bring the system down by exhausting any one of these resources. This feature helps you fend off some DoS attacks. This feature helps in running containers as multi-tenant citizens in cloud environments to ensure their uptime and performance. Any kind of exploitation by other containers are identified proactively and nipped in the bud so that any kind of misadventure gets avoided.

The root privilege – impacts and best practices

The Docker Engine efficiently protects the containers from any malicious activities by leveraging the recently mentioned resource isolation and control techniques. Nonetheless, Docker exposes a few potential security threats because the Docker daemon runs with the root privilege. Here, in this section, we list out a few security risks and the best practices to mitigate them.

Another important principle to adhere to is the least privilege. Each process within a container has to run with the minimal access rights and resources in order to deliver its function. The advantage here is that if a container gets compromised, the other resources and data can escape from further attacks.

The trusted user control

Since the Docker daemon runs with the root privilege, it has the capability to mount any directory from the Docker host to the container, without limiting any access rights. That is, you can start a container, where the /host directory will be the / directory on your host, and the container will be able to alter your host filesystem without any restriction. This is just an example among a myriad of malicious uses. Considering these activities, the latter versions of Docker restricts the access to the Docker daemon through a UNIX socket. Docker can be configured to access the daemon through the REST API over HTTP if you explicitly decide to do so. However, you should ensure that it will be reachable only from a trusted network or VPN or protected with stunnel and client SSL certificates. You can also secure them with HTTPS and certificates.

Non-root containers

As mentioned previously, the Docker containers by default run with the root privilege and so does the application that runs inside the container. This is another major concern from the security perspective because hackers can gain root access to the Docker host by hacking the application running inside the container. Docker provides a simple yet powerful solution to change the container's privilege to a non-root user and thus thwart malicious root access to the Docker host. This change to the non-root user can be accomplished using the -u or --user option of the docker run subcommand or the USER instruction in the Dockerfile.

In this section, we will demonstrate by showing you the default root privilege of the Docker container and then continue to modify the root privilege to a non-root user using the USER instruction in the Dockerfile.

First, demonstrate the default root privilege of the Docker container by running a simple `id` command in a `docker run` subcommand, as shown here:

```
$ sudodocker run --rm ubuntu:16.04 id
uid=0(root) gid=0(root) groups=0(root)
```

Now, let us perform the following steps:

1. Craft a `Dockerfile` that creates a non-root privilege user and modify the default root user to the newly-created non-root privilege user, as shown here:

```
############################################
# Dockerfile to change from root to
# non-root privilege
############################################
# Base image is Ubuntu
FROM ubuntu:16.04
# Add a new user "peter" with user id 7373
RUN useradd -u 7373 peter
# Change to non-root privilege
USER peter
```

2. Proceed to build the Docker image using the `docker build` subcommand, as depicted here:

```
$ sudo docker build -t nonrootimage .
```

3. Finally, let's verify the current user of our container using the `id` command in a `docker run` subcommand:

```
$ sudo docker run --rm nonrootimage id
uid=7373(peter) gid=7373(peter) groups=7373(peter)
```

Evidently, the container's user, group, and the groups are now changed to a non-root user.

Modifying the default root privilege to a non-root privilege is a very effective way of containing malevolent penetration into the Docker host kernel.

So far, we discussed the unique security-related kernel characteristics and capabilities. Most of the security holes can be closed down by understanding and applying those kernel capabilities. Security experts and exponents, having considered the faster and widespread adoption of the raging containerization idea in production environments, have brought forth a few more additional security solutions, described as follows in detail. These security methods need to be given utmost importance by developers as well as system administrators while developing, deploying, and delivering enterprise-class containers in order to nullify any kind of inside or outside security attacks.

SELinux for container security

Security-Enhanced Linux (**SELinux**) is a brave attempt to clean up the security holes in Linux containers and is an implementation of a **Mandatory Access Control** (**MAC**) mechanism, **Multi-Level Security** (**MLS**), and **Multi-Category Security** (**MCS**) in the Linux kernel. There is a new collaborative initiative, referred to as the sVirt project, which is being built on SELinux, and this is getting integrated with Libvirt to provide an adaptable MAC framework for VMs as well as containers. This new architecture provides a sheltered separation and safety net for containers, as it primarily prevents root processes, within the container, from interfacing and interfering with other processes running outside this container. Docker containers are automatically assigned to an SELinux context specified in the SELinux policy.

SELinux always checks for all the allowed operations after the standard **Discretionary Access Control** (**DAC**) is completely checked. SELinux can establish and enforce rules on files and processes in a Linux system and on their actions based on defined policies. As per the SELinux specifications, files, including directories and devices, are referred to as objects. Similarly, processes, such as a user running a command, are being termed as subjects. Most operating systems use a DAC system that controls how subjects interact with objects and one another. Using DAC on operating systems, users can control the permissions of their own objects. For example, on a Linux OS, users can make their home directories readable, giving users and subjects a handle to steal potentially sensitive information. However, DAC alone is not a fool-proof security method and DAC access decisions are solely based on user identity and ownership. Generally, DAC simply ignores other security enabling parameters, such as the role of the user, the function, trustworthiness of the program, and the sensitivity and integrity of the data.

As each user typically has the complete discretion over their files, ensuring a system-wide security policy is difficult. Further, every program run by a user simply inherits all the permissions granted to the user, and the user is free to change the access to their files. All this leads to a minimal protection against malicious software. Many system services and privileged programs run with coarse-grained privileges so that any flaw in any one of these programs can be easily exploited and extended to gain the catastrophic access to the system.

As mentioned at the beginning, SELinux adds MAC to the Linux kernel. This means that the owners of an object have no control or discretion over the access to an object. The kernel enforces MAC, which is a general-purpose MAC mechanism, and it needs the ability to enforce administratively set security policies to all the processes and files in the system. These files and processes will be used to base decisions on labels containing a variety of security-centric information.

MAC has the inherent capability to sufficiently protect the system. Further on, MAC ensures application security against any willful hacking and tampering. MAC also provides a strong separation of applications so that any attacked and compromised application runs separately.

Next in line is MCS. It is mainly used to protect containers from other containers. That is, any affected container does not have the capability to bring down other containers in the same Docker host. MCS is based on the MLS capability and uniquely takes advantage of the last component of the SELinux label, *the MLS field*. In general, when containers are launched, the Docker daemon picks a random MCS label. The Docker daemon labels all of the content in the container with that MCS label. When the daemon launches the container process, it tells the kernel to label the processes with the same MCS label. The kernel only allows the container processes to read/write their own content as long as their MCS label matches the filesystem content's MCS label. The kernel blocks the container processes from reading/writing content that is labeled with a different MCS label. This way, a hacked container process is prevented from attacking different containers. The Docker daemon is responsible for guaranteeing that no containers use the same MCS label. The cascading of errors among containers is prohibited through the adroit usage of MCS.

SELinux is not installed by default in Ubuntu 16.04, unlike, Red Hat Fedora or CentOS distribution, so install SELinux by running the `apt-get` command, as shown here:

```
$ sudo apt-get install selinux
```

Then continue to enable the SELinux mode by running the following `sed` scripts:

```
$ sudo sed -i 's/SELINUX=.*/SELINUX=enforcing/' /etc/selinux/config
$ sudo sed -i 's/SELINUXTYPE=.*/SELINUXTYPE=default/' \
/etc/selinux/config
```

Application Armor (AppArmor) is an effective and easy-to-use Linux application security system. AppArmor proactively protects the OS and applications from any kind of external or internal threats and prevents even unknown application flaws from being misused by any hackers. AppArmor is being made available for guaranteeing Docker containers and applications present inside the containers. Policies are turning out to be a powerful mechanism for ensuring container security. Policy formulation and the automated enforcement of policies go a long way in guaranteeing the safety of containers. AppArmor comes by default with Ubuntu 16.04, so this is always recommended to be used.

On Docker versions 1.13.0 and later, the Docker binary generates this profile in TMPFS and then loads it into the kernel. On Docker versions earlier than 1.13.0, this profile is generated in `/etc/apparmor.d/docker` instead.

The `docker-default` profile is the default one for running containers. It is moderately protective while providing wide application compatibility. When you run a container, it uses the `docker-default` policy unless you override it with the `security-opt` option. For example, the following explicitly specifies the default policy:

```
$ docker run --rm -it --security-opt \
        apparmor=docker-default hello-world
```

Secure computing mode (seccomp) is supported by the Docker Engine, a security feature made available in the Linux kernel. This allows the administrator to restrict the actions available within a container down to the granularity of a single system call. This capability greatly restricts the access that an application container has to the host system to perform actions. Enterprises can configure seccomp profiles accordingly and apply them to the Docker environment.

The default seccomp profile provides a sane default for running containers with seccomp and disables around 44 system calls out of over 300. It is moderately protective while providing wide application compatibility.

The vast majority of applications will be able to operate without any issue with the default profile. In fact, the default profile has been able to proactively protect Dockerized applications from several previously unknown bugs.

This is enabled by default on Ubuntu 16.04:

```
$ cat /boot/config-`uname -r` | grep CONFIG_SECCOMP= CONFIG_SECCOMP=y
```

SCONE: Secure Linux Containers with Intel SGX, is described by Sergei Arnautov and his team as a secure container mechanism for Docker that uses the SGX trusted execution support of Intel CPUs to protect container processes from outside attacks. The design objectives of SCONE are fixed as follows:

- Firstly, it attains small **Trusted Computing Base (TCB)**
- Secondly, it has to have a low-performance overhead

SCONE offers a secure C standard library interface that transparently encrypts/decrypts I/O data to significantly reduce the performance impact of thread synchronization and system calls within SGX enclaves. SCONE supports user-level threading and asynchronous system calls. As per their research paper, the evaluation of SCONE is greatly appreciated by Docker fans.

Loading the Docker images and the security implications

Docker typically pulls images from the network, which are usually curated and verified at the source. However, for the purpose of backup and restore, the Docker images can be saved using the `docker save` subcommand and loaded back using the `docker load` subcommand. This mechanism can also be used to load third-party images through unconventional means. Unfortunately, in such a practice, the Docker Engine cannot verify the source and, hence, the images can carry malicious code. So, as the first shield of safety, Docker extracts the image in a *chrooted* subprocess for privilege separation. Even though Docker ensures the privilege separation, it is not recommended to load arbitrary images.

Using container scanning to secure Docker deployments: Docker Content Trust (DCT) gives publishers an easy and expedited way to guarantee the authenticity of containers that are getting published in web-scale repositories such as Docker Hub. However, organizations need to take pragmatic measures to access, assess, and act accordingly for ensuring the security of their containerized applications throughout their complete life cycle. Precisely speaking, DCT is a means by which you can securely sign your Docker images that you have created to ensure that they are from who they say they are from.

Managing container security with Black Duck Hub: Black Duck Hub is a vital tool for managing the security of application containers throughout the full application life cycle. Black Duck Hub allows organizations to identify and track vulnerable open-source applications and components within their environment. Assessments draw on Black Duck's KnowledgeBase, which contains information on 1.1 million open-source projects and detailed data on more than 100,000 known open-source vulnerabilities across more than 350 billion lines of code. Through a partnership with Red Hat, Black Duck's ability to identify and inventory open source and proprietary code production environments is now being applied to containerized environments. Red Hat has launched **Deep Container Inspection (DCI)**, an enterprise-focused offering that wraps container certification, policy and trust into an overall architecture for deploying and managing application containers. As part of DCI, Red Hat is partnering with Black Duck to give organizations a means of validating the contents of a container before, during, and after deployment.

Integration of Black Duck Hub's vulnerability scanning and mapping capabilities enables OpenShift customers to consume, develop, and run containerized applications with increased confidence and security, knowing that these applications contain code that has been independently validated and certified. The integration also provides a means to track the impact of newly disclosed vulnerabilities or changes related to container aging that may impact on security and risk. Black Duck Hub's application vulnerability scanning and mapping capability give Docker customers the ability to identify vulnerabilities both before and after deployment and spot issues that arise as containerized applications age or become exposed to new security vulnerabilities and attacks.

Image signing and verification using TUF

The Docker community expects to have a strong cryptographic guarantee regarding the code and versions of the Dockerized software. DCT is the new security-related feature associated with the 1.8 version of the Docker platform. DCT intrinsically integrates **The Update Framework (TUF)** into Docker using Notary, an open source tool that provides trust over any content.

TUF helps developers to secure new or existing software update systems, which are often found to be vulnerable to many known attacks. TUF addresses this widespread problem by providing a comprehensive and flexible security framework that developers can integrate with any software update system. A software update system is an application running on a client system that obtains and installs software. This can include updates to software that is already installed or even completely new software.

Protection against image forgery: Once trust is established, DCT provides the ability to withstand a malicious actor with a privileged network position also known as a **Man-in-the-Middle (MitM)** attack.

Protection against replay attacks: In the typical replay attacks, previously valid payloads are replayed to trick another system. In the case of software update systems, old versions of signed software can be presented as the most recent ones. If a user is fooled into installing an older version of a particular software, the malicious actor can make use of the known security vulnerabilities to compromise the user's host. DCT uses the timestamp key when publishing the image, providing protection against replay attacks. This ensures that what the user receives is the most recent one.

Protection against key compromise: If a key is compromised, you can utilize that offline key to perform a key rotation. That key rotation can only be done by the one with the offline key. In this scenario, you will need to create a new key and sign it with your offline key.

Other security-enhancing projects include the following:

- **Clair**: This is an open-source project for the static analysis of vulnerabilities in application Docker containers (`https://github.com/coreos/clair`). It audits the Docker image locally and also checks vulnerability in container registry integration. Finally, during the first run, Clair will bootstrap its database with vulnerability data from its data sources.

- **Notary**: The Docker Notary project is a framework that allows anyone to securely publish and access content (for example, Docker images) over a potentially insecure network. Notary allows a user to digitally sign and verify content.

- **Project Nautilus**: Nautilus is Docker's image scanning capability, which can examine images in Docker Hub to help vulnerabilities that may exist in Docker containers. Today, Nautilus only works with Docker Hub. It does not support private or on-premises registries.

- **AuthZ Plugins**: The native Docker access control is all or nothing—you either have access to all Docker resources or none. The AuthZ framework is Twistlock's contribution to the Docker code base. AuthZ allows anyone to write an authorization plugin for Docker to provide fine-grained access control to Docker resources.

- **Docker Trusted Registry (DTR)**: This is Docker's enterprise version of Docker Hub. You can run DTR on-premises or in your virtual private cloud to support security or compliance requirements. Docker Hub is open source, whereas DTR is a subscription-based product sold by Docker. Communications with the registries use TLS, to ensure both confidentiality and content integrity. By default, the use of certificates trusted by the public PKI infrastructure is mandatory, but Docker allows the addition of a company internal CA root certificate to the trust store.

The emerging security approaches

As we all know, the Docker platform makes it easy for developers to update and control the data and software in containers. Similarly, Docker enables efficiently ensuring all the components that make an application are current and consistent at all times. Docker also innately delivers logical segregation of applications running on the same physical host. This celebrated isolation perfectly promotes fine-grained and efficient enforcement of security policies. However, as in the traditional environment, data at rest is susceptible to various attacks ceaselessly from cyber and internal attackers. There are other negative opportunities and possibilities for Docker environments to be subjected to heavy bombardment. Consequently, there is an insistence for proper safeguards to be in place. The faster and easier proliferation of containers and data can significantly expand the number and types of threats targeting containerized clouds.

About Vormetric transparent encryption

Organizations can establish strong controls around their sensitive data in Docker implementations in an efficient manner. This solution enables data-at-rest encryption, privileged user access control, and the collection of security intelligence logs for structured databases and unstructured files. With these capabilities, organizations can establish persistent, strong controls around their stored Docker images and protect all data generated by Docker containers when the data is being written to the Docker host storage on an NFS mount or a local folder.

The best practices for container security

There are robust and resilient security solutions to boost the confidence of providers as well as users toward embracing the containerization journey with clarity and alacrity. In this section, we provide a number of tips, best practices, and key guidelines collected from different sources in order to enable security administrators and consultants to tightly secure Docker containers. At the bottom line, if containers are running in a multi-tenant system and you are not using the proven security practices, then there are definite dangers lurking around the security front.

The first and foremost advice is, don't run random and untested Docker images on your system. Strategize and leverage trusted repositories of Docker images and containers to subscribe and use applications and data containers for application development, packaging, shipping, deployment, and delivery. It is clear from past experiences that any untrusted containers that are downloaded from the public domain may result in malevolent and messy situations. Linux distributions, such as **Red Hat Enterprise Linux** (**RHEL**), have the following mechanisms in place in order to assist administrators to ensure the utmost security.

The best practices widely recommended by Docker experts (Daniel Walsh Consulting Engineer, Red Hat) are as follows:

- Only run container images from trusted parties
- Container applications should drop privileges or run without privileges whenever possible
- Make sure the kernel is always updated with the latest security fixes; the security kernel is critical
- Make sure you have support teams watching for security flaws in the kernel
- Use a good quality supported host system for running the containers, with regular security updates

- Do not disable security features of the host operating system
- Examine your container images for security flaws and make sure the provider fixes them in a timely manner

As mentioned previously, the biggest problem is that everything in Linux is not namespaced. Currently, Docker uses five namespaces to alter the process's view of any system: process, network, mount, hostname, and shared memory. While these give the users some level of security, it is by no means a comprehensive one such as KVM. In a KVM environment, processes in a VM do not talk to the host kernel directly. They do not have any access to kernel filesystems. Device nodes can talk to the VMs kernel, not the hosts. Therefore, in order to have a privilege escalation out of a VM, the process has to subvert the VM's kernel, find an enabling vulnerability in the hypervisor, break through SELinux controls (sVirt), and attack the host's kernel. In the container landscape, the approach is to protect the host from the processes within the container and to protect containers from other containers. It is all about combining or clustering together multiple security controls to defend containers and their contents.

Basically, we want to put in as many security barriers as possible to prevent any sort of break out. If a privileged process can break out of one containment mechanism, the idea is to block them with the next barrier in the hierarchy. With Docker, it is possible to take advantage of as many security mechanisms of Linux as possible. The following are the possible security measures that can be taken:

- **Filesystem protection**: Filesystems need to be read-only in order to escape from any kind of unauthorized writing. That is, privileged container processes cannot write to them and do not affect the host system too. Generally, most of the applications need not write anything to their filesystems. There are several Linux distributions with read-only filesystems. It is, therefore, possible to block the ability of the privileged container processes from remounting filesystems as read and write. It is all about blocking the ability to mount any filesystems within the container.
- **Copy-on-write filesystems**: Docker has been using the **Advanced Multi-Layered Unification Filesystem (AUFS)** as a filesystem for containers. AUFS is a layered filesystem that can transparently overlay one or more existing filesystems. When a process needs to modify a file, AUFS first creates a copy of that file and is capable of merging multiple layers into a single representation of a filesystem. This process is called copy-on-write, and this prevents one container from seeing the changes of another container even if they write to the same filesystem image. One container cannot change the image content to affect the processes in another container.

- **The choice of capabilities**: Typically, there are two ways to perform permission checks: privileged processes and unprivileged processes. Privileged processes bypass all sorts of kernel permission checks, while unprivileged processes are subject to the full permission checking based on the process's credentials. The recent Linux kernel divides the privileges traditionally associated with the superuser into distinct units known as **capabilities**, which can be independently enabled and disabled. Capabilities are a per-thread attribute. Removing capabilities can bring forth several positive changes in Docker containers. Invariably, capabilities decide the Docker functionality, accessibility, usability, security, and so on. Therefore, it needs a deeper thinking while embarking on the journey of adding as well as removing capabilities.

- **Keeping systems and data secure**: Some security issues need to be addressed before enterprises and service providers use containers in production environments. Containerization will eventually make it easier to secure applications for the following three reasons:

  - A smaller payload reduces the surface area for security flaws
  - Instead of incrementally patching the operating system, you can update it
  - By allowing a clear separation of concerns, containers help IT and application teams collaborate purposefully

The IT department is responsible for security flaws associated with the infrastructure. The application team fixes flaws inside the container and is also responsible for runtime dependencies. Easing the tension between IT and applications development teams helps smooth the transition to a hybrid cloud model. The responsibilities of each team are clearly demarcated in order to secure both containers and their runtime infrastructures. With such a clear segregation, proactively identifying any visible and invisible endangering security ordeals and promptly eliminating time, policy engineering and enforcement, precise and perfect configuration, leveraging appropriate security-unearthing and mitigation tools, and so on, are being systematically accomplished.

- **Leveraging Linux kernel capabilities**: An average server (bare metal or VM) needs to run a bunch of processes as root. These typically include `ssh`, `cron`, `syslogd`, hardware management tools (for example, load modules), and network configuration tools (for example, handling DHCP, WPA, or VPNs). A container is very different because almost all of these tasks are being handled by the infrastructures on which the containers are to be hosted and run. There are several best practices, key guidelines, technical know-how, and so on in various blogs authored by security experts. You can find some of the most interesting and inspiring security-related details at `https://docs.docker.com/`.

Secure deployment guidelines for Docker containers

Docker containers are increasingly hosted in production environments to be publicly discovered and used by many. Especially, with the faster adoption of cloud technologies, the IT environments of worldwide organizations and institutions are getting methodically optimized and transformed to deftly and decisively host a wider variety of VMs and containers. There are new improvements and enablements, such as Flocker and Clocker, in order to speed up the process of taking containers to cloud environments (private, public, hybrid, and community). There are recommendations that have to be followed while deploying containers. As we all know, containers remarkably reduce the overhead by allowing developers and system administrators to seamlessly deploy containers for applications and services required for business operations. However, because Docker leverages the same kernel as the host system to reduce the need for resources, containers can be exposed to significant security risks if not adequately configured. There are a few carefully annotated guidelines to be strictly followed by both developers and system administrators while deploying containers. For example, `https://github.com/GDSSecurity/Docker-Secure-Deployment-Guidelines` elaborates in a tabular form with all the right details.

An indisputable truth is that the software flaws in distributed and complex applications open the way for intelligent attackers and hackers to break into systems that host critical, confidential, and customer data. Therefore, security solutions are being insisted and ingrained across all the layers in the IT stack, and hence, there arise many types of security vulnerabilities at different levels and layers. For example, the perimeter security that solves only part of the problem because the changing requirements are mandated for allowing network access to employees, customers, and partners. Similarly, there are firewalls, intrusion detection and prevention systems, **Application Delivery Controllers** (ADCs), access controls, multifactor authentication and authorization, patching, and so on. Then, for securing data while in transit, persistence, and being used by applications, there are encryption, steganography, and hybrid security models. All these are reactive and realistic mechanisms, but the increasing tendency is all about virtual businesses insisting on proactive and preemptive security methods. As IT is tending and trending toward the much anticipated virtual IT, the security issues and implications are being given extra importance by security experts.

The future of Docker security

There will be many noteworthy improvisations, transformations, and disruptions in the containerization space in the near future. Through a host of innovations and integrations, the Docker platform is being positioned as the leading one for strengthening the containerization journey. The following are the prime accomplishments through the smart leverage of the Docker technology:

- **Strengthening the distributed paradigm**: While computing is going to be increasingly distributed and federated, the MSA plays a very decisive and deeper role in IT. Docker containers are emerging as the most efficient ones for hosting and delivering a growing array of microservices. With container orchestration technologies and tools gaining greater recognition, microservices (specific as well as generic) get identified, matched, orchestrated, and choreographed to form business-aware composite services.

- **Empowering the cloud paradigm**: The cloud idea is strongly gripping the IT world to bring in the much-insisted IT infrastructure rationalization, simplification, standardization, automation, and optimization. The abstraction and virtualization concepts, the key ones for the unprecedented success of the cloud paradigm, are penetrating into every kind of IT module. Originally, it started with server virtualization and now it is all about storage and networking virtualization. With all the technological advancements around us, there is a widespread keenness to realize software-defined infrastructures (software-defined compute, storage, and networking). The Docker Engine, the core and critical portion of the Docker platform, is duly solidified in order to bring in the necessary eligibility for containers to run on software-defined environments without any hitch or hurdle.

- **Enabling IT elasticity, portability, agility, and adaptability**: Containers are emerging as the flexible and futuristic IT building blocks for bringing in more resiliency, versatility, elegance, and suppleness. Faster provisioning of IT resources for ensuring higher availability and real-time scalability, the easy elimination of all kinds of frictions between the development and operation teams, the guarantee of native performance of IT, the realization of organized and optimized IT for enhanced IT productivity, and so on, are some of the exemplary things being visualized for Docker containers toward the smarter IT.

Containers will be a strategic addition to VMs and bare metal servers in order to bring in deeper IT automation, acceleration, and augmentation, thereby the much-hyped and hoped for business agility, autonomy, and affordability will be achieved.

Summary

Security is definitely a challenge and an important aspect not to be sidestepped. If a container gets compromised, then bringing down the container host is not a difficult task. Thus, ensuring security for containers and then hosts is indispensable for the flourishing of the containerization concept, especially when the centralization and federation of IT systems are on the climb. In this chapter, we specifically focused on the sickening and devastating security issues on Docker containers and explained the ways and means of having foolproof security solutions for containers that host dynamic, enterprise-class, and mission-critical applications. In the days to unfurl, there will be fresh security approaches and solutions in order to guarantee impenetrable and unbreakable security for Docker containers and hosts, as the security of containers and their contents is of the utmost importance for service providers as well as consumers.

12
The Docker Platform – Distinct Capabilities and Use Cases

Without any doubt, IT is the most happening and highly visible domain at any point in time. As every kind of enterprising business (small, medium, and large) is being enabled through the delectable advancements in the IT space, there is a direct and decisive relationship between IT and business. With the IT budgets being pruned by business behemoths year after year due to the stagnant, even sliding, world economy, it is a clear-cut mandate and timely reminder for IT professionals to do more with less. That is, there is a continued insistence for deeper and deft automation of various business operations by methodically leveraging the proven and promising technologies, tools, and tips. Infrastructure optimization through hybrid clouds, process excellence through integration and orchestration techniques, the fast spread of the DevOps culture, the foundational aspect of compartmentalization through virtualization and containerization approaches, the penetrative, pervasive, and persuasive nature of APIs, the fast emergence of MSA, the cognitive analytics, and so on, are being overwhelmingly recognized and reaped as the dominant and prominent ways forward toward business agility, affordability, adaptivity, and autonomy.

Docker-enabled containerization is an intensely reviewed mechanism that has the innate strength to bring in certain critical disruptions for the field of software engineering. The Docker paradigm is all about optimal packaging of any kinds of software applications along with their dependencies to be shipped, deployed, and executed across any on-premise and off-premise environments. Containerized applications (applications and their execution containers) are extremely lightweight, portable, scalable, reproducible, and repeatable packages compared with the currently available options in the software industry.

The Docker idea facilitates many purposeful innovations. Docker (through its unique packaging format and the highly integrated platform) simplifies and accelerates the formation of publicly discoverable, network accessible, and remotely deployable containerized applications that are easily composable, consumable, and configurable. Further, there are software solutions for robust monitoring, measuring, and managing containers. In this chapter, we will discuss how the accelerated maturity and stability of the Docker paradigm ensures the much-needed business transformations. The literature talks about several game-changing implications of the Docker technology toward the next-generation IT and this chapter aims to unravel the Docker mystery.

Describing containers

Compartmentalization that comprises both virtualization and containerization is the new norm for IT agility. Virtualization has been the enigmatic foundation for the enormous success of cloud computing. Now with the containerization idea becoming ubiquitous and usable, there is a renewed focus on using containers for faster application building, deployment, and delivery. Containers are distinctively fitted with a few game-changing capabilities and hence there is a rush in embracing and evolving the containerization technologies and tools.

Containers are very hot in the industry. Essentially, a container is lightweight, virtualized, and portable, and the **Software-Defined Environment** (**SDE**) in which software can run is in isolation of other software running on the same physical host. The software that runs inside a container is typically a single-purpose application. Containers bring forth the much-coveted modularity, portability, and simplicity for IT environments. Developers love containers because they speed up the software engineering, whereas the operation team loves containers because they can just focus on runtime tasks such as logging, monitoring, managing the life cycle, and utilizing the resource rather than managing deployment and dependency.

Distinguishing Docker containers

Precisely speaking, Docker containers wrap a piece of software in a complete filesystem that contains everything that is needed to run: source code, runtime, system tools, and system libraries (anything that can be installed on a server). This guarantees that the software will always run the same, regardless of its operating environment.

The main motivations of Docker-enabled containerization are as follows:

- Containers running on a single machine share the same operating system kernel. They start instantly and use less RAM. Container images are constructed from layered filesystems and share common files, making disk usage and image downloads much more efficient.
- Docker containers are based on open standards. This standardization enables containers to run on all major Linux distributions and other operating systems such as Microsoft Windows and Apple Macintosh.

There are several benefits being associated with Docker containers, as listed here:

- **Efficiency**: As mentioned earlier, there can be multiple containers on a single machine leveraging the same kernel so they are lightweight, can start instantly, and make more efficient use of RAM.
    - **Resource sharing**: This among workloads allows greater efficiency compared to the use of dedicated and single-purpose equipment. This sharing enhances the utilization rate of resources.
    - **Resource partitioning**: This ensures that resources are appropriately segmented in order to meet the system requirements of each workload. Another objective for this partitioning is to prevent any kind of untoward interactions among workloads.
    - **Resource as a Service (RaaS)**: Various resources can be individually and collectively chosen, provisioned, and given to applications directly or to users to run applications.
- **Native performance**: Containers guarantee higher performance due to their lightweight nature and less wastage.
- **Portability**: Applications, dependencies, and configurations are all bundled together in a complete filesystem, ensuring applications work seamlessly in any environment (VMs, bare metal servers, local or remote, generalized or specialized machines, and so on). The main advantage of this portability is that it is possible to change the runtime dependencies (even programming language) between deployments.

The following diagram illustrates how containers are being moved and swapped across multiple hosts:

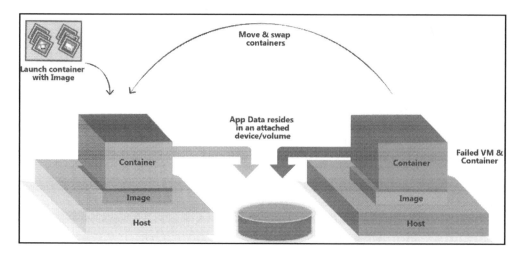

- **Real-time scalability**: Any number of fresh containers can be provisioned in a few seconds in order to handle the user and data loads. On the reverse side, additionally provisioned containers can be knocked down when the demand goes down. This ensures higher throughput and capacity on demand. Tools such as Docker Swarm, Kubernetes, and Apache Mesos further simplify elastic scaling.
- **High availability**: By running with multiple containers, redundancy can be built into the application. If one container fails, then the surviving peers—which are providing the same capability—continue to provide service. With orchestration, failed containers can be automatically recreated (rescheduled) either on the same or a different host, restoring full capacity and redundancy.
- **Maneuverability**: Applications running in Docker containers can be easily modified, updated, or extended without impacting other containers in the host.
- **Flexibility**: Developers are free to use the programming languages and development tools they prefer.
- **Clusterability**: Containers can be clustered for specific purposes on demand and there are integrated management platforms for cluster-enablement and management.
- **Composability**: Software services hosted in containers can be discovered, matched for, and linked to form business-critical, process-aware, and composite services.
- **Security**: Containers isolate applications from one another and the underlying infrastructure by providing an additional layer of protection for the application.

- **Predictability**: With immutable images, the image always exhibits the same behavior everywhere because the code is contained in the image. This means a lot in terms of deployment and in the management of the application life cycle.
- **Repeatability**: With Docker, one can build an image, test that image, and then use that same image in production.
- **Replicability**: With containers, it is easy to instantiate identical copies of full application stack and configuration. These can then be used by new hires, partners, support teams, and others to safely experiment in isolation.

Briefing the Docker platform

Linux containers are hugely complicated and not user-friendly. Having realized the fact that several complexities are coming in the way of massively producing and fluently using containers, an open-source project got initiated with the goal of deriving a sophisticated and modular platform comprising an enabling engine for simplifying and streamlining the life cycle phases of various containers. This means that the Docker platform is built to automate the crafting, packaging, shipping, deployment, and delivery of any software application embedded inside a lightweight, extensible, and self-sufficient container. Docker is positioned as the most flexible and futuristic containerization technology in realizing highly competent and enterprise-class distributed applications. This will make deft and decisive impacts on the IT industry, as instead of large monolithic applications distributed on a single physical or virtual server, companies are building smaller, self-defined and sustainable, easily manageable, and discrete ones. In short, services are becoming microservices these days in order to give the fillip to the containerization movement.

The Docker platform enables artistically assembling applications from disparate and distributed components and eliminates any kind of deficiencies and deviations that could come when shipping the code. Docker, through a host of scripts and tools, simplifies the isolation of software applications and makes them self-sustainable by running them in transient containers. Docker brings the required separation for each of the applications from one another as well as from the underlying host. We have been hugely accustomed to VMs that are formed through an additional layer of indirection in order to bring the necessary isolation. This additional layer and overhead consumes a lot of precious resources and is hence an unwanted cause of the slowdown of the system. On the other hand, Docker containers share all the resources (compute, storage, and networking) to the optimal level and hence can run much faster. Docker images, being derived in a standard form, can be widely shared and stocked easily for producing bigger and better application containers. In short, the Docker platform lays a stimulating and scintillating foundation for optimal consumption, management, and maneuverability of various IT infrastructures.

The Docker platform is an open-source containerization solution that smartly and swiftly automates the bundling of any software applications and services into containers and accelerates the deployment of containerized applications in any IT environments (local or remote systems, virtualized or bare metal machines, generalized or embedded devices, and so on). The container life cycle management tasks are fully taken care of by the Docker platform. The whole process starts with the formation of a standardized and optimized image for the identified software and its dependencies. Now the Docker platform takes the readied image to form the containerized software. There are image repositories made available publicly as well as in private locations. Developers and operations teams can leverage them to speed up software deployment in an automated manner.

The Docker ecosystem is rapidly growing with a number of third-party product and tool developers in order to make Docker an enterprise-scale containerization platform. It helps to skip the setup and maintenance of development environments and language-specific tooling. Instead, it focuses on creating and adding new features, fixing issues, and shipping software. "Build once and run everywhere," is the endemic mantra of the Docker-enabled containerization. Concisely speaking, the Docker platform brings in the following competencies:

- **Agility**: Developers have the freedom to define environments and the ability to create applications. IT operation teams can deploy applications faster, allowing the business to outpace the competition.
- **Controllability**: Developers own all the code from infrastructure to application.
- **Manageability**: IT operation team members have the manageability to standardize, secure, and scale the operating environment while reducing overall costs to the organization.

The evolving Docker platform components

Docker is a platform for developing, shipping, and running powerful applications crafted out of distributed microservices. The platform is in the expansion mode with the persistent support rendered by a number of third-party product vendors and start-ups in the Docker space. For different use cases, additional automation tools are being built and released to the marketplace:

- Docker Hub
- Docker Trusted Registry
- Docker Engine
- Docker Kitematic
- Docker Toolbox

- Docker Registry
- Docker Machine
- Docker Swarm
- Docker Compose
- Docker Cloud
- Docker Datacenter

With the ongoing requirements, we can safely expect new additions to the preceding list in the days ahead. The Docker team is proactively and preemptively working on various tools in order to bring in the desired automation and simplicity for lessening the workloads of IT professionals.

Implications of the Docker technology

With the systematic and sagacious usage of the Docker idea, enterprising businesses and organizations across the globe are bound to benefit immensely for their business transformation needs. This section will describe the paramount and potential impacts of the Docker paradigm. Without any doubt, containers are a hot topic these days. Corporates, service providers (cloud, communication, and so on), and consumers are pursuing the Docker dream. Docker has been creating multifaceted impressions and implications for enterprise and cloud IT. The systematic leverage of the Docker technology is assuredly accentuated to pour in delectable advancements for businesses.

Modern enterprise development

Conceptually, a container image can be thought of as a snapshot of a container's filesystem that can be stored on disk. The container filesystem is typically arranged in layers and every change gets carefully captured in a separate layer. This allows the container image to indicate from which parent image it is derived. The Docker images, being represented through a standardized and simplified format, can ultimately lead to the rapid and rewarding deployment and execution of software applications. Containers are portable. This means that building images once and running them everywhere is the crux of the portability goal. Containers can run on any hardware that runs the relevant operating system.

There are challenges too. As there can be many containers in a single Docker host, there can be the issue of the container sprawl in a cloud environment (private, public, and hybrid). For effective monitoring and management, the concepts of clustering and orchestration are being leveraged in order to find and bind different and distributed containers. Further on, for constructing distributed applications through containerized applications, service composition through the orchestration technique is encouraged. Docker Compose is the key solution for making composite applications. For working at the container level, there are automated monitoring, measurement, management, and orchestration software solutions (Docker Swarm, Kubernetes, and Mesos). In the following sections, we explain how containers are the best fit for agile and adroit businesses. This does not mean that virtualization is out of business. There are certain situations and scenarios wherein the mixed and merged usage of virtualization and containerization is posted for wonders.

Combining these special powers with container images, resulting in a viable and venerable abstraction, enables a clean isolation between applications from the underlying operating systems. This neat decoupling of image and OS makes it possible to deploy software applications in development, testing, staging, and production environments without any hurdle or hitch. This Docker-enabled uniformity and ubiquity improves deployment reliability and speeds up modern enterprise development by decimating all kinds of inconsistencies and unnecessary frictions. The widely expressed recommendation is to have an airtight container image that can encompass and encapsulate all of an application's dependencies into a package. This then can be deployed into a container to enable shipping to run anytime anywhere.

MSA and Docker containers

The service-enablement has been going on successfully for a number of reasons and objectives. Every system (physical, mechanical, electrical, and electronic) is systematically enabled with easily consumable interfaces. RESTful interfaces and services have become pervasive due to their simplicity. In the recent past, with the surging popularity of the web, enterprise, mobile, and cloud applications, the REST idea has clearly captured a lot of attention and attraction. It has been quickly discovered that splitting out business functions into reusable services is very effective; however, at the same, it introduces a risk point. This means that every time a service gets updated, then all the other services that make use of the updated service have to be subjected to a variety of formal verifications and validations. This is because services inevitably have to find, bind, and leverage other services and their unique capabilities and data points to be right and relevant. This unbridled sharing can happen locally or with remote ones over networks.

Basically, the microservices approach, in a nutshell, dictates that instead of having one giant code base that all developers touch, that often becomes perilous to manage, it is better to have numerous smaller code bases managed by small and agile teams that sit across different time zones. Every code base has to interoperate through well-intended and defined APIs. Every code base is small in size but also totally decoupled from one another. The dependency is gone totally, resulting in better security, reliability, simplicity, scalability, availability, and so on. The code base is termed as microservices. The motives for the unprecedented take off of microservices are definitely many; specifically, the granular scaling, easy manageability, maneuverability, reconfigurability and extensibility, strong security through API access, the appropriateness of containers as the optimal runtime environment, and so on, are the widely articulated ones. Microservices can be independently deployable, horizontally scalable, supported by any backend databases (SQL, NoSQL, NewSQL, In-Memory, and so on), and built by any programming languages.

Docker containers are the best fit for hosting microservices. This intentional containerization of single services or processes makes it very simple to manage, update, and scale out these services. Now with the number of microservices in any IT environment growing very rapidly, the management complexity is to zoom. This means that the challenges include how to manage single services in a cluster and how to tackle multiple services spread across distributed and different hosts. Kubernetes, MaestroNG, Mesosphere, and Fleet spring up to answer this growing need.

In summary, one prominent reason is the onset and rollout of microservices in droves and this has brought out the indispensability of containers. The various targets expected out of microservices are being fulfilled by stuffing microservices within containers. This interesting combination is bound to play a very stellar role for the IT teams of worldwide enterprising businesses. Practically speaking, the widespread usage of the containerization tenet has laid a stimulating foundation for the explosion of purpose-specific as well as agnostic microservices.

Case study

SA Home Loans faced challenges in development, as well as in production. SA currently has four scrum teams, each with a development and a system test lab. The team faced slow deployment times and was only able to build and deploy two applications in the dev labs, causing long deployment cycles and sometimes taking up to 2 weeks to get applications over to the testing environment. This issue got extended to production as well. The main home loan servicing software monolithic was built using legacy technologies.

The IT team made the conscious decision to adopt the MSA to gain the agility, portability, and extensibility, and the break-in resulted in 50 microservices. Having understood the significance of the blossoming Docker technology, the team could move all the microservices to containers.

The team also needed a production-ready orchestration service that could give it a single point from which to manage and distribute containers onto the nodes, as well as give the team a high-level oversight of all the containers. Docker Swarm is the orchestration tool. SA Home Loans now uses Docker Datacenter, the on-premises solution that brings container management and deployment services to the enterprise via a supported **Container as a Service** (**CaaS**) platform that is hosted locally. SA Home Loans now builds and deploys applications up to 20-30 times a day. **Universal Control Plane** (**UCP**) has embedded Swarm to give the production-ready container orchestration solution.

Infrastructure optimization

Virtualization has been the main mechanism for hugely optimizing and organizing various IT infrastructures (server machines, storage appliances, networking, and security solutions). The proven divide and conquer technique accomplished through VMs is the main target for IT optimization. In the recent past, Docker containers emerged as a blessing in disguise. Containers contain only what is necessary to build, ship, and run software applications. Unlike VMs, there is no guest OS or hypervisor necessary for containers. This allows enterprises to radically reduce the amount of storage and totally eliminate hypervisor licensing costs. The number of containers that can be accommodated in a physical host or in a VM is more compared to the number of VMs being stuffed in a physical machine. This means that containers are fine-grained whereas VMs are coarse-grained. The wastage of resources is very minimal in the case of containerization. Every bit of IT infrastructures and resources is being methodically used by containers.

Portability is another factor. This enables IT operations teams to move workloads across different cloud services, physical servers, or VMs without locking them into using a specific infrastructure tooling. Workload consolidation or optimization through containers is error-free because containers can run everywhere. In the case of VMs, VM placement is a tricky and tough affair considering the diversity of hypervisors / **Virtual Machine Monitors** (**VMMs**). The point here is that Docker allows enterprises to optimize infrastructure utilization and decrease the cost of maintaining existing applications, which is incidentally the number one challenge enterprise IT teams face every day.

Docker greatly reduces the amount of time it takes to install an application, scale to meet customer demands, or simply start new containers. This means, taking new offerings to market is exceedingly fast because the underlying infrastructure (virtual or physical) is being readied in a few seconds.

Case study

A client with the need to establish and provide **Database as a Service (DaaS)** capability has resolved that every database instance is provisioned and stationed inside its own VM. There can be occasions wherein there are 100 VMs running 100 databases. This is extremely inefficient, wasting a lot of expensive resources. Now the same number of database instances can be run on that number of containers, which in turn could run inside a few VMs. The result is huge cost savings. Another case study follows:

- **Customer details**: Swisscom is a Switzerland's leading telecom provider offering a range of enterprise and consumer services.
- **The business challenges**: This includes offering a reliable, easy-to-maintain DaaS to customers while achieving server density necessary to operate efficiently.
- **The solution approach**: Flocker by ClusterHQ provides the ability to programmatically manage persistent data for Docker containers stored in EMC ScaleIO.
- **The business outcome**: This solution has substantially increased the density of applications hosted per server, improved operational management of databases, and laid out a stimulating and sparkling platform for sustainable innovation in consumer and enterprise IT sectors.

Enabling DevOps

Agile development is being increasingly followed in the IT industry these days in order to elegantly ensure business agility, adaptivity, and affordability. This means that it is true that the much-demanded business agility is being fulfilled by stringently embracing the competent methods for IT agility. There is a growing array of viable and venerable mechanisms to realize IT agility. Primarily, IT agility is being driven through agile programming methods such as pair programming, **Extreme Programming (XP)**, Lean, Scrum and Kanban, **Test-Driven Development (TDD)**, and **Behaviour-Driven Development (BDD)**.

Now the software development process gets speeded up remarkably. However, there is a big disconnect between development and operation. This means that the real IT agility gets realized when the operation team also strictly follows agile, adaptive, and automated IT operations. Enterprise DevOps is the most promising way forward for establishing the beneficial connect between developers and operators so that the IT systems get up and running quickly. Containerization is the most positive development toward making DevOps pervasive, penetrative, and persuasive.

Docker is ideal for quickly setting up development and test environments as well as sandbox environments. Docker interestingly offers a better separation of concerns for guarantee-efficient DevOps; container crafters need to focus only on building Docker images and committing them to make them containers. The operation team could monitor, manage, and maintain the containers. Finally, Docker can be easily integrated into multiple DevOps tools to achieve better workflow automation and continuous integration. Also, it enables the DevOps teams to scale up development and test environments, quickly and cost-effectively, and to move applications from development, to test, to production in a seamless manner.

Continuous integration and continuous deployment

Continuous Integration (CI) and **Continuous Deployment (CD)** are the most sought-after technologies and tools for having agile IT. In the past, developers would automate their build process using any one of the build tools. Then they would hand over their code to the operation team to proceed with deployment, administration, management, and support. There are many configuration management and software deployment tools in order to automate the tedious and tough affair of software deployment and delivery. This segregated pattern brought forth a number of recurring issues. With containers, the operation team could build standard container images of the full stack that they want to deploy and deliver. Developers can use them to deploy their code to do unit testing. That same tested, refined, and hardened image can be used across all environments (development, test, stage, and production) to get the same results every time. This containerization-sponsored setup specifically accelerates the software deployment and delivery activities in a risk-free fashion.

As per the Docker site, CI/CD typically merges development with testing, allowing developers to build code collaboratively, submit it to the master branch, and check for any issues. This means that developers can build and test their code to catch bugs early in the applications development life cycle. Since Docker can integrate with tools such as Jenkins and GitHub, developers can submit code in GitHub, test the code, and automatically trigger a build using Jenkins, and once the image is complete, it can be added to Docker registries. This ultimately streamlines the process and saves times on build and setup processes, all while allowing developers to run tests in parallel and automate them so that they can continue to work on other projects while tests are being run. The environment dependencies and inconsistencies get eliminated with the containerization.

Continuous delivery

The **continuous delivery** approach involves fast software development iterations and frequent, safe updates to the deployed application. It is all about reducing risk and delivering value faster by producing reliable software in short iterations. Because Docker encapsulates both the application and the application's environment or infrastructure configuration, it provides a key building block for two essential aspects of a continuous delivery pipeline. Docker makes it easy to test exactly what you are going to deploy. The possibility of making serious errors during the handoff or bringing in any undesirable changes is less likely in this case. Docker containers encourage a central tenet of continuous delivery: they reuse the same binaries at each step of the pipeline to ensure no errors are introduced in the build process itself.

As indicated earlier, Docker containers provide the basis for immutable infrastructures. Applications can be added, removed, cloned, and/or their constituencies can change without leaving any residues behind. IT infrastructures can be changed without affecting the applications that run on them. The Docker tool ecosystem is the growth trajectory and hence a lot of delivery-related works get simply automated and accelerated to add business value. As Martin Fowler says, you actually do continuous delivery in the following situations:

- If your software is deployable throughout its life cycle
- If your team prioritizes keeping the software deployable over working on new features
- If anybody can get fast, automated feedback on the production readiness of their systems anytime somebody makes a change to them
- If you can perform push-button deployments of any version of the software to any environment on demand

Docker also easily integrates with CI and continuous delivery platforms enabling development and testing to deliver seamless updates to production. In the case of any kind of failure, it is possible to roll back to the previous working version.

Accurate testing

Docker accelerates DevOps by creating a common framework for building, testing, and administering distributed applications, independent of languages, development tools or environmental variables. Docker improves collaboration by allowing developers, **Quality Assurance (QA)** teams, and system administrators to efficiently share code, exchange content, and integrate applications. We can be confident that our QA environment exactly matches what will be deployed in the production environment.

Facilitating CaaS

We have been fiddling with IT infrastructure and **Platform as a Service (PaaS)**. Bare metal servers and VMs are the key computing resources in IT centers. Now with the successful proliferation of containers, **Container as a Service (CaaS)** is becoming hugely popular and tantalizing. There are certain issues with PaaS in traditional environments. CaaS is being touted as the solution approach for surmounting the prickling issues of PaaS:

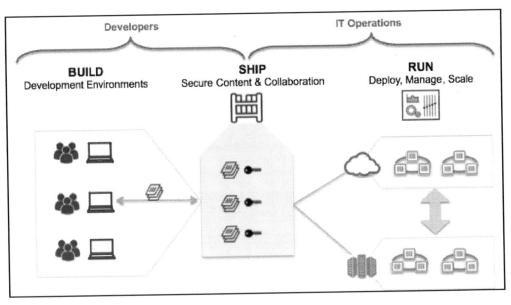

The high-level CaaS architecture

In the preceding figure, developers on the left-hand side are pulling and pushing application content from a library of trusted and curated base images. Operations teams on the right-hand side are monitoring and managing deployed applications and infrastructures. The two teams can collaborate through a toolset that allows for a separation of concerns while unifying the two teams through the application life cycle. The Docker platform is that toolset empowering to build a CaaS that fits varying business requirements.

Adding new technology components is greatly simplified. Let's say a company wants to add MongoDB to its portfolio. Now a certified image can be pulled down from Docker Hub and tweaked as needed, and then quickly deployed. This container can then be offered to developers for their consumption. Containers also allow for more experimentation. Since it is so easy to build and tear down containers, a developer can quickly compare the features of a stack component. For example, a developer wants to test the performance of three different NoSQL database technologies and they can simply fire up the appropriate container for each NoSQL technology without having to deal with the complexity of managing the infrastructure and the underlying technology stack. The developer could then run performance tests against each distinct container and select the appropriate one quickly.

Containers have the innate and incredible power to offer JVM-like portability in terms of completely abstracting the underlying infrastructure. A true CaaS model is to pave the way for the deployment of multi-container applications in multi-cloud environments.

Accelerating workload modernization

There are a variety of workloads in need of getting appropriately modernized and migrated to powerful environments (clouds) to be readily found, bound, and used by worldwide users for producing business-critical applications. Workloads typically represent software applications, middleware, platforms, and so on. In the past, **Service-Oriented Architecture (SOA)** was an enabler of software modernization through integration and composition. In the recent past, MSA is being touted as the best-in-class approach for modernizing legacy, monolithic, and massive applications. Applications are being fragmented accordingly in order to be easily manageable. The development, deployment, and management complexities are expected to go down with complex applications being expressed and exposed as a collection of interoperable, portable, and composable microservices. This means that application modules are being refactored and readied to be loosely or lightly coupled, even decoupled. Further, applications are recommended to be stateless to be scalable and independently deployable.

Some applications can take a "lift and shift" path to the cloud. This means that if some code modifications are brought in, they can be significantly refactored to take the distinct advantages of cloud centers. The applications are being redesigned, recoded, and repurposed for the specific cloud platform. This gives the legacy application a new life and a new purpose.

Containers are the highly optimized and organized runtime for hosting and delivering microservices. Containers in conjunction with microservices are emerging as the most crucial combination for the IT world in many respects. The use of containers to "wrap" or containerize existing legacy applications comes with a few advantages. The containers take care of the underlying platforms and infrastructures and the complexities associated with them. Containerized applications are portable and enhances the speed in which legacy modernization is performed. The cloud migration is smoothened through the utilization of containers. Additional capabilities such as security, web and service enablement, and governance can be attached to containerized applications easily and quickly. Further, modernized legacy applications are a better fit for distributed computing.

A great way to modernize the current and conventional applications as we move them to the cloud is to leverage technologies such as Kubernetes and Mesos instead of building all of the **Non-Functional Requirements** (**NFRs**), such as scalability, security, and sustainability.

Docker for stateful applications

Containers are typically stateless. However, for several applications, stateful compute resources are needed. Docker does not natively provide storage volume management or data persistence when porting these compute resources between hosts. The Flocker solution by ClusterHQ addresses these needs and enables the containers to be used for stateful applications, such as databases, by providing a framework for volume management and data persistence when moving compute resources from one host to another. Flocker works with all the major container managers (including Docker Swarm, Kubernetes, and Apache Mesos).

Containers for edge computing

The security fear along with the lack of visibility and controllability is being touted as the widely articulated and accepted drawback of cloud computing. Private clouds and cloudlets are the viable options. Yet, they too face certain limitations. However, the recent phenomenon of edge or fog computing has been pronounced as the most successful computing paradigm for surmounting all the cloud weaknesses.

Edge computing is all about shifting the data processing and storage from the centralized locations (cloud) to the distributed and decentralized environments (local). This means that by bringing in compute, network, and storage competencies closer to the users, the **Quality of Service (QoS)** attributes / the NFRs are readily and rewardingly accomplished. Traditionally, all the computing and storage takes place in cloud environments (on-premises and off-premises). However, certain scenarios such as real-time analytics and faster responses insist for computing at the user end. It is not an exaggeration to say that the QoS and experience goes up significantly when IT becomes people-centric, context-aware, adaptive, real-time, and multimodal. Real-world and real-time applications and services invariably pitch in for computing at the edges. There have been several architectural complications even for edge computing, and now with the faster maturity and stability of application and volume containers, edge computing innately gets the much-needed fillip.

Devices networking, service enablement, and clustering

Generally, edge devices such as implantables, wearables, portables, gateways, mobiles, handhelds, consumer electronics, and robots may be primarily resource-constrained. Most of these devices are not static and typically nomadic. Establishing seamless connectivity among them for process, application, and data integration is a tedious and tough affair indeed. Geo-distributed computation on edge devices, therefore, requires a lightweight, intrinsically extensible, and intelligent platform to handle extremely fragile service deployment, delivery, and management. **Open Service Gateway interface (OSGi)** is an interesting framework for elegantly activating and administering resource-constrained, embedded and connected devices, and their unique services. Any service or application can be containerized and can be loaded with all kinds of participating devices. Then an instance of the OSGi package can be containerized and hosted in a reasonably powerful device stationed at the user environment in order to discover and manage all kinds of devices and their service containers inside. This kind of setup enables centralized (from the cloud) as well as decentralized monitoring, measurement, and management of device services. The Dockerized platform is a proven mechanism to install, configure, manage, upgrade, and terminate running services.

Device service registry for discovery

There may be thousands of edge devices in a particular environment. To discover, index, and manage heterogeneous, dynamic, and distributed devices in a systematic manner, the need for service registry and discovery capabilities is being insisted upon. The management platform has to have this feature in order to find, bind, and leverage multiple devices in an automated manner.

Fault tolerance

The platform must be fault-tolerant in order to guarantee high availability and reliability to ensure business continuity.

Caching

Caching can be performed on the edge devices to enable faster access and to improve the overall application performance. If Docker images are stocked and cached at the edge, then application provisioning can be speeded up sharply. Another use case is to store application data in a cache in order to remarkably increase application performance.

Bukhary Ikhwan Ismail and the team have built a testbed in order to examine Docker as one of the candidate technologies for edge or fog computing. The testbed consists of a data center and three edge sites to simulate the environment. At each edge site, a Docker Registry is set up to store Docker images locally at the edge. A Docker daemon at the edge site will be able to search and pull the Docker image from the Docker Registry. Docker Swarm is configured on each edge site to manage multiple Docker daemons. Docker Swarm acts as a clustering and orchestration tool. Based on the experimentation and evaluation, Docker is found to be providing fast deployment, small footprint, and good performance, which make it potentially a viable edge computing platform.

Marcel Grossmann and the team have developed **Hypriot Cluster Lab (HCL)**. This is an ARM-powered cloud solution utilizing Docker. Embedded systems and other **Single Board Computers (SBCs)** have gained tremendous computing power. With devices increasingly interconnected and web-enabled, a massive amount of machine data gets generated and the growing need is to collect and crunch them quickly in order to squeeze out real-time insights. As illustrated earlier, the era of edge/fog analytics is picking up fast. HCL can provide the basis for a virtualized edge because it runs on the ARM architecture, which behaves like a small data center and ships energy-efficient features by design.

The Docker use cases

Containerization is emerging as the way forward for the software industry as it brings forth a newer and richer way of building and bundling any kind of software, shipping and running them everywhere. That is the fast-evolving aspect of containerization that promises and provides software portability, which has been a constant nuisance for IT developers and administrators for many decades now. The Docker idea is flourishing here because of a number of enabling factors and facets. This section is specially prepared for specifying the key use cases of the Docker idea.

Integrating containers into workflows

Workflows are a widely accepted and used abstraction for unambiguously representing the right details of any complicated and large-scale business and scientific applications and executing them on distributed computing systems such as clusters, clouds, and grids. However, workflow management systems have been largely evasive in conveying the relevant information of the underlying environment on which the tasks inscribed in the workflow are to run. This means that the workflow tasks can run perfectly on the environment for which they were designed. The real challenge is to run the tasks across multiple IT environments without tweaking and twisting the source codes of the required tasks. Increasingly, the IT environments are heterogeneous with the leverage of disparate operating systems, middleware, programming languages and frameworks, databases, and so on. Typically, workflow systems focus on data interchange between tasks and are environment-specific. A workflow, which is working fine in one environment, starts to crumble when it is being migrated and deployed on different IT environments. All kinds of known and unknown dependencies and incompatibilities spring up to denigrate the workflows delaying the whole job of IT setup, application installation and configuration, deployment, and delivery. Containers are the best bet for resolving this imbroglio once and for all.

In the article, *Integrating Containers into Workflows: A Case Study Using Makeflow, Work Queue, and Docker, Chao Zheng* and *Douglas Thain* have done a good job of analyzing several methods in order to experimentally prove the unique contributions of containers in empowering workflow/process management systems. They have explored the performance of a large bioinformatics workload on a Docker-enabled cluster and observed the best configuration to be locally managed on containers that are shared between multiple tasks.

Docker for HPC and TC applications

According to Douglas M. Jacobsen and Richard Shane Canon, currently, containers are being overwhelmingly used for the web, enterprise, mobile, and cloud applications. However, there are questions being asked and doubts being raised on whether containers can be a viable runtime for hosting technical and scientific computing applications. Especially, there are many **High-Performance Computing (HPC)** applications yearning for a perfect deployment and execution environment. The authors of this research paper have realized that Docker containers can be a perfect answer for HPC workloads.

In many cases, users desire to have the ability to easily execute their scientific applications and workflows in the same environment used for development or adopted by their community. Some researchers have tried out the cloud option, but the challenges are many. The users need to solve how they handle workload management, filesystems, and basic provisioning. Containers promise to offer the flexibility of cloud-type systems coupled with the performance of bare-metal systems. Furthermore, containers have the potential to be more easily integrated into traditional HPC environments, which means that users can obtain the benefits of flexibility without the added burden of managing other layers of the system (that is, batch systems, filesystems, and so on).

Minh Thanh Chung and the team have analyzed the performance of VMs and containers for high-performance applications and benchmarked the results that clearly show containers are the next-generation runtime for HPC applications. In short, Docker offers many attractive benefits in an HPC environment. To test these, IBM Platform LSF and Docker have been integrated outside the core of Platform LSF and the integration leverages the rich Platform LSF plugin framework.

We all know that the aspect of compartmentalization is for resource partitioning and provisioning. This means that physical machines are subdivided into multiple logical machines (VMs and containers). Now on the reverse side, such kinds of logical systems carved out of multiple physical machines can be linked together to build a virtual supercomputer to solve certain complicated problems. *Hsi-En Yu* and *Weicheng Huang* have described how they built a virtual HPC cluster in the research paper, *Building a Virtual HPC Cluster with Auto Scaling by the Docker*. They have integrated the autoscaling feature of service discovery with the lightweight virtualization paradigm (Docker) and embarked on the realization of a virtual cluster on top of physical cluster hardware.

Containers for telecom applications

Csaba Rotter and the team have explored and published a survey article with the title, *Using Linux Containers in Telecom Applications*. Telecom applications exhibit strong performance and high availability requirements; therefore, running them in containers requires additional investigations. A telecom application is a single or multiple node application responsible for a well-defined task. Telecom applications use standardized interfaces to connect to other network elements and implement standardized functions. On top of the standardized functions, a telecom application can have vendor-specific functionality. There is a set of QoS and **Quality of Experience (QoE)** attributes such as high availability, capacity, and performance/throughput. The paper has clearly laid out the reasons for the unique contributions of containers in having next-generation telecom applications.

Efficient Prototyping of Fault Tolerant Map-Reduce Applications with Docker-Hadoop by *Javier Rey and the team* advocated that distributed computing is the way forward for compute and data-intensive workloads. There are two major trends. Data becomes big and there are realizations that big data leads to big insights through the leverage of pioneering algorithms, scripts, and parallel languages such as Scala, integrated platforms, new-generation databases, and dynamic IT infrastructures. MapReduce is a parallel programming paradigm currently used to perform computations on massive amounts of data. Docker-Hadoop1 is a virtualization testbed conceived to allow the rapid deployment of a Hadoop cluster. With Docker-Hadoop, it is possible to control the characteristics of the node and run scalability and performance tests that otherwise would require a large computing environment. Docker-Hadoop facilitates simulation and reproduction of different failure scenarios for the validation of an application.

Regarding interactive social media applications, Alin Calinciuc and the team have come out with a research publication titled as *OpenStack and Docker: Building a high-performance IaaS platform for interactive social media applications*. It is a well-known truth that interactive social media applications face the challenge of efficiently provisioning new resources in order to meet the demands of the growing number of application users. The authors have given the necessary description on how Docker can run as a hypervisor, and how the authors can manage to enable the fast provisioning of computing resources inside of an OpenStack IaaS using the `nova-docker` plugin that they had developed.

Summary

At this point in time, Docker is nothing short of an epidemic and every enterprising business across the globe is literally obsessed with the containerization mania for their extreme automation, transformation, and disruption. With the blossoming of hybrid IT, the role of Docker-enabled containerization is steadily growing in order to smartly empower IT-enabled businesses. In this chapter, we discussed the prime capabilities and contributions of the Docker paradigm. We described how a typical software package can be containerized. Further, you can come across industrial and enterprise-scale use cases.

Index

Made in the USA
Middletown, DE
29 May 2018